REVIEWS OF SOCIAL INC.

Zukis's observations are very thought provoking and it's nice to have someone finally explain social in terms a CEO can relate to.

–Dave Yarnold, CEO ServiceMax

I agree with Bob Zukis that social technology is a game changer. Organizations must build in business processes and policies to safely embrace it—or they will be left behind.

–Gene Hodges, former CEO Websense

Bob is one of the few who is able to clearly envision and articulate the up and coming era of enterprise computing. This is like the Renaissance Age that replaced austere medieval practices with humanitarian inspiration. The new era of enterprise computing is no longer solely about process and efficiency.

–David Chen, President Pactera

Zukis's vision around social technology, online freelancing and changing labor models bring new light to why today's workplace is being revolutionized.

–Fabio Rosati, CEO Elance

Social Inc. provides boards, management teams and their employees with the key strategies needed to emerge stronger and more competitive in this big shift from transactions to engagement.

–Ray Wang, CEO Constellation Research

SOCIAL INC.

WHY BUSINESS IS THE NEXT SOCIAL OPPORTUNITY WORTH TRILLIONS

@Bob Zukis

Edited by Anna F. Doherty & Leslie F. Peters

Under no circumstances shall any of the information provided herein be construed as investment advice of any kind.

Social Inc.
Why Business Is the Next Social Opportunity Worth Trillions
Bob Zukis

Copyright © 2013 Bob Zukis

Published by Kauffman Fellows Press
855 El Camino Real, Suite 12, Palo Alto, CA 94301, United States
www.kauffmanfellows.org

Library of Congress Control Number: 2013930412
ISBN-13: 978-1-939533-99-9
Printed in the United States of America

Editing and design by Together Editing & Design, Inc.
www.togetherediting.com

First Edition: February 2013
9 8 7 6 5 4 3 2 1

For Kimberly. You're my girl.

Contents

Tables & Figures

FOREWORD
BY MARC BENIOFF
CHAIRMAN & CEO, SALESFORCE.COM

For several years, one of my favorite maxims—and one that's especially true in the technology industry—is that people overestimate what they can do in one year, and underestimate what they can do in a decade. I've certainly experienced this in the first ten-plus years building salesforce.com.

While there were critics who initially doubted our vision to deliver business applications over the internet, in just a bit over a decade, the idea now known as *cloud computing* exploded into a $100+ billion phenomenon and revolutionized the software industry. Our startup, launched in a one-bedroom apartment, grew into the largest tech employer in San Francisco, the first cloud computing company to reach a $3 billion run rate (Kerner 2012, para. 1) and the most innovative company in the world the last two years, according to *Forbes* (2012).

Most significantly, cloud computing (and the multi-tenant technology that leverages the efficiencies of sharing, which we evangelized) has changed how we live and how we work—and it's only the beginning. Nicholas Carr, an influential thinker in the IT industry, has suggested that "utility-supplied" computing will have economic and social impacts as profound as the ones that took place one hundred years ago, when companies "stopped generating their own power with steam engines and dynamos and plugged into the newly built electric grid" (n.d., para. 1).

Ten years ago we talked about the "End of Software" revolution (e.g., *BloombergBusinessweek Magazine* 2003),but even I underestimated how quickly massive change could take root. Now—at the start of an exciting new era in computing—I am heeding lessons from the past ten years and infinitely inspired by what's possible. This time, I am not underestimating the potential for change in the coming decade: *I am predicting it's going to be bigger than anything we've seen before.*

I also know now that the mantra I believed during the last decade about overestimating what we can do in one year is no longer true. We cannot overestimate what can we do in one year—this notion may have held up in the past, but it doesn't anymore. There is no such thing as overestimating; we are now in a time where anything is possible. It's all being fueled by social technology and delivered by companies that embrace the transformative power of these new social tools.

As businesses of all kinds evolve to embrace practices that are more social, mobile, and open, we've seen a profound shift where new parties possess power. While many people fear this shift—after all, change is hard—we need to understand that there are actually far more benefits than risks associated with the adoption of these new social tools and technologies. Besides, we have no choice: The world is moving forward and we have to move with it. The rapid adoption of new technologies does not stop for anyone. It's simple: If your employees and customers are using social technology, you and your company have to be as well.

Managers in companies (the "elite") no longer control the conversation. We've already seen the world change with the Arab Spring (Lam 2012). If we do not find a better way to create more authentic and meaningful relationships with customers and employees, a Corporate Spring and a CEO Spring will be next.

Over the past three years at salesforce.com, we embraced new thinking and new technologies to transform our company into a *social technology-enabled business*—one that uses social technologies and social business practices to engage with customers, employees, and data differently—and we have been blown away by the results. With the connectivity, communication, community, and collaboration opportunities available in the cloud, we have found a way to work much faster, become smarter, and exceed every one of our expectations. We have had to change the way we forecast: We no longer talk about what we'll accomplish in the next quarter, but about what we'll accomplish in the next week. We're able to listen, learn, share, and innovate better than even we imagined. We excel at things we've never even tried before—things people told us we would never be able to do. See Part 3 of *Social Inc.*: "Toyota Drives toward a Social Destiny" for the fantastic story behind how salesforce.com helped a customer with their social destiny, and in the process we helped ourselves. We are constantly learning how to delight customers and employees in new ways, and we are receiving the benefits of their engagement, their loyalty, and their commitment. We've achieved more— and it's been easier, less expensive, and more fun—than I would have predicted even a few years ago. *To sum it up: I have spent thirty years in the technology industry, and I've seen the most profound and most exciting changes in the past two.*

Today, everything is becoming social and moving to the cloud. Apps are moving to the cloud. Platforms are moving to the cloud. Databases are moving to the cloud. Collaboration platforms—which had not been re- imagined for decades—are becoming social and moving to the cloud.

Unlike traditional shifts in computing that were only accessible to the biggest enterprises, this shift benefits everyone. The cloud serves companies of every size, even companies that don't seem inherently social. Toyota, the largest car company in the world, which can afford any service, is pioneering with social technology and choosing the cloud because it provides a better alternative. Toyota is reinventing the experience of car ownership and driving with social technology. Coca Cola is becoming a social company and reinventing the experience around consuming their products with these new tools. These companies are showing that anything and everything can be a social experience—this is the new competitive playing field, and it's only possible because of these recent developments. The most exciting part is that the exact same benefits are available and affordable for every organization, including very small companies and even nonprofits.

I'm so passionate about social because of its democratizing powers. I remember that Steve Jobs, who personally inspired and influenced me and changed all of our lives for the better with his visionary thinking, would often talk about how the information revolution would empower individuals and democratize everything. As far back as his visionary 1985 interview with *Playboy*, he said, "This revolution, the information revolution, is a revolution of free energy as well, but of another kind: free intellectual energy" (Sheff 1985, para. 13). This democratization is happening all around us now and at a scale never before possible, and I believe we are only at the beginning of this phenomenon. Much as the internet has given a voice to people around the world who once went unheard, the cloud and social technology have leveled the business playing field, giving all companies the same access to tools that can increase their capabilities, competitive advantages, and power to unleash innovation. We already know that technology becomes lower in cost and easier to use every day. Each day brings more value for more users. Now we are working on entirely new opportunities, ways to engage we never before imagined, all powered by the power of social—and all with ramifications far more impactful than just reducing costs. It is a spectacular time.

Bob Zukis, one of our early customers and an advocate of cloud computing long before it was fashionable, stood on stage ten years ago at our Freedom From Software customer event in New York City and talked about the benefits his business was receiving from our cloud-based technology. Bob got it then, and he gets it now. *Social Inc.* takes you on a fascinating journey that explains why social technology is changing business as we know it, and what each of us should be doing about it as CEOs, directors, managers, employees, customers, and investors.

The social technology-empowered company is enabling significant developments in business management that are only possibly because of the recent advancements in these technologies. The future that is now possible for your company is much different than only a few years ago. How will you thrive, and what will you now achieve with these powerful tools? I, for one, am excited to find out. Read on to discover what's possible.

–Marc Benioff
San Francisco, California

PREFACE

Over the past thirty years, across 20 countries and 4 continents my clients hired me for my experience, knowledge, and expertise to help them solve a range of problems, from the strategic to the tactical. The irony of my thirty years as a "management consultant" is that the many companies I worked with, or more accurately the individuals within them, could have fixed their own problems. Almost without exception the solution resided within the company itself. The problem was that the organization got in its own way—it prevented its employees from fixing what they knew was broken.

The reality behind why things weren't working was smothered and stuck in a quagmire of institutional sludge. The human collective of the modern corporation stifled the truth that would set their problems free—mostly (though not always) inadvertently.

I came in as a liberator of the truth, working outside the artificial boundaries of the corporation. As a consultant I did not have to follow the rules of the organization: its management hierarchies, organizational structures, matrix management systems, job titles and descriptions, performance management approaches to nowhere, rigid IT systems, antiquated policies, inefficient procedures, and so on. None of that applied to me, which let me be the emancipator—releasing the truth and telling the company what was broken, and why. I was brought in to wade through organizationally imposed oppression and set the truth free. Although I have relished this role, social technology and the companies that embrace it are making me redundant, putting me out of business—and it's about time.

Every company has been built on a century of trial-and-error in business management theory and practice. As employees, customers, and investors, we've been making this up as we go along. For the past hundred years, it's been one huge experiment.

The last thirty years of my own experiment have taught me that whether you are an employee, customer, or investor, you know when things are broken in companies. You want the truth to be free as well—you want to make things better, and you usually know how. Unfortunately, the modern corporation has failed you. You know that the companies you work for, invest in, and buy from could be doing things much better than they are today.

Finally, because of today's social technology, you can do something about fixing things: Social technology makes all of us liberators of the truth. Business management theory and practice is now being open-sourced. Unprecedented levels of engagement and transparency are disrupting and reinventing how companies do business and how customers and workers experience them, their products, and their services. The biggest business-management revolution of our lifetime is here, because the biggest social technology-enabled disruption to human behavior has also arrived.

A new chapter in business is at our doorstep because of today's social technology—one where the truth is reality, not perception. In this new chapter, the truth has been set free. The social technology-empowered world and the companies that inhabit it will be what we all want them to be, and what we all make them.

Each of us can be an active and willing participant in this next chapter of the business management experiment—and each of us needs to be. Because of you—the leaders, employees, customers, and investors in every business around the world—I believe in the future of the social technology-empowered business. I know that you want things to be better, and I know that you know how to fix them.

–Bob Zukis
Manhattan Beach, California
February 2013

THE BUSINESS MANAGEMENT OPPORTUNITY OF THE CENTURY

You know, we just don't recognize the most
significant moments of our lives while
they're happening. Back then I thought,
"Well, there'll be other days."
I didn't realize that that was the only day.

–Moonlight Graham
Field of Dreams (1985)

A Revolution—By the People, for the People

Social technology in the workplace is changing your company as you know it...whether you want it to, or not. The future anticipated at the dawn of the millennium has been altered forever by breakthrough technology developments in social software, mobile devices, the cloud, and the many related innovations that make this new social technology-empowered world possible.

These advancements have arrived just in time. Distrust in government and business is rampant and growing; people's confidence levels in CEOs are abysmally low (Edelman Trust Barometer 2012, slide 21); employees everywhere are woefully disengaged (Gallup 2010, p. 2); and economic growth, while projected to return (albeit at lower levels), is on very shaky footing (IMF 2012, p. xv). The overall economic assessment is reflected in 2012 headlines: "growth will remain weak" and "unemployment will remain high for some time" (p. xiii).

However, a significant moment in the history of business management is currently unfolding that could change this troubling landscape. Today's social technology has brought a revolution to the doorstep of the modern corporation through the "creative destruction" described by Joseph Schumpeter, named the "most influential economist of the 20th century" by business management guru Peter Drucker (Schumpeter 2008, back cover). Schumpeter describes *creative destruction* as a form of "industrial mutation" (p. 83) that "incessantly revolutionizes the economic structure from within, incessantly destroying the old one, incessantly creating a new one" (p. 83). He believes that certain types of competitive disruptions, like "new technology" or a "new type of organization" (p. 84), can create revolutionary surges followed by periods of absorption.

The moment facing business today is one of creative destruction, absorption, and revolution brought about by social technology. With revolution, there is money at stake for business—a lot of money. The McKinsey Global Institute values this next chapter in the story of social technology at over a trillion dollars annually for businesses globally (Chui et al. 2012, p. 1).

Social technology started to gain tremendous consumer momentum through the iPhone's explosion onto the market in 2007 (Kerris & Dowling 2007), the Zynga and LinkedIn IPOs,[1] the movie *The Social Network* (2010), and the buzz that escalated around Facebook's much-anticipated public debut. Acceleration increased through 2011 with massive VC investment into anything "social" (Lerner 2012, para. 5) and Twitter's role in political and social uprisings around the world (O'Donnell 2012). By 2012, everything had become all social, all the time—2012 was the year that "social" finally went big time with Facebook's massive, albeit now-infamous IPO.[2]

So far, social technology adoption has been driven by rampant consumer use and acceptance, and businesses have largely seen this trend as a narrow marketing issue—but not anymore. Business is the next killer social opportunity because major leaps forward in social technology have two consistent effects over time: They make us smarter and they make us more productive (see Part 2 of *Social Inc.* for the history). This perfect storm of benefits drives revenue growth and profits to the bottom line —in big ways.

However, this is not a book about how to use Facebook, Twitter, LinkedIn, Chatter, or the other social technology tools out there. This is also not a book about social media marketing. *Social Inc.* is the story of the biggest business management development we'll experience in our lifetimes—the story of why and how social technology will transform or destroy your company, if you let it.

The unstoppable power of social technology controls the future of business. Companies that use this power to run their business and socially engage their customers, partners, investors, and employees are creating the next chapter in business management history. These companies recognize that if they

---

[1] More on the Zynga "IPO that fell flat" can be found in Spears and MacMillan (2011), Rushe (2011), and Hof (2011). LinkedIn's offering, including its post-IPO price run-up, is discussed in detail in Baldwin and Selyukh (2011) and Rusli (2011).

[2] For more on the Facebook IPO, see Pepitone (2012); Sandler, Womack, and MacMillan (2012); and Blodget (2012).

What is "social technology"?

Social networking, social media, and social technology—because this is still an emerging and evolving area, many different terms are being used interchangeably and in different ways to define and describe today's phenomenon of "social." For the purposes of *Social Inc.*, I primarily refer to and use the term *social technology*, of which social networking and social media are essentially component parts.

Early use of the term *social technology* is traceable back to the end of the 19th century in the *American Journal of Sociology*. It was used in 1898 by Albion Small, who founded the first Department of Sociology at the University of Chicago (p. 131), and in 1901 C. R. Henderson offered this definition: "social technology deals with both: with what exists as a revelation of what ought to be, and of the method of realizing what ought to be" (p. 468).

Social media has been described as a "tool for sending, receiving, storing, and retrieving information" (Poe 2012, p. 11). Social networking sites like Facebook comprise a broader social media landscape that includes Twitter, Chatter, and other tools being used to change the ways people connect and communicate. People are using these tools to realize what "ought to be" (Henderson 1901, p. 468). McKinsey uses social technology to refer to "the products and services that enable social interactions in the digital realm, and thus allow people to connect and interact virtually" (Chui et al. 2012, p. 4).

Social technology is therefore a broad term that encompasses all of the various tools, devices, software, hardware, infrastructure, and so on that people use and leverage to connect, communicate, collaborate, and establish community. As this toolset is constantly evolving, *Social Inc.* focuses not on the actual tools, but on how we use them—that is, I define social technology according to the human behaviors that the tools capture, change, and amplify. Peter Drucker shares this view when he says "Technology is not about tools, it deals with how Man works" (2011, p. vii).

Social technology therefore refers to the broader universe of tools that people invent and use to enable and alter the core behaviors of connecting, communicating, collaborating, and establishing community—realizing the world that ought to be (Henderson 1901). Services or products like Facebook, Twitter, Chatter, Pinterest, and the iPhone are component, albeit integral, parts of the overall social technology landscape, enabled and delivered by the internet and the cloud.

succeed, they will also benefit all their stakeholders in a consequential way, expanding the pie for all.

The *Social Inc.* Roadmap

Social technology tools do not promise incremental improvements. They deliver game-changing breakthroughs—massive improvements in intellectual and workforce productivity. These are competitive advantages that can deliver knockout blows.

Because hindsight offers a focused perspective, in the chapters that follow I use humanity's past to frame today's transcendent moment against the backdrop of traditional business management theory and practice. Social technology has a history that business leaders and their employees can learn from. More importantly, *Social Inc.* also looks forward in time to envision what can—and will—be next as a result of these tools.

Revolutions often start quietly, with a small spark that smolders, lingering, waiting for the right catalyst to arrive. Once the catalyst arrives, the revolution erupts uncontrollably, often violently, and pushes change and upheaval into the world—sometimes for better, sometimes for worse. The billions of people using social technology are that catalyst for business.

This is a significant moment in the history of business—and I am committed to making sure you realize why and understand what you need to do about it. So get ready to go social.

In the remainder of Part 1, I introduce the first two of 10 "*Social Inc.* Rules" that collectively define the essence of this opportunity. I also frame the social technology opportunity in terms that every business leader can relate to: financial opportunity.

In Part 2, I explain the history behind today's social technology revolution in order to frame today's social explosion in a context that is easy to relate to: prior social technologies and how they changed business and society over time. Questions such as "Why is social technology exploding onto the scene now and where are its roots?" and "How will the past influence the future?"

are addressed. With this background, I discuss the history of social technology adoption, deployment, and impact on human behavior. From this discussion, you will be able to envision how your company is changing and will continue to change as social technology spreads like the wildfire it is.

In Part 3, I address the nuts-and-bolts of how business management is changing. Concepts and thinking from some of the greatest minds in business management history—Taylor, Drucker, Maslow, Deming, and others—tell the story of where business management theory and practice has led companies over the past hundred years. Marc Benioff, Chairman and CEO of salesforce.com, also shares a story from one of his key customers that changed their future, as well as his company's.

In Part 4, concepts from one of today's leading business management thinkers, Michael Porter, are "mashed-up" with social technology to illustrate how strategy, competitive advantage, and creating value are being impacted through these new tools. Your company's social technology-driven destiny is revealed here.

Part 5 dives into the essence of why these tools are so disruptive and so valuable. I address the economics behind the use and adoption of social technology—or what I call the "Social Inc-onomics."

Part 6 covers the important issue of social technology governance for CEOs and boards. Social technology has a life all of its own that CEOs and boards are struggling to understand. Your company will not find its social goldmine—or avoid social disasters—without a better understanding of social technology risks and opportunities. I include several examples of how CEOs and boards are addressing this rapidly changing risk environment, as well as recommendations and some tools that boards and CEOs can use immediately.

Part 7 is my antidote to Lewis Carroll's *Alice in Wonderland* (1865) suggestion that if you don't know where you are going, any path will get you there. I offer a roadmap for an integrated social technology and business management approach. The game has changed, and social technology is rewriting the rules.

Part 7 is your company's action plan to fully enable the social technology-empowered business.

I close in Part 8 by presenting ten predictions for 2020 to stretch your thinking around the magnitude of what is unfolding. What will the business world look like eight short years into the future? What impact will social technology have on industry structures and on how firms compete? How will the economics behind social technology change businesses and impact economies? The predictions I offer will challenge your thinking, open your eyes, and get you excited—or scared—about a *Social Inc.* future.

You can ignore social technology, but it won't ignore you or your company, much less your company's employees, investors, products, services, and most importantly, customers. So get your *Social Inc.* game face on.

The New and Social Future of Business

A curious thing has been happening throughout all of the social hype: Business has been far slower than individuals in embracing and understanding this technology. Most businesses are still struggling to understand what is sweeping over them. Chatter, Jive, Twitter, and mobile smart phones are just the tip of the iceberg of new cloud and socially designed tools that embody, enable, and amplify new human behaviors. Rule 1 of *Social Inc.* anchors this issue where it belongs: to the things people do, and want to do, through these tools. This new social technology is now forever intertwined in the mentalities and actions of a global workforce, customer base, and investor pool.

Social Inc. Rule 1
Social technology is about human behavior.

How humans communicate, interrelate, engage, and collaborate has permanently been altered. Thanks to the role these tools played in real-world revolutions from Cairo to London to Wall Street (e.g., Srinivasan 2012; Firger 2012), social technology officially lost its novelty status in 2011 and became recognized as a powerful new force for disruption. This technology has turned countries upside down because it has turned human behavior upside down. Just think what it can do to—or for—your company.

The billions of people who validated today's social technology through their ravenous adoption and use have created a crisis of relevancy for business. These people are all customers, employees, and investors in some way, shape, or form for business. Business is no longer the early adopter of new technology—individuals are. Customers have business on the ropes, playing defense, and so far playing it poorly. Business is just now starting to wake up, starting to realize that customers, employees, and investors are behaving differently because of this new technology—and that business needs to catch up, fast.

A Behavior-Led Revolution

In his 2009 book *The Nature of Technology*, W. Brian Arthur defines *technology* as "a collection of phenomena captured and put to use" (pp. 50–51). *Social Inc.* is a book about the unique social phenomena behind social technology—the changes these phenomena have made to human behavior and our relationship with our environments, as well as the impact that these latest developments are having on business as we know it.

When human behavior changes, business changes. Personal infatuation with and rampant adoption of social technology is now the "tail wagging the [corporate] dog." This is a people-led revolution. Employees and customers will not—and are not—waiting for a management edict to be handed down to embrace the power of social technology. We have taken control and are changing the rules, reinventing the future of business in real-time.

In one respect, we've done business a big favor. For the first time we have climbed up the technology learning curve on our own individual time and dime. The business status quo is primed for disruption because of our adoption and fascination with this technology. Unfortunately, most companies are struggling with how they should respond. Fortunately, this technology is exactly what business needs—the answer to those struggles is the technology itself.

You as an employee are the solution to the very challenge that you as a customer have created for business. As a socially empowered consumer who has leaped ahead, you now need to solve this dilemma as a socially empowered employee. As employees, we need to transform our companies to be social technology-inspired and driven, to save them from the institutional sludge of their own existence.

The Social Company recognizes that it must adopt the tools and technology its markets, customers, employees, and investors are using. Furthermore, Social Companies know that this technology changes their traditional thinking around business management: from what their strategy is to who their customers are, how they engage with their markets, how they organize themselves, and how they compete and make money.

The rules of business are changing before our very eyes—for better and for worse. Leaders who understand social technology recognize that business management is evolutionary, and that they are in a major period of disruption because of how their markets want to use these new tools to get things done. This dramatic level of change is okay, though—business has been through it before (which might be surprising) and the good news is we can learn from the past (see Part 2 of *Social Inc.*).

There's money on the table with this technology, and a once-in-a-lifetime opportunity to take your company and your business to new heights. For the first time, business changes are being driven and paced by the outside forces of customer, employee, and investor empowerment. The way that companies create and capture value is changing because of the new rules of engagement that customers are putting in place. As customers, we know businesses can be improved, and as employees, we know how to make things better.

Business Is the Next Killer Social Technology Opportunity

Companies are finally seeing social technology as something other than just a marketing tool. Today's social technologies have defined an entirely new category of tools that have introduced new techniques for connecting, communicating, collaborating, and creating community.

What is a Social Company?

Social enterprise, *social business*, and *social company* are terms often seen as interchangeable, but they are starting to emerge as different things. "Social enterprise" was a term that salesforce.com was trying until recently to trademark, to label and define the market proposition around their products.

However, *social enterprise* has been in use for a relatively long time to define organizations that use commercial approaches to primarily address a human or environmental initiative; these organizations are not necessarily not-for-profits, but their operational and bottom line mandates are primarily focused on driving and supporting their human or environmental well-being agenda. These entities may be using social technology, or they may not be, but the benefits of social technology still apply to them and they will eventually integrate these tools into their missions.

Social business and *social company* are labels being used to describe typical for-profit, capitalist companies or organizations that are early adopters of this new technology to run and manage their businesses. Eventually, most companies will be *Social Companies*: designed to operate through social technology to deliver a unique experience to their markets.

Social technology will not change the fact that for-profit companies maximize investor value, which means maximizing profits, but I do believe that the stakeholder communities in which for-profits operate can no longer be underserved. Social technology will force a trend toward greater accountability in this respect.

In their book *Unleashing the Killer App: Digital Strategies for Market Dominance* (1998), authors Larry Downes and Chunka Mui define a killer application, or *killer app*, as a "new good or service that establishes an entirely new category" (p. 4) and state that "the primary forces at work in spawning today's killer apps are both technological and economic in nature" (p. 4). Today's social technology applications, tools, and devices are a new category that is creating killer opportunities for businesses to generate and capture new sources of value, through the behaviors and economics altered by these tools.

The broader adoption and application of social technology is the proof that these tools are not some trivial diversion or toy for a new generation, but an honest-to-goodness business tool and competitive weapon that can create business value. Where value can be created, it can be captured—this is a social gold rush for business, and the story is not about Facebook. This current stage of social technology evolution ups the ante and puts every business, every business model, and every industry at risk—at risk of becoming irrelevant or indispensable, and at risk of surviving or thriving into the near future.

Our expectations around engagement as consumers and investors now far exceed the experiences currently offered by most companies. The tools employers provide workers to do their jobs dramatically lag behind what we are using in our personal lives. Seemingly, in the blink of an eye, corporate information technology (IT) and the vast sums of money companies have spent on "legacy" IT have become largely irrelevant—because employees have moved on. We've "leapfrogged" the legacy IT our employers provide us—jumped over it, because we found something much, much better.

The Social Technology "Arms Race" Is On

Companies now teeter precariously between legacy IT-imposed irrelevance and breakthrough social technology-driven reinvention. Social technology offers a chance at business model and economic reinvention for those that understand and embrace its potential—it's a new strategic and tactical weapon in the battle for competitive advantage. Social technology also underscores how legacy IT has lost its ability to add value to the business, because it is not adding value for customers, investors, or employees.

Companies are dying faster than they used to because of technology-driven disruption and the advancing "grim reaper" of marketplace irrelevancy. Denial, a still seemingly common approach to social technology in the workplace, is a strategy for guaranteed failure. Imagine ignoring the development of the landline telephone in the early 1900s, an advancement that drove massive increases in business productivity. For business today, a phone number is just "table stakes" or part of the ante needed to enter the game—like today's social technology needs to be for your company. Inability or unwillingness to understand why and how today's social technology works and how it is shaping and influencing human behavior will prove fatal for many businesses.

Social technology changes how companies find, reach, engage, incentivize, serve, sell, and market to customers. This is not just a marketing or customer service tool, though—it changes how employees get recruited, evaluated, and rewarded and how work gets done. Collaboration with these tools is an entirely new ball game that changes every aspect of how a company does business, including how to work with suppliers and innovate through R&D. From strategy to every facet of operations, all bets are off. Governance and risk management also become entirely new challenges—ones that boards are ill-prepared to handle.

❮ The Business Opportunity Worth Trillions

It's been quite a while since there was a groundbreaking advancement in business management theory and approach—something foundational that alters the nature of competition and the economics of business. Social technology is now enabling the biggest business management development of our lives. How big? For starters, how about the GDPs of Hong Kong, Israel, Ireland, Chile, and New Zealand—combined (World Bank Group 2012, 2011 GDP data).

The McKinsey Global Institute recently estimated that there is between $900 billion and $1.3 trillion in value that could be released by business through social technology (Chui et al. 2012, p. 3). The four sectors that they analyzed represented about 20% of global revenues, at a trillion dollars of potential (p. 3). What's at stake is a multiple of this amount across all industries—trillions.

How does social technology deliver this value? As *Social Inc.* Rule 2 states, social technology makes people smarter and more productive (as history teaches—see Part 3). Being smart and productive is good for business—indeed, great for business according to McKinsey's analysis (Chui et al. 2012, p. 3). The story that unfolds in *Social Inc.* explains why and how these trillions will be realized.

Social Inc. Rule 2

Social technology makes people smarter and more productive.

This is the most disruptive corporate IT development I have seen in my 30-year career—bigger than the PC, bigger than e-business. Social technology is different than those advancements because it is accelerating and amplifying at a different pace and scale and in a different way. The PC, internet, mobile, and the cloud have been the raw materials for what is now possible—they are the forge and flame that can now transform the world. The really impactful things are what we can now create with these raw materials. The foundation has been established, and it is now time to exploit it.

The forces at play in business are being altered because of these developments. MIT Professor Erik Brynjolfsson and Andrew McAfee, associate director at the MIT Center for Digital Business, think that business is now in an information and communications technology super-fueled Great Restructuring (2011, p. 9). Not just doing more with less (although social technology takes business to a different productivity plateau as well), social technology means doing *new things* extremely effectively and efficiently. It's about changing the rules, both competitive and economic. As Brynjolfsson says, "Our technologies are racing ahead but many of our skills and organizations are lagging behind" (p. 9).

Furthermore, figuring out what to do with these tools no longer progresses at a snail's pace, incrementally, from some central IT or executive group. The application and use of this technology is now open-sourced by the billions who are using it. The masses are now leading and innovating beyond anything business has had to deal with or contemplate before.

Technology helps us do many things better, and do many new things. The opportunities are limitless. Intercepting customers at your competitor's point of sale? Making your customers into salespeople and rewarding them for their effort? Making your employees 20%, 30%, or 60% more productive?

Understanding what customers want before they know it? Transforming physical products into an engaging experience? Getting people to work for you, for free? Getting customers to line up to do business with you, and having them pay you a premium for the unique experience? The early adopters of social technology are currently accomplishing all of this, as you'll read in the coming chapters.

Trillions? At a minimum. Table 1-1 lists some of the things that information technology has enabled business to do over the last one hundred years, and outlines where social technology is now taking us.

Table 1-1: Historical IT and Expected Social Technology Impact to Business

Technology effect	Historical IT impact	Social technology impact
AUTOMATING ROUTINE TASKS	Out of the gate, a productivity boost came with the shift from manual processes to automated workflow. Work became less menial. The nature of work shifted into new domains. Greater efficiency meant fewer jobs overall, unfortunately.	Efficient automation of non-routine tasks through social technology collaboration will change everything all over again and establish a new productivity plateau. This short-term, productivity-driven economic benefit will disrupt markets as it increases competition. Social technology early-adopters have a new and powerful weapon, one that truly releases the power of their workforce. A coordinated government and business response will be required to address the ongoing threat to overall employment levels.
ALLOWING WORKERS TO DO MORE THINGS AT THE SAME TIME	Multitasking was a labor productivity enhancer—but also a distraction.	With share-tasking, tasks and work can be carved up differently than before because these new tools largely eliminate most transaction and engagement costs. A collaboration explosion contributes to redefining productivity levels and opens new channels of innovation.
IMPROVING THE OPERATIONAL EFFICIENCY OF COMPANIES	Business could and did crank out anything, at scale, and at high quality.	A focus on innovation and creating value through social technology defines the next major step forward in business management.

Technology effect	Historical IT impact	Social technology impact
IMPROVING THE OPERATIONAL EFFICIENCY OF COMPANIES (cont'd)	Supply-side productivity growth now exceeds demand-side consumption growth: we can produce faster than we consume. Management has been overly focused on value-redistribution strategies instead of value creation. Focus moved to cost reductions, as business became commoditized.	Disruption will increase as wildly creative and unique propositions emerge and enthrall millions through the velocity and reach of this technology. Expanding the economic pie by increasing value disrupts the nature of direct competition and industry structures, and also has the potential to create new sources of economic growth.
RESTRUCTURING SUPPLY CHAINS	Transaction costs between parties slowly declined. Supply chain strategies focused on cost-reduction tactics, such as offshoring and outsourcing.	With engagement and transaction costs virtually eliminated through social technology, the supply chain can be reimagined, including employment models. The potential of collective action threatens existing industry power structures. How the collective of an industry drives value and who profits will be realigned, as different social technology adoption cycles create asymmetry that the Social Company can exploit, at the expense of their socially challenged competitors.
SUBSTITUTING DIGITAL THINGS FOR PHYSICAL ONES (I.E., BITS FOR ATOMS)	Worked like a charm. Now, what do we do with the explosion of digital data we're buried under?	Competition is now being driven by information supply, not consumer demand. Winners are those with the ability to understand and interpret what the market is telling them, in real time, and to change the ways that their markets experience their company, products, or services. Value-creation reigns supreme, and disruption is the norm. Resistance is futile, and fatal.
ENABLING SELF-SERVICE	This definitely worked— remember talking to airline reservation agents? Technology altered the economic equation and made engagement easier for the consumer.	Social graphs, or the interrelationships and expanse of an individual's network, will start to take on new tasks: selling, influencing, working, informing, innovating, and delivering content, information, and an experience. The interaction, integration, and flow of information will create new self-service opportunities.

Technology effect	Historical IT impact	Social technology impact
ENABLING SELF-SERVICE (cont'd)	Value can be created this way, but if done poorly can backfire.	New interactions between people—and between people and things—will reinvent anything and everything and alter how we experience the world.
ALLOWING FOR RESOURCE SHIFTING	In theory, technology-displaced labor resources are moved to other domains, or excess labor resources are moved to where there was labor demand. Unfortunately, it has proven easier to simply eliminate the resource.	Shifting is now achievable both internally, and for more fluid external resource coupling and decoupling into a Social Company. Organizational structures and the nature of jobs and work will morph. Social technology will lower barriers to learning, and simplify and reduce the engagement costs of connecting into and out of networks and corporate ecosystems—both within a company and beyond its borders.
PROVIDING TOOLS FOR BETTER DECISION-MAKING	Having more reliable information, more quickly meant that more decisions could be made—even bad ones. Luckily, humans did generally get smarter along the way.	Do diminishing returns to data volume and velocity kick in? Is too much data a bad thing? There are no right or obvious answers anymore, as today's experiment unfolds in real time. Business and markets are in a constant state of evolution, and real-time engagement with markets will define success. Iterating with a fickle market is the new differentiator of the Social Company. The real-time flow of information will drive a different approach to strategic planning and business management overall. The Social Company lives in the present, and invents the future by using information to engage with its markets to shape the future and to quickly fix the mistakes of today.
MAKING MARKETS MORE EFFICIENT	New markets were created and old markets made more efficient through internet technology and its ability to lower transaction costs.	Social technology takes market efficiency to new heights. Business models will be created and be destroyed. Disruption will occur at a much faster pace. Transaction costs will be virtually eliminated with social technology, creating many more transactions and new markets.

Technology effect	Historical IT impact	Social technology impact
MAKING MARKETS MORE EFFICIENT (cont'd)	New markets were made and the long-tail[3] of many markets was reached efficiently.	The nature of a market in a social context also starts to morph because of this technology.
IMPROVING QUALITY AND SERVICE	Quality and consistency were improved, and the definition and nature of a "service" evolved as a result of technology. Huge productivity improvements created high quality/low cost product and service propositions everywhere. However, high levels of service consistency and quality have remained elusive.	Enter "the experience" as the next major business-management mantra and driver of competitive advantage. The *internet of things*[4] connects everything and enables experiences where there could be none before—not just between people, but between objects and people, or even between the objects. Service consistency and quality becomes achievable through this next iteration of social technology.
ELIMINATING TIME AND SPACE DISTORTIONS	Information flowed faster and more accurately, but gaps were still significant. Businesses were able to exploit knowledge asymmetries with their markets, and maintaining those asymmetries was an important part of many business models. The truth was what you made it.	The "last mile" of connectivity has been bridged: the world is largely distortion-free. Social technology closes the sizeable gaps between people, location, and time and has given us control over our spatial and temporal environments. When you know where your customers, employees, or investors are in real-time, information asymmetries collapse and truth and transparency are in the spotlight. The elimination of space and time between people—and between people and things—will continue to reinvent our world in dramatic fashion.

Note. Author's table.

---

[3] Chris Anderson, author of *The Long Tail* blog (2012), describes this succinctly:
> [O]ur culture and economy [are] increasingly shifting away from a focus on a relatively small number of "hits" (mainstream products and markets) at the head of the demand curve and toward a huge number of niches in the tail. (para. 5)

[4] A new and emerging phase, the *internet of things* refers to the ability of objects to connect to the internet. The Internet of Things Consortium (IoTC) (n.d.) supports and fosters the growth of internet-connected devices.

⋘ A Social Company-Led Renaissance

Is human destiny really just disagreement, non-stop debate, conflict, and warfare? Why can't we fix the things that are so obviously wrong with business, government, our societies, and the planet? It certainly feels like humanity is on the brink of something calamitous, not just in the United States, but also across Europe and the globe. Or are we about to embark upon a different path for business and for human societies as a whole?

Less than a decade ago, the world was reinvented before our very eyes because of social technology, and no one saw it coming. What will the world of business look like eight years from now, in 2020? How will Social Companies change business and the world around us as social technology, design, and engagement permeate every aspect of our lives?

Three themes drive my predictions for the future: collective action, overreaction, and collateral impact (which will include rapid disruption, and possibly chaos). Will customer uprisings take down entire businesses? Can employee or investor mutinies take down CEOs or boards? How do these developments impact financial statements, economies, and the balance of power globally? How will authority structures respond or react to the empowerment of the masses through these tools? What problems can the human collective now solve in business and in society?

After a century of luxuriating in a demand-driven consumption nirvana, businesses are now facing an information supply-driven change in human behavior that has caught most companies entirely off guard. But business moves fast when there's money involved, and a lot is now at stake because of social technology.

These changes are potentially rife with conflict and may be painful and disruptive at times, but I believe the potential path forward is through a business-led renaissance enabled with these tools. Humans seem to do a very poor job of fixing the foundational and obvious challenges in business and society throughout the world. Many of the problems are apparent (even obvious), acknowledged, and discussed and debated *ad nauseam*. Much like the companies I've consulted for throughout my career, we individually know what needs to be fixed throughout the world but we can't seem to collectively work through the sludge of human existence to get these challenges resolved.

A Leadership Moment

What's the role of business in our global dilemmas? Confidence in government and business has reached new lows of late (Edelman Trust Barometer 2012, slide 8), but business nonetheless has an opportunity and expectation to lead. This time, something is different: Each of us has the ability to play a much bigger role because of social technology. An individual voice can now make a difference when amplified through social technology; a collective voice, enabled through this technology has already changed the world.

Harry S. Truman once said,

> Men make history and not the other way 'round. In periods where there is no leadership, society stands still. Progress occurs when courageous, skillful leaders seize the opportunity to change things for the better. (Robbins & Robbins 1959, p. 8)

The need for business to lead in order to seize this opportunity is, in fact, not a new challenge. Sixty-five years ago, Peter Drucker had an opinion on the role of the corporation in society, which he expressed in his 1946 book *Concept of the Corporation*. Drucker commented: "[The corporation] should be so organized as to fulfill automatically its social obligations in the very act of seeking its own best self-interest" (p. 17).

Klaus Schwab, founder of the World Economic Forum in Davos, first introduced his "stakeholder" theory of management into this forum in 1971 (Pigman 2007, pp. 9–10). According to this theory, to maximize its potential a firm must consider the interests of a very broad stakeholder group beyond its customers, employees, investors, and managers. This group also includes the communities that the firm operates within, its geographic neighbors, governments, and the shared environment. In his own words in 2010, he commented:

It [stakeholder theory] is based on the principle that each individual is embedded in societal communities in which the common good can only be promoted through the interaction of all participants—and business success is also embedded in this interaction. (Schwab 2010, para. 4)

Marc Benioff, the CEO of salesforce.com and author of the introduction to this book, called out the inevitability of a "Corporate Spring" in September 2011: "When will we see the first corporate CEO fall for the same reason because his or her customers are rising up or not listening to their employees, not paying attention?" (video at 9:10). Benioff has also been a pioneer in corporate philanthropy, baking his famous 1/1/1 model into the founding of salesforce.com (his model deploys 1% of product, 1% of equity, and 1% of his employee time into community efforts). His book titled *Compassionate Capitalism: How Corporations Can Make Doing Good an Integral Part of Doing Well* (Benioff & Southwick 2004) chronicles his views.

In June 2012, Apple gave its retail-store workers (two-thirds of its workforce) a 25% raise. These employees are Apple's first line of engagement in their delivery of a unique experience, making this move a very worthwhile investment. Jonathan Blum, a contributor for *TheStreet*, commented as follows: "A golden age is at hand. All we have to do is decide we want to invest in it" (2012, last para). His "golden age" is one where companies reinvest in all of their stakeholders, which creates demand for the products of their own company and others and expands the economic ecosystem for all. This concept has been espoused since the days of Frederick Taylor—Blum even points out Henry Ford's belief in this model (para. 9).

Business is not a zero-sum game where the only goal is to gain at the expense of others in the supply chain, although this has been a prevalent practice for many years. The creation of value requires more from business leaders, as some of today's business leaders and companies realize.

Over the U.S. July 4th holiday in 2012, Starbucks CEO Howard Schultz wrote an open letter to the nation that included the following:

> I love America, but we all know there is something wrong. The deficits this country must reconcile are much more than financial, and our inability to solve our own problems is sapping our national spirit. We are better than this. (para. 5)

Using the Twitter hashtag #indivisible, he encouraged those living in the United States to "come together and amplify our voices" (para. 6). Schultz talked more about this initiative over the holiday break:

> Starbucks has always tried to manage its business by balancing profitability with a social conscience; for more than twenty years since going public, that has served us well. If you look at the history of companies "doing the right thing," most have performed extremely well. Really we are witnessing a seismic change in consumer behavior. The amount of information and transparency means we can see so much more, we have more choices and you can see what a company does in terms of what it stands for. (Serwer 2012, para. 4)

Peter Drucker, Karl Schwab, Marc Benioff, Henry Ford, and Howard Schultz... that's good company. I believe social technology will help us figure these issues out, and business will lead the way. But before we make the future, there's a past to learn from.

SOCIAL TECHNOLOGY'S
802,013-YEAR EVOLUTION

Information is the oxygen
of the modern age.
It seeps through the walls
topped by barbed wire,
it wafts across the electrified borders.

–Ronald Reagan
(Associated Press 1989, para. 11)

≺ The "Secret Sauce"

It's no secret that people are flocking to social technology in unprecedented numbers. What has driven one billion users to Facebook? Why do 85% of people on this planet (6+ billion individuals) now have a mobile phone, while landline telephone penetration never reached more than 20%? About 46% of Indian households have lavatories, while 53% have a mobile phone.[5] In a society where many lack basic amenities, state-of-the-art technology that lets people connect and communicate is widespread.

What are people trying to achieve when they collectively tweet 400 million times a day? Why are people clicking "like" over 2.7 billion times a day on Facebook?[6]

Without any central direction, mandate, or coordination, people have been drawn to this technology like moths to a flame. Individuals are doing things differently because of this technology, and these tools are amplifying what they were already doing.

Studies of why people use social networking sites conclude that they engage two very basic and primary human needs: (1) the need to belong and (2) the need for self-presentation (Nadkarni & Hofmann 2012). Researchers at Cornell found that self-esteem increased when people viewed their online profiles (Shackford 2011). Ph.D. student Rachel Meyerson (2012) summarized this phenomenon succinctly:

> Sharing news, personal observations, status updates, and photos on social networking sites are merely more sophisticated platforms for communication and social bonding than town squares, Roman baths, and French salons. Playing on our most basic psychological tenets, social networking sites, whether it's Facebook, Twitter, Google+, or a site not yet born, are here to stay. (last para.)

In short, we can't help ourselves; using these tools is intrinsic to who we are.

---

[5] Sources for these statistics are as follows: Mobile and landline phones (International Telecommunication Union 2011, Fixed telephone lines and Mobile cellular subscriptions); percentage of Indian households with plumbing and mobile phones (based on data from D. Nelson 2012, para. 1).
[6] Sources for these statistics are as follows: Tweets per day (Farber 2012, para. 1); Facebook "likes" per day (Tam 2012, para. 6).

A recent survey by the Pew Research Center also provides some clues behind why we participate in social activity online: It's fun! Pew asked users for one word to describe their experiences using social networking sites. "Good" was the most common response, and the words "fun," "great," "interesting," and "convenient" were used much more frequently than negative or neutral words (Madden & Zickuhr 2011, last para.).

Social technology-driven change is always a people-led movement—individuals flock to these tools and then figure out what to do with them. We're innovative, creative, mischievous, resourceful, and determined. We usually figure out a way to get what we want—and because of this latest version of social technology, we are finally in charge. Not everyone has figured this out yet, but some of us have. Social technology is about you, it's about us, and it's about how we engage and experience the world—as social consumers, social employees, and social investors.

Meanwhile, governments and businesses have struggled to anticipate or predict the emergence of these tools and how they can and will be used in their markets. They are better at reacting (although some might even argue with that), but once they do see what's happening they jump in with both feet, and not always for the better. Social technology has become impossible to ignore.

What's foundationally at work here? What power is pulling people to adopt these tools at such an exponential pace? Why can't we put this technology down? What do we eventually want to accomplish with these tools? Why is "social" so important?

If I extend economist W. Brian Arthur's (2009) definition of *technology*,[7] *social technology* can be defined as something that captures and exploits certain phenomena that are "social" in nature. For me, the Wikipedia description captures the essence of what users are experiencing with this technology today:

---

[7] "a collection of phenomena captured and put to use" (Arthur 2009, pp. 50–51).

The term *social* refers to the characteristic of living organisms as applied to populations of humans and other animals. It always refers to the interaction of organisms with other organisms and to their collective co-existence, irrespective of whether they are aware of it or not, and irrespective of whether the interaction is voluntary or involuntary. (wiki "social", para. 1, December 5, 2012)

This emphasis on interaction reflects the core of what I believe is being "captured and put to use" (Arthur 2009, p. 51) with social technology. Enabling interaction is about engagement, and engagement is about how we experience someone or something. New ways of interacting and different types of engagement are changing the world around us, both directly and indirectly by creating new ways to experience things.

Human behavior has changed and will continue to evolve through social technology, and when human behavior fundamentally changes, business-as-usual gets disrupted. The key to understanding social technology's impact on business is to understand the new behaviors and experiences that can be enabled and empowered by these interactions.

One good way to understand and predict what the social future may hold is to learn from the past. While Facebook's arrival onto the scene may seem to have occurred unexpectedly, I see a logical evolution taking place—however, this pattern only emerges when looking at these trends through the lens of human and social technology history. As we contemplate what is now possible, the lessons of history are very valuable, as reflected in Rule 3 of *Social Inc.*

Social Inc. Rule 3

You can learn from social technology's history.

Understanding social technology's past and its impact on human behavior and society will demonstrate why today's social technology is an integral and inevitable part of your company's evolution and social destiny. As these tools move from outside the company (e.g., Facebook) to inside (e.g., Chatter), they have the potential to impact many, if not all, aspects of any organization—in every industry from technology to services to manufacturing. Whether yours is a business-to-consumer (B2C) or a business-to-business (B2B) company, today's social technology matters. The past can guide our future, but only if we listen to its message closely enough.

◄ Homo Erectus and the First Social Technology

Most people think social technology is a recent phenomenon driven by the developments of the last several years, but major advancements in social technology were occurring a hundred years before Facebook was founded in 2004. What's more, the first social technology is much older than you might think—more than 800,000 years old, in fact.

The foundation for today's explosion in social technology has been there for a very long time, and this explosion in our personal lives is the catalyst for a business management revolution that has also been smoldering for a very long time. Understanding the disruptive potential for business requires some grounding in our ancestors' experience with prior iterations of social technologies. Powerful lessons can be learned from understanding the roots of human use, adoption, and exploitation of social technology tools and how those tools have impacted the generations of employees, consumers, and investors that have come before us.

Humans have been exploiting social technology since the beginning of recorded time. This first tool provided a range of social benefits and some social risks as well, much like it does today. It was unpredictable, feared, and difficult to bring under control—much like Facebook and Twitter have already proven to be. But the first social technology also yielded enormous benefit once it could be managed, and it literally changed the world in many favorable yet sometimes-destructive and cataclysmic ways.

We still use this ancient technology today and it's all around us, although its presence is often hidden, muted—abstracted out of the way. We couldn't live without it, but we've tamed it for the most part and leveraged its power.

Fire was the first social technology. It was discovered, controlled, and put to human use more than 800,000 years ago (Alperson-Afil & Goren-Inbar 2010, p. 1).

Fire and Facebook have more in common than you think. The evolution and use of fire and people's early experiences with today's social networking sites like Facebook are surprisingly similar.

The *International Encyclopedia of the Social and Behavioral Sciences* commented that "control [of fire] has played a far more important part in human history and social evolution than is generally acknowledged in the literature of the social sciences" (Gouldsblom 2004, p. 5672). Under-appreciated and taken for granted as an agent of change, fire as a technology went through an evolution that I believe is mirrored by today's social technology. Fire altered our behavior and changed the world around us—a tale of social technology-driven disruption.

Whether as a metaphorical or literal ancestor, fire represented the first stage of humanity's experience with a social technology. Stephen J. Pyne, often recognized as the world's leading expert on the history of fire, comments in his 2001 book *Fire: A Brief History*: "without fire humanity sinks to a status of near helplessness, a plump chimp with a scraping stone and digging stick, hiding from the night's terrors, crowding into minor biotic niches" (p. 25). I tend to think we'd be a lot less plump without fire, but you get the point.

The technology of fire changed everything. The ability to harness and exploit this tool allowed humanity to make a major step forward, and quite literally freed us from the physical world. With fire, the cold could be kept at bay and night turned into day. Land that couldn't previously sustain us became productive, as our ancestors opened up large areas for cultivation by burning off existing vegetation. Crops could be transformed with cooking and fire could be used to control other animals, which ushered in the practice of scale animal husbandry. Humans could now wander and occupy otherwise inhospitable territory. Modern industry was born from control of the flame.

Fire also had some uniquely social impacts that changed how people connected, communicated, created community, and got things done—a lot of things, and much, much differently than before. Stephen J. Pyne assessed its impact by writing, "[Fire] affected not only fields, farms, woods and wildlands, but cities, manufacturing, trade, capitalism, politics, technology, and social order—all on a planetary scale" (2001, p. 156).

Fire wasn't invented by humans; it was a randomly occurring event in nature most frequently started by a random lightning strike (Pyne 2001, p. 5). In some respects Facebook and Twitter were "stumbled upon"—they were experiments that tapped into latent desires and proved wildly popular and engaging. Their founders built them because they could, and people responded in droves because those tools tap into something instinctual, something inherent in who we are as humans.

From fire's initial discovery, it was used for light and warmth. Those were pretty obvious applications even for ancient humans, but more foundationally, something more social started to happen. People started to gather around the fire, and it became a social hub of interaction, communication, and community. Over time, fire itself has also been used as a communication medium. Both the Chinese (Lovell 2007, p. 227) and Native Americans (M. Lewis & Clark 1805) used fire and smoke signals to send messages across large distances. A burning candle in a window (Brox, 2010, p. 27) and lit fires on a rocky coast also served as ways to communicate a message (Pollard & Reid 2006, p. 90); the Vatican still uses smoke to signal when a new Pope has been chosen.

Sustainability quickly became a problem—fire had to be managed in order to stay lit. It had to be watched, much like today's social networking tools must be regularly used to stay relevant and meaningful. By watching fire, humans started to understand it and be able to control it. They kept it from going out and from spreading and releasing its destructive powers. Because it was a valuable source of light and warmth, humans also needed to keep the fire from being stolen, as fire started to create social hierarchies. Stephen A. Pyne commented that "fire's possession altered social relationships. Groups defined themselves by their shared fire. Domestication itself most likely began with the tending of the flame" (2001, p. 24).

Exactly when humans learned how to create fire is still debated, but the discovery of the Gesher Benot Ya'aqov site in northern Israel in 2008 puts these estimates at 790,000 years ago (Alperson-Afil & Goren-Inbar 2010, p. 1). Once ancient humans were able to initiate fire, they started to work with it and learned how to exploit its power. Control led to exploitation as its use proliferated across different domains.

This technology quickly became the center of the community, and human behavior was organized around the fire. Pyne describes our relationship with fire as a "Faustian pact," commenting, "If fire freed humanity, it is also true that humanity unshackled flame. Every place humans visited, they touched with fire" (2001, p. 25). Tribal or communal fires were maintained collectively, and individual fires were lit from the communal fire. Fire occupied a central spot in the community, and eventually smaller fires dispersed through the villages and towns as control over the flame evolved (Goudsblom 2004, p. 5673).

As a community hub, the fire pit became a gathering spot and natural nexus for communication (Burton 2009, p. 11). Is Facebook the equivalent of a large communal fire that we are all gathered around today? Is Pinterest an example of an emerging specialized use of what we learned from the communal hub of Facebook? According to TechCrunch and comScore, Pinterest was the fastest growing independent website to hit 10 million monthly unique users in the United States (Constine 2012, para. 1), passing this point in 2012. Are Pinterest users a niche demographic that is abandoning Facebook for a more contextual and specialized social experience focused on interest groups and visual communication? Are products like Chatter and Yammer examples of how the first generation of social tools (e.g., Facebook) morph and then embed themselves into the fabric of business?

Returning to the lessons of our past, communities began to be less nomadic but individuals were able to wander more and expand their domains. Scale agricultural pursuit and animal husbandry were enabled by fire, and changed how societies organized themselves. As these communities grew, the number of discrete fires within the community also grew—and specialty uses started to emerge around this social technology. Once this happened, how humans got things done started to change dramatically (Goudsblom 2004, p. 5674).

Once fire started to disseminate across different domains, it became exploited for different niche purposes, which launched a new era of rapid evolution and widespread social technology-fueled disruption, especially for commerce. Different craftspeople and professions started to tailor the technology of fire to their specific purposes. Eventually, the Industrial Revolution emerged and the steam engine, combustion engine, food production and preparation, electricity, incandescent lights, steel, glass, warfare, home and office heating, and countless other direct and derivative applications owe their very existence to the human ability to control and manipulate fire.

New products, services, and industries were created and flourished once the technology was understood and could be exploited. The technology of fire itself became a tool that other tools integrated with and leveraged, evolving in incredibly abstract ways to create entirely new applications that let people do things they didn't even consciously know they wanted to do.

Fear, Control, and Innovation

Today, humans interact with fire daily but no longer notice it because it is woven into our existence and largely taken for granted. However, the piercing sirens of fire engines remind us of our inability to completely master it. In human history, the proliferation of fire technology also brought the risk (and the reality) that a massive conflagration would destroy a home, a settlement, or city.

Fire increased both the productive and destructive potential of humankind, and so far, today's social technology has done the same. Given the negative publicity around social media missteps and the role played by these tools in civil uprisings, some might argue that its destructive capacity has so far outweighed its productive capacity—but this might have been the initial experience with fire as well.

In this context, control has two primary dimensions—the ability to understand and then exploit a social technology, and the desire to restrict or regulate the use of it. These two opposing forces usually emerge together. Once the ability to exploit a technology is understood and undertaken, authority and regulatory control start to impose constraints.

Can we control today's version of social technology? Who should control it? How should it be controlled? These discussions and debates have all started and are becoming more frequent and controversial as the destructive power of this technology becomes understood and exploited. But the story of fire teaches that control of social technology is a major part of its evolution, and that issues of control are a sign that a major period of social technology-fueled disruption is upon us. Regulatory control signals that these tools work, and that authority frameworks have finally woken up to the threat that social technology poses to the status quo.

Does today's social technology capture our need for community in the same way that fire did? Does the massive proliferation of today's social technology raise the risk of a new kind of conflagration? From Wall Street to the uprisings in Egypt, it would certainly appear so.

The Egyptian government took a brute force approach to controlling social technology during the country's 2011 uprising—they shut it down. Christopher Williams, a technology correspondent for *The Telegraph* reported at the time:

> The ongoing attempt by the Egyptian government to shut down all online communication is, however, a new phenomenon. It not only prevents ordinary Egyptian internet users from accessing any websites, it cripples Tor, an anti-censorship tool that technical experts and activists were using to circumvent the Facebook and Twitter blocks. The action puts Egypt, temporarily at least, in the company of North Korea, which has never allowed its citizens access to the internet. (para. 8)

In 2012, China's leading micro blogging site bowed to pressure and started to watch and control its content. CNN reported that Sina Weibo introduced new contract terms that "[seek] to prevent posts that 'spread rumors, disrupt social order, or destroy social stability'" (Hunt 2012, para. 6).

Google maintains a Transparency Report that summarizes the requests it gets from governments to remove data from its services. In the six months ending December 2011, they received over a thousand individual requests from 28 countries. They comply with some, and ignore others. Some of the recent summaries and Google's responses include the following.

> **India.** We received requests from different law enforcement agencies to remove blog and YouTube videos that were critical of Chief Ministers and senior officials of different states. We did not remove content in response to these requests. (Breakdown by Reporting Period, July–December 2010)

> **Vietnam.** We received a request from the Vietnamese government to remove search results on a particular word that generated results that contained allegedly unflattering depictions of past Vietnamese leaders. We declined the request. (Breakdown by Reporting Period, July–December 2010)

> **Canada.** We received a request from the Passport Canada office to remove a YouTube video of a Canadian citizen urinating on his passport and flushing it down the toilet. We did not remove content in response to this request. (Breakdown by Reporting Period, July–December 2011)

> **Thailand.** We received four requests from the Ministry of Information, Communication and Technology in Thailand to remove 149 YouTube videos for allegedly insulting the monarchy in violation of Thailand's lèse-majesté law. We restricted 70% of these videos from view in Thailand out of respect for local law. (Breakdown by Reporting Period, July–December 2011)

The OpenNet Initative (2012) tracks and analyzes the level of control being imposed by different governments over the internet and third-party social sites. OpenSite.org declared China, Iran, and Syria as the "Top 3" enemies of the internet in 2012, noting that Iran was the first country to sentence citizens to death for their online activity (infographic). Even regulators in the United States have been active with the proposed SOPA and PIPA (Stop Online Piracy Act, Protect IP Act) regulations that were eventually shot down in 2012 (Newman 2012).

However, control is a natural part of the progression of all social technology, and it indicates an important pivot point in the cycle of social technology adoption. Attempts to impose control signal the start of a period of innovation and the oncoming of disruption across many different domains.

Two dimensions of control drive innovation: The ability to exploit social technology extends and enables people's desire for things that are better, faster, and cheaper, while regulation feeds people's insatiable desire to work around the boundaries imposed by others. Control is required to drive innovation and the specialized use of any social technology. Fire's productive capacity was only realized once humans were able to exert some level of influence and control over it—to start it, stop it, move it, protect it, and use it. The ability to exploit the power of these technologies requires an understanding of how and why they work, and how to manipulate them.

Business's approach to controlling the risks associated with social technology has been similar to that of some governments: ignoring the tools or denying their employees access. These knee-jerk reactions are diminishing as a business practice, however.

Businesses that chose the path of denial quickly realized that while they could ignore social technology, it would not ignore them or their customers, employees, or investors. These technologies tap into fundamental instincts that are natural to humankind. Business isn't like government—employees, customers, and investors can vote with their feet and their wallets. These businesses soon realized that ignoring this latest social technology incarnation also meant ignoring the behavioral instincts of the people who matter most to their companies.

Censorship finds its way into any communication medium and has been the initial control reaction from governments and companies; but not all regulation is bad—building codes and flame-retardant clothing are good things, for example. There is no doubt that policies and governance over social technology will become more structured and formal, from companies and governments alike. Today's social technology is very much a force of nature, much like fire. The information security approach that companies deploy is changing because of the specific risks around these new tools. As a result, corporate governance is also changing and boards need to adapt to understand the new strategic and risk environments in which they now operate.

Once a social technology can be controlled and is distributed throughout niche domains, a curious thing starts to happen: It starts to disappear, becoming a part of the fabric of our lives that we no longer think about discretely. Fire has long been abstracted into the background of our lives.

Most people don't think of the incandescent light bulb as a use of fire, but it is a reflection of the high level of control humans achieved over this primitive tool. The humble light bulb was mastered by Thomas Edison in 1879; this development and refined control over the combustion process further allowed the technology of fire to diffuse, directly and indirectly, across society. (Ironically, the incandescent light bulb is now on the decline. The much greater energy efficiency of compact fluorescent lamps and LEDs is forcing the reliable, although comparatively inefficient, incandescent light bulb into regulatory extinction (Koeppel 2011).)

As the LED reinvents the incandescent light bulb, it is also morphing as a social technology. Phillips Hue LED is a "personal wireless lighting" system that can be controlled by a mobile smart phone (Phillips 2012). Without even a light switch, users can turn lights on remotely, change lighting colors to suit a mood, or share their lighting choices. Through social technology, Phillips is taking something as ordinary as the light bulb and making it into social experience. Once 5 billion of these social LEDs are part of the infrastructure, will there be large-scale, social, energy-management ramifications for the way people interact and experience their worlds from something as innocuous as a light bulb?

The unending quest for efficiency, greater productivity, and ways to experience our world spares nothing and no one. Old technology is constantly under threat and will always be replaced by new technology that is more efficient and effective, either voluntarily or eventually by external forces. For this reason, legacy IT environments in many companies are doomed—it's just a matter of time whether a company pulls the plug itself or market forces do it from the outside.

For CEOs, executives, managers, and employees, how will the distribution of today's social technology and social business management concepts be adopted and applied in different markets, functional areas, or within different teams throughout a company? Customers have flocked to this technology; that's the obvious and immediate challenge. Now companies have to figure out how this technology affects and interacts with every aspect of doing business. Today's social technology has already proven to be as unpredictable to human behavior as fire was, and its path will reach a similar destiny—disruption of the status quo. This is inevitable.

The history of fire as a social technology is a lesson about disruption, for good and bad. The lesson also teaches that changes in human behavior brought about by new social tools and technologies are the fulcrum for the resulting disruption. There is much to learn from observing the important role that control plays in the overall cycle of transformation and innovation, as well.

✄ The 4 Cs: Connecting, Communicating, Collaborating, and Community

Fire as a historical frame for social technology introduces the behavioral context of these tools. There are four core phenomena that all social technologies exploit in some way, shape, or fashion: connecting, communicating, collaborating, and community (Figure 2-1). These effects are

Figure 2-1. The 4 Cs of *Social Inc.* Author's image.

present and exploited by the major social technologies that humankind has experienced throughout our evolution (discussed below). The way that new technologies "capture and put to use" (Arthur 2009, p. 51) these effects changes with the nature of a specific social technology. These behaviors all circle the human desire to interact and engage with one another and the world around us, and that's why we're uncontrollably drawn to these tools— and always will be.

Really "sticky" social technologies engage all four behaviors. For example, some analysts think LinkedIn will outlive Facebook because LinkedIn's context is much deeper, which relates to community and collaboration. People on

LinkedIn know it is used for career and business purposes and connections (Wallace 2012).

For the most part, people on LinkedIn are representing their professional achievements to others in the business community and maintaining an active business network through this technology. They can update their network with what they are doing at any point in time, join groups with common backgrounds, find and meet new people with similar interests, and get introduced to useful people they don't know who may be a world away. Users tell others about their travels, job changes, and achievements, and even show others who else is in their business network.

The context of work, career, and employment is extremely focused and compelling for many people; people who opt into LinkedIn self-select themselves into this kind of contextual community. Because there is specific context for the entire community, the actions that derive from this particular social technology can be more specific and meaningful. Facebook, so far, has a broader context and is less of a community that is driving toward a collaborative and common objective.

The widespread personal adoption and application of today's social technology has done business an enormous favor by teaching billions how to use these tools. As individuals, we have learned the mechanisms of engaging by connecting, sharing, liking, poking, friending, tweeting, pinning,[8] and so on.

Even more important than our advancement up the learning curve, using this social technology has expanded our thinking about what is potentially possible with this unprecedented level of connectivity and interaction. It is now business's turn to figure out how to leverage these tools, and the 4 Cs are the key to understanding why and how social technology will take hold across the business landscape.

---

[8] "Pinterest is a social network…[that] fits into the category of 'visual bookmarking.'…[It] lets you 'pin' any photo from the Internet to a 'board' on its site" (Madrigal 2012).

Connecting

Establishing connections is the starting point for any social technology. In one way or another, social technologies bring us together—sometimes in person, sometimes just by voice, sometimes by connecting us over large distances or even through time. Social technologies create new ways for people to establish and sustain relationships as well as helping to keep us engaged with one another, or with our surroundings. They deliver an experience around relationships and our desire to interact. They connect us to the people we know, and to those whom we don't yet know. They give us access to each other; sometimes this is welcomed and sometimes it's not.

Once we're connected to each other, many fascinating things start to happen as we expand our interactions and engagement. Connections are also not necessarily just between people. As we start to connect with our entire environment (i.e., with things and with those things that connect to other things) everything can and will be reimagined once again. The "internet of things" is a concept that is starting to become a reality. Credited to Kevin Ashton back in 1999, this vision contemplates an internet where objects gather data without human intervention (Ashton, 2009). This data then creates or drives an interaction with human customers, or with other things through the internet. Until now, social technology has been about human-to-human interaction—introduce a new dimension of object-driven engagement, and the social concepts of connecting, communicating, collaborating, and community can and are being rethought once again.

Communicating

Social technology is a great facilitator and enabler of communication. With social technology we communicate in new and more efficient ways and we communicate more—and humans love to communicate. Frequently, the technology itself is a new communication mechanism that lets people express themselves in a different way than they have been able to before. Human horizons expand and the realm of what is possible starts to broaden through these new communications. People learn, understand, and think of new things.

We leverage the lessons of others, and advance our intellect. However, people can start to confuse each other as well and conflict can arise—our similarities as well as our differences get exposed, and we can also be manipulated and deceived. Making sense out of what is being communicated and filtering the good from the bad becomes a new challenge.

The domain of communication between people and things (and between things and things) is also being stretched in new ways. Innovation around the human–machine interface through social technology will recast the nature of content and impact our communication and collaboration approaches in many new ways.

Collaborating

Effective collaboration means getting things done together, enabling collective action, and being better than any one could be individually. The best social technology drives people to act, to do something—to evolve. Collaboration is different than cooperation. *Cooperation* is a hierarchical division of labor, or in other words, the typical design of business. *Collaboration* is "a coordinated, synchronous activity that is the result of a continued attempt to construct and maintain a shared conception of a problem" (Roschelle & Teasley 1995, p. 70), and social technology makes collaborating easier and more efficient. Business, for the first time with today's social tools, can now scale and sustain collaboration in ways never before possible. Collaboration is not necessarily hierarchical; in fact, it usually works better without hierarchy.

Collaboration can overthrow governments (and it has, recently). Collaboration makes social technology powerful, massively disruptive, and feared by authority frameworks everywhere. The need to get things done with ever-increasing levels of efficiency pulls social technology into business, broadly and deeply, where every business niche will adapt and apply it for a specific purpose.

Community

Community brings context to humans connecting, communicating, and collaborating. Once we start connecting and communicating, communities arise. A business is inherently contextual because it's a community. The missions and objectives of companies are usually pretty clear to most employees, investors, or customers—although, I realize, not always.

Social technologies create community where there was none before. People organize themselves around and through this technology; it not only brings us together but also acts as the glue that can keep us together. Social technology changes how we live and how we behave and with whom. People can start to think as a group, in unison. Communities can organize, act, and engage at scale and do things that individuals on their own could not accomplish.

The community itself can become important and can take on its own identity, and the individual can become subordinated to the group identity. This dynamic can have its downside, as individuals can choose sides and stop thinking for themselves.

Back to the Social Technology Future

As the example of fire demonstrates, social technology has a past—a turbulent, traumatic, and unexpected past—which surprises a lot of people. The 4 Cs of connecting, communicating, collaborating, and community are four core phenomena that define the essence of what is being captured with social technology.

Understanding the 4 Cs and the history around how social technologies have exploited and shaped the world is the start to understanding the potential impact of today's social technology on the future of business. Today's internet, the cloud, mobile devices, and social software tools like Chatter—these tools exploit the 4 Cs in new ways. Businesses can do things very differently than they have before, and additional lessons from history can help us understand what is happening and what's at stake.

◆ Gutenberg Prints Up 385% Faster Economic Growth

In 1436, Johannes Gutenberg invented a major social technology: movable type printing, commonly referred to as the printing press (Man 2009). This technology freed people from their information environment, and the world has thankfully never been the same.

Who thinks about the written word anymore? It is entirely taken for granted today, but the world was a vastly different place before writing was scalable. Before the printing press, written information was a rare and valuable commodity. With mass-produced words, the 4 Cs of social technology were exploited in new and astounding ways. Buringh and van Zanden (2009) refer to books as "a crucial part of the information infrastructure and, in a way, the 'hardware' which stored all ideas" (p. 410).

Gutenberg's social technology liberated information by providing a means to efficiently replicate the hand-written word. Once words could be copied, they could be distributed. Once distributed, they could be learned from. No longer was knowledge limited to what those in close proximity shared, taught, or laboriously reproduced by hand. Information and knowledge started to flow across vast distances between people who had never met, and between the living and the dead. People were able to document and share their thinking; others could learn from prior efforts and build upon that work without being neighbors. The quality of information transfer also improved considerably.

Economic changes in the cost of information acquisition and exchange also inevitably produced social changes. Because of Gutenberg's technology, the price of books declined rapidly (Buringh & van Zanden 2009, p. 433), which directly increased the consumption of books by those who were literate and dropped the cost barriers to becoming literate. Not only did Gutenberg's invention allow for the mass distribution of information, but it did so through economies of scale which were then passed on to readers. Lower book prices—estimated by as much as 67% (p. 441)—also lowered the costs of knowledge acquisition and directly drove demand for more books.

Knowledge acquisition is price-sensitive—that is, when the price to acquire it drops, demand for knowledge increases. Literacy rates improved as a result of the printing press, and the world moved on, better informed and smarter than it had been.

Gutenberg's invention also had a positive economic impact in the centuries before 1800. Advancements in human capital formation attributable to relative levels of book production (i.e., literacy) played a significant role in the wealth and poverty of nations (Baten & van Zanden 2008, p. 219): Those countries with higher levels of human capital formation were able to leverage it by initiating or participating in the Industrial Revolution of the 19th century (p. 231).

The history of the printed word (i.e., the book) as a social technology illustrates several foundational issues. As a communication vehicle, the printing press was a major leap forward in the efficiency and effectiveness of conveying information. Communities morphed and human behavior changed around the printed word: Learning institutions, libraries, and newspapers all became central to the human experience. The printed word pulled people together and created community, much like the communal fire pit of ancient times. The printed word both brought context and shaped context—the mass-produced word created action in a big way. The macroeconomic forces at play improved the future for those who understood them, and held back the progress of those who did not.

Prior to Gutenberg's invention, the creation or transcription of manuscripts was a time-consuming and labor-intensive process. The written word was in scarce supply as were those who could read it. As a result, it was a valuable and closely controlled medium that the "elite" protected to establish and maintain power. Marshall Poe (2010) describes this by saying,

> Because they and they alone could write, the princes and priests of the Manuscript Era could conduct their business (which, as it happened, was everyone's business) and control the *lingua sacre* [sacred language] in private, out of the view of their ordinarily illiterate subjects. (p. 123)

These overt restrictions constrained how freely data, information, and knowledge were developed and shared, with whom they were shared, what people learned, and what they thought. Because of these limitations, the information and knowledge between a manuscript's covers diffused slowly among people. Human evolution was stunted and knowledge limited by an individual's specific geography. Knowledge could not be captured or transferred quickly or efficiently over distance or over time, and the limitations of oral knowledge transfer made physical proximity a major constraint. Power was maintained by those who controlled and monopolized writing and reading. Printing, however, both set the truth free and turned up its volume (Poe 2010, p. 120).

After Gutenberg, knowledge-acquisition became much more efficient than it had been before. Social technology in the form of the mass-produced printed book and related texts put a stake partway into the heart of an immense, inefficient information market. Once information and knowledge could be reproduced and distributed, there was a profound impact on human behavior and business through its productivity benefits: "Print offered traders compelling efficiencies" (Poe 2010, p. 109). The printing press has been declared as "the most important invention between the invention of writing itself and the computer" (Butler 2007, last para.) and it created an enormous wave of social technology disruption that continues to wash over us today.

Social technologies have a tendency toward rapid diffusion and adoption, and printed books were no different. They proliferated across Europe, faster than the spread of fire technology, but nothing like the pace of social technology adoption today. In the 6th and 7th century, an average total of 120 books a year were produced annually in Western Europe—in 1790, total production was more than 20 million books (Buringh & van Zanden 2009, p. 439). This diffusion occurred despite the fact that literacy rates were low and physical distribution was laborious, expensive, and cumbersome.

An Information Explosion Pulls Business into the Future

As we also saw with fire, this major leap forward in social technology also brought disruption. The Protestant Reformation at the beginning of the 16th century is largely recognized as the first revolutionary mass movement spurred on by the social technology of the printed word (MacCulloch 2005, p. 147). When the Catholic Church controlled the handwritten manuscripts, early books were largely religious texts. But with the printing press, books eventually broadened to many subject areas and society started to change in profound ways. This expansion bred the creative and widespread adoption of this social technology into daily human life.

Mass production of the written word in its many different forms (books, newspapers, brochures, pamphlets, etc.) freed humanity from the inefficiencies of person-to-person communication. Communication speed and quality increased; learning accelerated, quite literally. Verbally exchanged information travels at less than half the speed of written communications: The average adult speaking English in the United States speaks at about 100 words per minute, can listen comfortably at 150-160 words per minute, but can read at 250-300 words per minute (Bailey 2000, items 3, 2, and 1).

Verbal communications are also prone to distortion. As a child, I played the game "telephone" in which ten people line up and the first one whispers something into the second one's ear. The message then passes down the line, with each person whispering to the next what they just heard, until the tenth person repeats the message aloud. An original message such as "The big brown bear swam the raging river, and caught a big fish" comes out as "The bear swam the brown river with angry fish."

A written message passed down the same line would come out exactly as it started—no communication distortion. However, "garbage in, garbage out" remains a problem; if the original message is inaccurate, it stays inaccurate. Today's social technology has the ability to address both of these quality issues (see Part 3). In business, social accountability around the quality of information that gets shared in a more open forum is improving through the use of tools like Chatter, Jive, or Yammer. Better information quality and flow is a workplace productivity enhancement in any century.

Today we take the written word for granted. Electronic media like text messaging, blogs, wikis, tweets, and email are ingrained in our daily lives. The written word has been abstracted into the background of our existence, but this much data, information, and knowledge has never travelled so far, so fast.

In 2010, Google estimated that 129,864,880 book titles had been published in the history of the world (Taycher 2010, last para.). From 120 titles per year in the 7th century (Buringh & van Zanden 2009, p. 439) to 129,864,880 million total titles by 2010—Gutenberg would be proud. However, the total number of books in print is much greater than 130 million: In 2010 alone, 2.57 billion books of all formats were sold (Bosman 2011, para. 2), including 114 million e-books (para. 9).

As a way to capture and distribute information and knowledge accurately and efficiently, the printed word was a significant advancement in social technology. Before Gutenberg and the printed book, information did not move quickly. With the printing press, the book, and its derivatives, humankind had its first medium for mass communication and mass transformation. Through the impact of the printing press, Poe summarizes, "societies became, eventually, more productive, better governed, and more humane" (2010, p. 151).

Gutenberg 's invention raised humanity's collective intelligence, but as with fire, the book as a social technology had both a productive and a destructive capacity. With proliferation of the written word, people began to understand the power of this technology. Control and regulation soon followed, much like it did with fire. In 1559, Pope Alexander IV formalized his approach to censoring books when he published the *Index Librorum Prohibitorm*, or *Index of Prohibited Books*. The church abolished this practice over 400 years later, in 1966 (Newth 2010, para. 6). Control through censorship started to take hold.

What do all of the following books have in common?[9]

> Little Red Riding Hood
> Alice's Adventures in Wonderland
> The Color Purple
> Catcher in the Rye
> The Adventures of Huckleberry Finn
> The Harry Potter series

As you probably guessed, they have all been censored in some fashion in the United States. *Little Red Riding Hood*—really?

The practice of censorship by ruling parties and authority structures is a very old occurrence. Even Plato baked it into his grand social design, saying, "The rulers will need to use a quite considerable amount of falsehood and deception for the benefit of those ruled" (360 B.C.E., p. 161). In Plato's vision for society, the "elite" should govern the less-than-elite through this kind of censored approach, in order to protect them from themselves (p. 161).

History shows that control is a common denominator with social technology, as the liberation of communication invites control through censorship. The printed word connected people and their thoughts without regard to distance, discrimination, or familiarity. With this new, scalable way to communicate, community formed in multiple contexts from the physical library to the classroom, office, and church. Books brought people together, but they also tore us apart. Human behavior reacted unexpectedly to the social technology of the book—many viewed books and the knowledge they imparted as a threat, an occurrence and mindset that can still exist today.

The exploitation of these breakthrough social technologies changed the human relationship with the world around us. Fire freed us from our physical environment, and the book from our information environment, and inherent in this freedom is the empowerment of humankind over our physical and information domains.

---

[9] *Little Red Riding Hood* (Huffington Post 2011); *Alice's Adventures in Wonderland* (Baldassarro 2011); *The Color Purple, Catcher in the Rye*, and the *Harry Potter* series (American Library Association, 2012); *The Adventures of Huckleberry Finn* (Rawls 2011).

Empowerment drives disruption, and the way companies view, relate, engage, and manage interactions is fundamentally changing once again. Customer empowerment with today's social technology requires a shift in customer strategy and approach. Today's tools also change the dynamics between businesses and their employees, investors, competitors, and supply chain partners—with everyone. When people are empowered, human behavior evolves. When human behavior evolves, every business is impacted.

As the evolution of fire and the printed word and their impact on society have shown, human behavior is at the root of social technologies. The recent advent of e-books reflects the latest incarnation of the book as a social technology. What impact will e-books have on the growth rate of published titles? Will more published titles make humanity smarter? Will information flow faster? There will certainly be more information, that's obvious, but how much more and of what quality? The book as a 600-year-old social technology is morphing before our eyes, in real time.

The 600-year-old printed book has long been a social object and social technology in and of itself, and now it is being reinvented around today's social technology. In 2012, Apple announced that it was reinventing the textbook with iBook Author and iBooks 2 (Apple 2012a). No longer just digital representations of text, books are now becoming interactive and social experiences. As a result, the world is being (and will increasingly be) flooded with more specialized and nuanced content along with easier and more efficient ways to distribute, share, augment, and then consume that content.

Instinctively, one would surmise that the printing press had a positive economic impact. Economic research on its impact is scarce, but Jeremiah Dittmar, Assistant Professor of Economics at American University, explored this issue and concluded that cities adopting the printing press in the late 1400s "grew at least 20 percentage points—and as much as 78 percentage points—more than similar cities that did not [have the printing press] over the period 1500–1600" (2011, p. 22). Is our past teaching us that information freedom is a driver of economic growth?

Dittmar (2011) concludes "that major changes in the ways ideas can be stored and transmitted may have far reaching consequences" (p. 4) for humankind's intellectual development. Dittmar's research indicates that on average, cities that adopted Gutenberg's type of printing press had a 385% faster growth rate: 27% growth versus 7% for those cities that did not adopt the printing press (Dittmar 2011, Table II).

Information Supply and the New Competitive Landscape

What does this much information flowing this quickly mean for business in today's context? The challenge is very different today than in Gutenberg's time. Are humans collectively smarter than we were 600 years ago? Of course. Has business changed fundamentally? Has society? Absolutely. Now that information is flowing even more freely and with such velocity, how do we harness it? This is where today's social technology steps in—making sense out of the "noise" is where these tools truly excel.

The information spigot has turned into a fire hose, and information is only as good as the ability to make use of it. The challenge of the information fire hose is real time, massive amounts of data, evoking the image of a person dying of thirst in the middle of a vast salt-water ocean. The paradox of this challenge has monumental implications for business. Are there diminishing returns or are there increasing returns for a real-time, massive information flow?

This level of information flow is entirely unprecedented. If adoption of the printing press drove economic growth at a rate 3.85 times that of economies without this technology, what will these latest developments mean for economies and business? The mass printing of text was a productivity boon to business 600 years ago that made this tool a business necessity: "reading and writing became a cost of doing business in early modern Europe" (Poe 2010, p. 109). I believe today's information freedom and velocity will once again contribute to innovation and economic growth. As these tools are adopted and understood, their impact may be just as dramatic.

The micro-publishing platform of Twitter has taken Gutenberg's invention to the most extreme application yet—delivering a 140-character message instantaneously to a global audience, and then allowing that audience to share, amplify, explain, refute, support, change, or augment the message. Context is what makes sense out of the communication noise, which makes this ultra-short type of communication incredibly relevant for business. Twitter taught users the skill of brevity. Businesses need to figure out how to use this new type of information flow to connect, communicate, collaborate, and create community with employees, customers, investors, and partners. What can business do better, faster, or cheaper with this approach to information?

The niche application of social technology into individual businesses and ecosystems is only just beginning. Where technicians (e.g., refrigerator, copy machine, or industrial product support and service workers) need to travel to the device or location, does a collaboration tool like ServiceMax's ServicePulse for social field service management improve productivity, profitability, or sales growth? Frost and Sullivan's (2006) research on business collaboration indicates that globally, collaboration is the key driver of business performance—more so than strategic orientation or market dynamics (p. 7). Collaboration positively impacts each of the key areas of profitability: profit growth, sales growth, labor productivity, customer satisfaction, innovation, and quality. They estimate that 36% of a company's performance is due to its collaborative capability (as measured by their index, p. 7). They conclude their research with a strong message: "In short, the more collaborative enterprises are, the better they perform" (p. 18).

The story of the printing press shows that people want to communicate, to share what they know, and to learn from others, as well as demonstrating that information freedom is a good thing for economic growth. As people build upon each other's collective knowledge and collaborate in different ways through today's social technology, I believe business will start to innovate and solve problems that could not be solved before.

◂ Alexander Graham Bell Dials Up a New Social Technology

As a pivotal part of humanity's social technology journey, the telephone has done an incredible job of freeing people from their geographic environment. The first telephone call was made on March 10, 1876 (America's Library n.d., para. 1)—136 years ago. I've been alive for a little over a third of the time that this social technology has been in existence. This technology figuratively shrank the world. If I know a person's phone number, and increasingly even if I don't, I can pretty much talk or instantly communicate with that person—or just about anyone else—anywhere on the planet, whenever I want.

Once communication and information could travel quickly beyond the confines of personal geography, a big world became much, much more manageable. Communities started to change as people became more mobile because they could stay in touch with their immediate family from far away. Business changed: New markets on the other side of the planet could be managed and better understood with more regular communications. The telephone morphed into the telex, and fax machines and modems started to transmit digital information over vast distances. The spoken word was distributed, along with many other kinds of content. Local community started to become less of a hub of daily life, as each individual had an extended network that she could be in touch with easily and regularly.

Reinventing Life and Business through the Telephone

In his 2011 book, *The Master Switch: The Rise and Fall of Information Empires*, Tim Wu described how the telephone started to change behavior and expand relationships beyond the physical confines of people's rural communities in the early 1900s: "With a telephone in the house comes a new companionship, new life, new possibilities, new relationships, and attachments for the old farm by both old and young" (p. 47). He goes on to explain that in 1904, as the telephone began to take hold across the United States, local independent phone companies started to wire rural areas, closing the geographic gap between neighbors and communities and opening up new worlds where information flowed in different ways and at a different pace.

By 1880—four years after the invention of the landline telephone—there were 133,000 telephones in use (Farley 1998–2006, Part 4, para. 15). Here's a fantastic first-person account of the early days of the telephone, from a woman born in 1907.

The Telephone Reinvents Society

Years before there were big telephone systems, many very small companies were in use in our area of Indiana. It was not uncommon for neighbors to have different lines, and be unable to communicate by phone unless they had both lines. The more affluent had at least two phones. We had only one, and it served our need well except at cherry-picking time, when Auntie took calls on one of her two lines and then relayed them on her second phone, which was on the same hook-up as ours.

How did they work? There were always six or seven on one line. To reach the operator you turned one long crank of the little handle on the side of the phone box, a lady answered and asked who you wanted, and she rang them. If she wasn't busy, sometimes she would chat a bit before ringing the number desired. No one on your line heard you call the operator, but if a call came to someone on your line, all line members heard.

How did they distinguish who the calls were for? There was a system of rings—as two short–one long, one short–one long, etc.—and neighbors soon learned who was being called by the code of rings. If someone wanted to know what was going on at some home, all that was necessary was to listen for the ring, and quietly slip down the receiver off the hook and listen in. This was such common practice that a third party (listener) often joined in the conversation making it three-way, or, at times, four-way, if another decided to join in, not far different from the modern day coffee break.

In case of illness neighbors seldom phoned the home, but depended on the neighborhood listening service for information.

While there was much non-essential talk, there was a dearth of boy–girl conversation or even girl–girl talk. Who wanted to whisper sweet nothings, or have the talk about "him" literally broadcast over the community?

It was complicated, inefficient, often out of service, but it did form a link of togetherness that scattered farm families would not otherwise have.

There was a class distinction of a sort because those who could afford two phones were considered in a higher socioeconomic group, but in the case of emergencies those who had, shared willingly with those who had not. Thus the community was bound together by a myriad of wires and brown boxes with a hand crank on one side. Another time, another era—but definite progress in the evolution of communication. (reprinted with author's permission from Miller 2009)

Is the Telephone an Asset or Liability?

There is no doubt that the invention of the landline telephone significantly impacted people's personal lives, but by today's standards personal adoption started very slowly with only about 40% of U.S. households having telephone service by 1942—65 years after its invention (Fischer 1992, p. 255). The telephone was initially adopted largely as a tool for business: "The telephone began as a novelty, became business's substitute for the telegraph, and then evolved into a mass product" (p. 23).

While broad consumer adoption was partly constrained by the pace with which far-flung communities could be wired together, along with cost, consumer adoption was also constrained by a lack of understanding of what this technology could be used for. This was the case for business and individuals alike. Significant effort was spent on educating the public about this social technology, "convincing people that their [Alexander Graham Bell and his backers'] 'toy' was a useful tool" (Fischer 1992, p. 65).

This situation is not dissimilar to what is happening today, with businesses struggling to understand what today's social technology can be used for. However, unlike with the landline phone, today's consumers are adopting the new technology in droves—forcing companies to figure out how these tools can be used for business.

Much like fire, which blazed the path for the industrial revolution, the telephone laid the groundwork for the information age. As the telephone penetrated businesses, companies discovered some unexpected consequences. The marketing and sales pitch offered up by the early telephone salesman promised that it would "increase efficiency, save time and impress customers" (Fischer 1992, p. 66). Early advertisements for business telephony highlighted the productivity enhancements that this social communication device could bring, such as immediate savings of "over a week per year of the time of every telephone user from the $10 a week clerk to the $100,000 a year executive" (Automatic Electric Co. 1916, p. 1870).

In this same advertisement, a footnote at the bottom of the page references a manual to help executives understand the telephone and its impact for their businesses. Its title, *Your Telephone—Asset or Liability*, suggests that executives at the time questioned whether the telephone was a positive or negative influence in the workplace (Automatic Electric Co. 1916, p. 1870). This sounds like many of the discussions I have heard in boardrooms about today's social technology.

The telephone became an indispensible productivity tool, changing the way that companies marketed to, sold to, and serviced their customers—often for the better, but sometimes for worse. The telephone connected people in new ways, changed the pace of business, speeding up communications, creating new communities, and changing collaboration as mail and meetings gave way to telephone calls.

While fire and the printed word provided two key building blocks for today's social technology revolution, it was the telephone that truly took the concept of social networking beyond the community and created global connectivity and interaction. However, global fixed landline telephone penetration has never been above 20% and peaked in 2005 (Türk Telekom Group 2012, Figure 1.6). In contrast, mobile telephone penetration rates were only slightly above 30% in 2005 (Figure 1.6) but 87% globally by mid-2012 (Ericsson 2012, p. 5). Moreover, Ericsson projects that mobile subscriptions will reach 9 billion by 2017, far in excess of the human population, because machine-to-machine connections will continue to increase the number (p. 6).

The human experience of being globally connected as a species through the social technology of the mobile telephone is a very recent phenomenon. Ericsson summarizes what they see as the impact of this social technology: "[mobile] changes how people behave and how they leverage mobility to communicate and to improve their daily lives, through new and existing services. Users now demand connectivity anywhere and anytime" (2012, p. 3).

While there are few, if any, humans who do not use fire today, its many abstracted forms do not reach every citizen of the earth. For those who do not know how to read, books are irrelevant. The global adult literacy rate is 84%, which means there are about 775 million adults on the planet who cannot read (UNESCO 2012a, p. 1). These people can, however, speak and listen—and with global mobile phone penetration rates at 85% and rising (International Telecommunication Union 2011, Mobile cellular subscriptions), today's social technology offers them increased participation in knowledge sharing as well as the possibility of increased literacy. However, everyone does not progress at the same pace—this is true in society, and it's true in business. Unfortunately for business, the Darwinian inevitability of the for-profit, capitalist model destroys those that cannot or will not evolve, faster and more mercilessly than society does.

Herein lies the lesson for business—time is not on your side. Social technology-driven evolution and revolution is disrupting the business status quo once again. Those who ignore today's social technology in their businesses are losing competitive ground to those who have embraced it. Laggards will face an enormous—and potentially impossible—uphill battle to reclaim lost ground.

Because of the social technology of the telephone, this planet feels like and is experienced like a much smaller place, and people want information to flow even faster. Today's social technology phenomenon allows information-exchange that can be instantaneous and the world—and everyone and everything in it—is potentially at our fingertips.

⪻ The Arrival of Spatial and Temporal Relevance

To say that social technology has longevity is an understatement. Fire, the printed word, and the telephone—three ancestors to today's developments—still impact daily human life. Each owes its existence in some part to the technologies that preceded it. Whether evolutionary or revolutionary, disruption is an indisputable result of new social technology, as reflected in Rule 4 of *Social Inc.*

Social Inc. Rule 4
Changes in human behavior disrupt the business status quo.

Major social technologies impact humanity for a very long time because they foundationally alter behavior and the way we experience our environments. Fire liberated people from the physical environment, the printed word from the information environment, and the telephone from the geographic environment.

Distortions and inefficiencies due to distance and time are now vanishing because of today's social technology. The last mile has been bridged. A degree of intimacy and immediacy never before possible is now at hand because space- and time-based relevancy can influence anything, and everything. Knowing where people and/or things are relative to each other, and at a particular point in time—these are new factors in creating a value proposition for companies.

Information flow has generally been an inefficient market. People heard about things long after they happened in many cases, and sometimes didn't ever hear about them. I might hear about an event on the evening news or in the newspaper, sometimes days later—sometimes never. Getting a message to someone used to consume a lot of time and was expensive, at least compared to today. Fire had to be seen in order for a person to be able to read or understand its message. The Pony Express was not "express" by our standards today, but at the time this technology was revolutionary. In 1860, messages sent by Pony Express traveled between the coasts of the United States in about 10 days (Pony Express National Museum n.d., April 14, 1860 timeline). Early telephones were a major improvement but still required an operator to connect the caller to another person. Thanks to Twitter and mobile devices like the iPhone and tablets, people can now know instantaneously when most things happen, regardless of where they happen.

One area of improved information flow is very publicly affecting business management: Customer dissatisfaction or satisfaction can now be aired immediately and amplified exponentially. Companies can reach their customers, employees, investors, and partners wherever they are, anytime.

For example, South Korean manufacturer LG recently released their Smart ThinQ line of appliances that use home wi-fi to connect to the internet. LG (2012) says that with a smartphone, users can know what is inside their refrigerator and when each food item will expire. Follow this capability through the entire supply chain, and it's easy to imagine the ability to connect to your grocery store of choice and have them deliver what you need, exactly when you need it—or to have your Smart ThinQ refrigerator conduct a weekly scan and complete a grocery list that gets fulfilled automatically. Your refrigerator could even tell you if you have the ingredients for a particular recipe, and any missing items could be delivered by roving grocery trucks. Moreover, how does the grocery supply chain adapt? Do large grocery stores disappear? Does spoilage go down because we're procuring and then consuming non-durable goods on a real-time basis? The implications are not only individual—if you and your neighbors both have this technology, you could potentially save by making group purchases or sharing as a community. These somewhat obvious ramifications, and many more abstract ones, alter the nature of the entire industry.

Today's social technology also gives the power of collective action to customers, at a scale never before possible. A company's brand can be "occupied" in an instant by a collaborative effort that can mobilize millions around the world. What would happen if a million customers decided to go on strike against a particular company, brand, product, or service? What if customers quickly organized a massive boycott, a collective action to not buy from a company for a period of time—or to abandon it altogether and go to a competitor? This will happen. There are already skirmishes occurring along these lines (see Part 5: Tropicana Turns Oranges into Lemons and Back Again). The "petition platform" service Change.org is already rallying hundreds of thousands for various causes including corporate accountability.

Up until now, the inefficiencies around customer information-flow could be a friend to business, as companies could wear down complaints over time and service problems could dissipate. Not anymore.

Space and *time*—the distance between you as a consumer and a particular product or service—has evaporated. What can business do with this intimacy and immediacy? What new risks emerge? How does the experience that consumers, employees, investors, and business partners have with a company change with this new dynamic? As individuals, our expectations continue to rise as a result of what we are already experiencing daily in our personal lives through these tools—the bar keeps getting higher for business.

Corporate leaders need to recognize that new market efficiencies can be realized between their company and customers, employees, investors, and business partners. Businesses have the ability to know where their stakeholders are and engage them immediately. Their stakeholders can also engage each other or your competitors, in the same fashion.

Interactions are changing: Engagement has a different meaning when coupled with spatial and temporal relevancy, and the experiences that businesses choose to provide are different when they integrate this social technology into their value proposition. Can companies define their own unique offering by changing what it's like to do business with them on these terms? Michael Porter argues that strategic competition is about being unique (Magretta 2012, pp. 29, 31), which means thriving on innovation. Can you create value in your markets through today's social technology tools and techniques and then, of course, capture some of it for yourself? I think that you not only can, but you must.

Reinventing Business, All Over Again

Fire, the book, and the telephone—Part 2 describes periods of social and business disruption brought about by other social technologies. I believe that a natural progression occurs between generations of social technology tools that amplify and advance the way that humans have behaved, interacted with each other, shared information, and experienced the world. The common ground between these social technology generations is found in the phenomena they capture, while the specific behaviors enabled have varied with each generation and advancement. People exploit these behaviors differently depending on what actions the technology enables and how information flows; therefore, there is a highly unpredictable and wildly disruptive impact each time we experience a major breakthrough such as the one we are going through today.

As of this writing, there are an estimated 3.1 billion social media accounts worldwide, with that figure growing to almost 5 billion by 2016, representing 2.3 billion users (Radicati & Yamasaki 2012, p. 4)—driving an unprecedented level of global connectivity, engagement, and interaction. By 2017, Ericsson (2012) estimates there will be over 5 billion mobile broadband subscriptions (vs. a total of 9 billion mobile subscriptions), up from less than 1.5 billion in

2012 (p. 11, Figure 13). Along with this connectivity, data traffic will grow 1,500% between now and 2017 (p. 13), while voice traffic remains relatively flat. What will people do with this level of connectivity and sharing?

This is the first time in human history that so many of us have been connected in real time. This amazing change is happening right now—and it's why we are at a defining moment in business management history.

History teaches that people get smarter with social technology and that these tools are valuable productivity-enhancers. Humans have 800,000 years of evidence to this effect. In the next chapter, I examine why today's tools are the next killer opportunity for business and what that's worth.

Business
Is the Next Killer
Social Opportunity

What's important is that
you have a faith in people,
that they're basically good and smart,
and if you give them tools,
they'll do wonderful things with them.

—Steve Jobs
(Goodell 2011, para. 57)

❮ Toyota Drives toward a Social Destiny

I spent nine years living and working in Tokyo, Japan (1994–2003), and that's where I first met Marc Benioff, salesforce.com's Chairman and CEO. Marc took salesforce.com into the Japanese market shortly after he started his company—and my firm was one of his early customers.

Japan is a fascinating country and a microcosm of human behavior that yields some interesting insights when closely examined. The population density, economic might, and maturity of the country combine to create a hotbed of innovation. Pour about half of the population of the United States into a landmass the size of California, and you've got Japan: Controlling, managing, feeding, and entertaining that kind of population density doesn't happen without a plan or without some creative thinking.

I often recommend to other non-Japanese executives that if they want to see what the next big thing is, they should spend some time in Japan. For example, mobile telephony in Japan in the late 1990s far exceeded the rest of the world. Things as mundane or inane as reality television existed in Japan long before they made their way to the West. Some Japanese companies were also early adopters of the business management concepts taught and espoused by Peter Drucker and Dr. W. Edwards Deming (Drucker 1993, p. 302; Aguayo 1990, p. 6).

The following story told by Marc Benioff, Chairman and CEO of salesforce.com, is no exception to the Japanese market's ability to innovate. This is the story of Marc's experience with one of his Japanese customers, Toyota; the impact their relationship had on salesforce.com's future; and the change in Toyota's future shaped by social technology. Here's how he tells it…

Toyota has never been our biggest customer, but it is the one that has impacted us the most. Toyota taught us how to become a Social Company and how to help our customers transform as well. That understanding changed everything for salesforce.com and allowed us to maintain both our fast-paced growth and our leadership position.

In 2010, Toyota executive Shigeki Tomoyama came to my office in San Francisco looking for what his company could learn from salesforce.com. I didn't initially know why he came to see me. There was no set agenda, so I told him what I was finding most interesting—bringing social technologies into the enterprise—and showed him what we were doing with Chatter.

He went back to Japan and told his boss, Akio Toyoda, President and CEO of Toyota and the grandson of Toyota's founder (the family changed the spelling of the company's name for "greater euphony" (A. Taylor 2009, para. 6)), and the next time we heard from the Toyota executives, we learned they were coming back to the United States to meet with two companies: Microsoft and salesforce.com. Times had changed. I remember when our employees pitched potential customers in the supermarket check-out line, and now we were competing directly against Microsoft for the business of the biggest car manufacturer (OICA 2011) in the world.

However, as some things change, others stay the same. We still saw the world very differently than Microsoft did. We were interested in a different story at salesforce.com—one about enabling businesses to do more, not one about selling decades-old software. Toyota wasn't interested in "business as usual" either.

We had to show Toyota the transformative powers of the cloud, the mobile revolution, and the social technologies that were changing everything for consumers. We had to help them stay closer to their customers and move faster. But, most importantly, we had to listen to Toyota. What could we learn? What were their concerns? What was their future?

I was at a fundraiser for College Track, a nonprofit organization started by Laurene Jobs that helps prepare underserved youth for higher education. I was in an elevator talking with my friend, musician will.i.am, and our chief creative officer, Bruce Campbell. We were discussing some of Bruce's previous projects, including the car company Saturn, and Will expressed how he had loved that car.

Bruce wasn't surprised; he'd heard this before. "Buying a car is an emotional process," he said. "At Saturn, we saw cars as friends." I thought, "Toyota Friend"—that's what this is all about. That's what we had to bring to Toyota.

We had so many new ways—created long after Saturn ceased to exist—to make cars our "friends." We could use Twitter or Chatter to communicate with cars (see below), and social technologies could make all products more collaborative.

Toyota, the maker of the Corolla, the Tacoma, the Lexus, and the Prius, is an incredible company but it had experienced a very difficult few years. Some of its vehicles were found to have faulty braking systems, which resulted in Congressional investigations and, eventually, a recall. During this time, Toyota lost trust with customers (Steinberg 2010).

Toyota needed to change its customers' perception, and to do so, it needed to change the way it operated. It needed to be closer to its customers, closer to its dealers, closer to its vendors and partners, and closer to its cars to know what was happening with them. Everything needed to be interconnected—that was the future. That was the way for Toyota to regain trust, and that was the way for Toyota to go faster.

In January 2010, right after a meeting in Seattle with Microsoft, the Toyota team flew to Hawaii to see me. As it turned out, their guesthouse was next to mine on the Big Island, which I considered interesting karma.

We had anticipated a small meeting, but Toyoda-san brought his entire management team. We met their plane at the airport and brought them Hawaiian shirts and swimsuits, which we imagined they'd use during their stay—they wore them to the meeting. That was only the beginning of how we would be working very differently than either company had before.

"What is the most exciting thing happening?" Toyoda-san asked me. "How can I go faster?"

"Facebook," I told him. "Facebook is where I look for inspiration. The most exciting thing happening is how we are using social technologies to make everything in our lives connected," I explained. "At salesforce.com, we are using our own product, Chatter, that we built for the enterprise to connect to one another. It's how we share ideas and content, and how we collaborate. It allows us to go faster than I had ever imagined."

Social media is so widely adopted and understood in Japan. Toyota had a popular Facebook page. Toyoda-san had a Facebook page. Both had Twitter accounts. Why couldn't individual cars have a Facebook page or Twitter feed? Why couldn't customers be friends with their cars, and "follow" them to see how they were doing? Why couldn't a car "tweet" to its users what was wrong: When it needed air in the tires, or the battery on an electric vehicle had to be recharged, or when it needed maintenance or to schedule an appointment via a link to the service center.

As we talked, I realized we were talking about fundamentally changing the way people experience their car and their relationship with Toyota. We were envisioning a new business model, not focused around a product, but around an experience that was only possible through social technology tools.

The salesforce.com team had built a prototype on top of Chatter and customized it so it looked like Toyota's own system. I gave the demo on my iPad. "Why is my car not my friend?" I asked. "Why isn't there Toyota Friend?"

"...You've got me," Toyoda-san replied.

When the Toyota executives noted that they liked the icon we came up with—it looked like a smile—I knew Toyota saw business the way we did, with the customer's success as the most important business value. "The customer's smile is the thing we want the most," said Tomoyama-san. "Toyota deeply values building long-term relationships of trust with customers and the communities they belong to. Going beyond the limitations of time and space, social networking makes it possible to achieve this."

For more than a decade, Toyota had been engaged in developing technologies and producing concept cars that "humanize" vehicles, but they had been focused on more of a one-on-one conversation between driver and vehicle. Social networks unlock other capabilities—and according to Tomoyama-san are "capable of revolutionizing the automotive business." In Toyota Friend, the vehicle's tweets are shared with the owner as well as with friends, dealership staff, and engineers. For example, the vehicle could say, "I'd like a check-up," and another owner with the same model could see this communication and could tweet some advice to the owner. In the meantime, someone at the dealership could post a message offering a "free oil-change for a limited time," and the owner could then decide to book a service appointment for the car. The vehicle could then thank its owner with another tweet.

Toyota is building Toyota Friend into its cars in the automobile production line, which means that the vehicle could start tweeting to the customer the moment the order is sent to the production plant (Paladino 2012). That's important. Toyota knows the expectations of customers are at their highest level while waiting for the vehicle to be delivered. Now, while waiting, the vehicle can talk frequently to its future owner, informing him or her, "Construction of my body line has started," or "I'm being painted now—the color is silver, right?" Tomoyama-san says this kind of participation will put considerable pressure on the production engineers and the manufacturing site because their work will be transparent to customers—and the corporation. He believes that this new openness will specifically encourage manufacturers to be more just-in-time and competitive. "The communication created from this is capable of revolutionizing the automotive business," he concluded.

Toyota Friend, which was officially launched at the Tokyo Motor Show in 2011 (Toyota 2011), has made an impact far beyond what Toyota had initially expected. It has changed the way Toyota operates its business. "Frankly the past two to three years have not been a happy time for me. We had the natural disaster and the recall problem. We caused many people a lot of concern," says Toyoda-san. "At the same time, over the past two years I learned exactly what my role is. As CEO, my job is to be decisive. Knowing how people are doing has become very important to me. In that sense, knowing what people are talking about through Chatter is enormously valuable to me. I discovered a whole new world, and my life has been changing in a big way ever since."

It's not often that a customer says we changed his or her life. The most interesting part of this story to us, however, is that in helping Toyota see things differently we began to see ourselves differently as well. If we could help the biggest car company in the world (OICA 2011) change the way it interacted with employees, customers, and products and connect everything together, we could help every company leverage the same ideas, connect everything together, and go faster.

With Toyota, we discovered something important about ourselves. Salesforce.com is about more than products; we are a new way to think about doing business. We started to think about providing end-to-end digital social solutions based on where our customers could go as, opposed to where we ourselves were going. This transformational moment became a transformational time in which we began working with other companies, like Coca-Cola, GE, and Burberry, to help them create their own social roadmaps. We also began to understand our path to becoming a Social Company that could grow faster and remain innovative.

Growing faster was our imperative. As we began our second decade in business, I knew we had to accelerate our growth trajectory. We had a mandate to reach $10 billion in revenue and to get there we need to increase our business by $1 billion every year (not over ten years as we did in the past decade). Becoming a Social Company illuminated that road for us.

Marc often shares this story at salesforce.com's Dreamforce and Cloudforce events around the world. The early adopters and leaders who understand the transformative power of this technology are rethinking the traditional concepts they've learned about the nature of business and how value gets created and captured. Business technology is moving beyond the automation of transactions to enable new levels of engagement, and ultimately, an overall experience—enabled by a perfect storm of social technology advancements. Marc and his team spent the last decade reinventing business software; these social technology tools are now reinventing business and the future of business management.

The 100-Year Business Management Experiment

Today's business management experiment started in the early 1900s; Frederick Taylor is usually credited with giving birth to business management theory with his publication of *The Principles of Scientific Management* (1911). Over the hundred years since then, business management theory and practice unfolded awkwardly through trial and error (Figure 3-1), expanding slowly, erratically, and experientially.

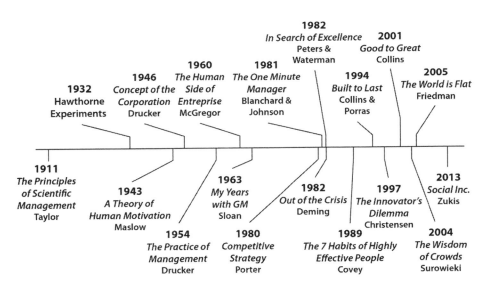

Figure 3-1. A Century of Business Management Thought Leadership. Author's image.

Those who followed and adopted these practices (i.e., nearly all companies, together with their managers and employees) have been guinea pigs for a poorly designed and executed behavioral, economic, and social experiment that has produced the modern corporation. The business thinkers, researchers, philosophers, and provocateurs of the last century include Frederick Taylor, Alfred Sloan, Peter Drucker, W. Edwards Deming, Stephen Covey, Tom Peters, Michael Porter, Jim Collins, Gary Hamel, and many others (Figure 3-1); their concepts and views have formed the backbone upon which the modern organization has been built. This real-time experiment has reacted, rebounded, and recreated itself with the agility of a hippo. Ideas have been mashed together, layered upon each other, and bolted together like a Frankenstein, birthed from the mind of a deranged MBA student. The result is a mosaic of strategies, philosophies, tools, techniques, and approaches all designed to accomplish one common goal: getting a group of people to work together to make as much money as possible.

The problem is that this experiment is not working; consumer trust in business is deteriorating, employee engagement is abysmal, and economic growth is lethargic at best.[10] The business management experiment needs help. These words, usually attributed to Peter Drucker, capture the problem in a nutshell:

> "So much of what we call management consists in making it difficult for people to work."

The experimentation hasn't been entirely without merit; in fact, the trials and tribulations of the past hundred years have set up the next evolutionary step for breakthrough success. The total body of this management experimentation includes hundreds of interpretations, tangential ideas, derivative thinking, and niche theories. Taken together, however, I argue that we have broadly transitioned through three different phases: starting with a focus on the work, moving to a focus on the organization and then to the individual. Social technology is enabling a fourth major stage—the experience (Figure 3-2).

---

[10] Data from Edelman Trust Barometer (2012, slide 7), Gallup (2010, p. 2), and the International Monetary Fund (2012, p. xv), respectively.

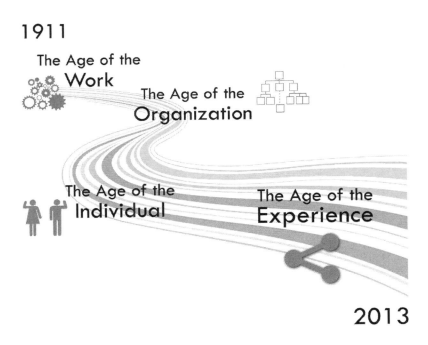

Figure 3-2. The 100-Year Business Experiment. Author's image.

The Age of the Work—Employees as Cogs

Frederick Taylor's *Principles of Scientific Management* in 1911 viewed workers as naturally lazy cogs in a machine, incapable of understanding the higher purpose and "science" of management. Taylor wrote,

> the workman who is best suited to actually doing the work is incapable of fully understanding this science, without the guidance and help of those who are working with him or over him, either through lack of education or through insufficient mental capacity. (p. 26)

F. Taylor (1911) felt that workers were naturally inclined to shirking and as a result were underproductive. He felt that with a more structured and scientific management system, industrial companies could double the productivity of their workforce (p. 142). This improvement in productivity would also flow to the workers in the form of wages that could be higher by 30-100% (p. 12). Taylor's model focused the worker on the strict performance of tasks under the watchful and benevolent eye of a smarter, more capable manager. Replaceable like parts in a machine, workers worked; they didn't think. In its time, this model seemed like a logical next step as it was one notch removed from servitude.

In addition, F. Taylor (1911) was an early proponent of best practices, standardized processes, performance management, task analysis, graphical data analysis, time and motion studies, on-the-job training, process improvement and reengineering, statistical analysis, and skills alignment. His approach focused on getting workers to do their work better and more efficiently, thereby increasing productivity, outputs, and growth.

He concluded that his model

> will enable the companies who adopt this management, particularly those who adopt it first, to compete far better than they were able to before, and this will so enlarge their markets that their men will have almost constant work even in dull times, and that they will earn larger profits at all times (F. Taylor 1911, p. 143).

Science, harmony, cooperation, and maximum output were the cornerstones of Taylor's management science (p. 140).

Frederick Taylor didn't contemplate the customer, and he didn't believe in worker empowerment. For the time, however, a business management philosophy with an assembly-line approach to work and the worker was called for. Wringing massive efficiency out of the production of consumer and industrial products was what drove profits during the Industrial Revolution. Much of the labor force was low- or un-skilled, manual work and labor was plentiful, and technology had not yet addressed many of the tasks that could be performed faster, better, and cheaper by automated means.

In more mature economies, the nature of work and the role of the worker have generally evolved well beyond Frederick Taylor's worker-as-cog model, but many of his concepts still survive and are regularly applied in today's context. The lesson is that traditional business management theory and practice continues to have foundational application, depending on the circumstances and context. Each theory or concept is not absolute, but is evolutionary in nature and in application. Thanks to Frederick Taylor, Henry Ford (see below), and others, humans are now experts at breaking down work into discrete component parts to produce or deliver something (anything, really) efficiently, consistently, and at scale. However, time has exposed the Achilles' heel of this model: rapidly changing markets, deviation from the standard blueprint, and ongoing technology-driven productivity gains.

The Age of the Organization—Bureaucracy Works for Government...Doesn't It?

Once workers could crank out any manner of product, the benefits of the scale corporation became apparent. In the mid-1940s, as companies continued to grow and grow, they had to figure out how to organize and manage much larger groups of people.

Peter Drucker's book, *Concept of the Corporation*, was published in 1946 and introduced his concepts and opinions around the organization, notably, centrally governed decentralization. His book was based on his detailed, insider's view into the world that Alfred P. Sloan created at General Motors (GM). Drucker examined the way GM was structured with a diagnostic eye, made some recommendations for GM, and applied those concepts to broader business management. GM's management model at the time could be compared to the other scale organizational models of that era: the Catholic Church and the U.S. government.

Drucker's work dissected how large groups of people within the GM model interacted with each other, with their work, and with the organization. His GM work started to highlight certain weaknesses in what had evolved since Frederick Taylor's time. In particular, he observed that low levels of worker satisfaction go along with "an assembly-line mentality among modern management which believes that a worker is the more efficient the more machine-like and the less human he is" (Drucker 1993, p. 154).

The irony of Drucker's invitation to study GM, which he did for 18 months, was that after he published his thoughts, his work was summarily ignored by GM's leadership (1993, p. 293). Nonetheless, Drucker's work did have an impact, just not with GM. His work at GM to understand the nature of the organization in business helped formalize management as a practice and field of study (p. ix), and organizations including Ford, General Electric, Toyota, the U.S. government, and many others studied this work and adopted his methods (pp. 291–292).

Drucker's 1946 work on *Concept of the Corporation* also revealed a subtle distinction relative to how he viewed business management compared to the views of GM and even Frederick Taylor some 35 years earlier. Whereas Taylor saw management as a "science," as evidenced by the title to his 1911 seminal work, *The Principles of Scientific Management*, Drucker viewed business management as a "practice" (1993, p. 297). Drucker attributes the rejection of his work by GM to this fundamental issue: GM's executives also viewed management as a science—something that they had figured out that was irrefutable (p. 296). There were "right" and "wrong" ways of doing things based upon principles that they themselves invented, and these principles were tried, true, and beyond reproach.

Throughout all his management work, however, Drucker maintained the view that management was a practice, something that was iterative and could change and evolve. In his own words, the management principles that GM and others maintained were "ways of identifying the right question rather than the one right answer" (1993, p. 296).

The organization as a massive bureaucratic and decentralized system of integrated moving parts did accomplish great things impossible for an individual or lesser-sized firm. This business management model and these beliefs lasted for a long time—until they stopped accomplishing great things, and then even mediocre things. The world that Sloan created at GM was utopian for its time. But we now know that bureaucracy breaks down under its own scale and weight, and bureaucratic corporations become their own weak link—especially when the needs and demands of a marketplace are rapidly evolving. GM was not built for agility, and it eventually fractured under the weight of its own management inadequacies—requiring a U.S. taxpayer bailout in 2008 (Sanger, Herszenhorn, & Vlasic 2008). Ironically, in GM's bailout and subsequent bankruptcy in 2009 (Isidore 2009), the bureaucratic ideal of GM collided with the very bureaucracy on which it was originally modeled: the U.S. government.

Drucker was right about management being a practice: It needs to evolve to adapt to the changes taking place in society and within its markets. In 1946, he knew that "the essence of the corporation is social, that is human, organization" (Drucker 1993, p. 21). Over 60 years ago Drucker had a vision of the organization that time has proven accurate; in hindsight, I suspect Alfred Sloan and GM's other executives wish they had seen this as well.

Drucker's final edition of *Concept of the Corporation*, in 1993, provides a running commentary and a rare opportunity to see the longevity of his vision around GM play out. His introduction to this edition points out "the reasons for General Motors's fumbling and inability to pull itself out of the mire, are largely the problems *Concept of the Corporation* pointed out fifty years ago" (p. xxi).

His comments then mirror my own words in the preface of *Social Inc.*: "By now everybody at General Motors knows that these are the crucial problems. And yet General Motors does not seem able to resolve them" (Drucker 1993, p. xii). In other words, the institutional sludge that plagued GM and that Drucker so keenly identified prevented them from fixing what they knew was broken.

Large, slow-moving organizations become progressively less relevant in a rapidly evolving market. They are constantly under attack from smaller, more agile firms able to bring more relevancy to the marketplace, more quickly. Time isn't on the side of business any longer: Change is the enemy of traditional business management thinking and practice. Leaders now need to recognize the inherent limitations in the traditional approaches to business management. Evolving to a new model that can be flexible and keep pace with the demands of changing markets is the mission of the Social Company.

Drucker's observations around GM have withstood the test of time. In the preface to his 1983 edition of *Concept of the Corporation*, he discusses more broadly where he thought business was heading.

With information technology and with manufacturing processes shifting increasingly to feedback control—that is, toward automation based on information and knowledge—the economics of scale may shift drastically. The optimum size may be the one that gives the greatest adaptability rather than the one that gives the greatest mass. (p. xxii)

The bureaucracy as an ideal organizational model was a business management idea that did not hold up over time, against scale or change. Once again, the weak spot was exposed when markets and customers became more unpredictable and volatile. Change, so far, is the enemy of the traditional approach to business management. While these types of corporations still exist, most (I would argue all) are fighting the rapidly rising tide of more agile competitors, changing consumer behavior and market relevancy.

Are all large corporations doomed, or is it possible to be a large, fast moving, and agile business? I believe the failure of this model lies not within its scale but within its design: The growing impracticality of hierarchy and the transaction costs associated with organizing and managing large numbers of people in this fashion are its weaknesses. This is a problem that I believe the Social Company can now solve.

Many corporations, especially larger ones, are victims of the artificial boundaries they put in place to try to organize and manage a workforce in this manner—incentive programs, rigid IT, management by objectives, matrix management, performance management, organization charts, job descriptions, pay scales, and so on. Well-intentioned they may be, but in my experience these tools and techniques are impossible to align or to administer efficiently and effectively. Trying to divide up today's work in this cooperative, assembly-line style breaks down at scale, or when markets change quickly. The system of the modern-day corporation is not working.

In my consulting work, I have always been amazed at the gap between the design of the corporation and its actual functioning in the companies I worked with. Management designed their company to work one way, and then there was a parallel universe for how they often functioned. These workarounds, unstructured teams, and paths of least resistance were the ways employees had found to actually improve upon the formal structures management had established. The lesson I learned was that employees know when things are broken, they know how to fix them and do them better—and more importantly, they want to fix them.

Drucker's 1983 epilogue to *Concept of the Corporation* also uncovered this point as he dissected why GM did not adopt his recommendations. He mentions an employee survey of almost 300,000 people that GM conducted, titled "My Job and Why I Like It." He presents survey responses such as, "What I like best in my job in that my supervisor expects me to tell him how to do the job better" and "What I dislike is that I know how to do a much better job but am never being asked" as capturing the overwhelming sentiment of the project (p. 300).

This history lesson, which mirrors my own experience, is that the truth is in the hands of employees and customers—social technology has now liberated it. The opportunity facing Social Companies is how to leverage transparency, openness, and accountability with these new tools and with a better management model.

Drucker is also known for introducing the concepts of management by objectives, knowledge workers, and the corporation as a human society with responsibilities extending beyond its walls and into the communities where it operates. He thought that workers were assets, he was disapproving of command and control, and he believed that the customer was the singular rallying point for every business (Byrne & Gerdes 2005).

He didn't realize it then, but Drucker was a man ahead of his time in envisioning a business approach that could be empowered through social technology. While his theory and conceptualization were many steps in the right direction, the information and social technology tools of the time were lacking. They could not effectively pull the entire system together; however, today's Social Company has deep roots in Peter Drucker's thinking and today's social technology is a new enabler for much of his vision. However, it will take more than just Drucker's views to help businesses with the opportunities and challenges that they face today.

The Age of the Individual—Power to the People

More than twenty years after Frederick Taylor's vision of the worker as an unthinking and naturally lazy cog motivated only by pay, the National Research Council and Harvard University conducted what would become known as the "Hawthorne Experiments" at the Western Electric Company in Chicago (Mayo 1933, 1945). The plant primarily manufactured the social technology of its day: the telephone.

The eight-year research project wrapped up by 1932 and ushered in a new era of corporate human relations acknowledging that people are more than just cogs, and that their motivation—and consequently their productivity—is influenced by more than just pay. With an emphasis on group behavior, the concepts of behavioral motivation and human relations started to enter the business management playbook after the Hawthorne Experiments (Mayo 1933).

Abraham Maslow then introduced his framework in "A Theory of Human Motivation" (1943), which became an oft-cited model for understanding this important aspect of human behavior. Often referred to as Maslow's "hierarchy of needs," his model is based on the concept that some human needs are more important than others, and will be fulfilled in relative order of priority. Maslow listed needs, in the order they will be fulfilled, from physiological, to safety, love, esteem, and finally, self-actualization (p. 394). For example, a person's physiological need for food, water, and sleep will be fulfilled before the need for love, or for family and belonging.

Douglas McGregor's "Theory X" and "Theory Y" also focus on trying to isolate the ideal way to get the most out of people. His Theory X views workers as naturally lazy, irresponsible, and craving security above all else (2006, pp. 45–46). His Theory Y views people as naturally hardworking, capable of self-direction, seekers of responsibility, naturally innovative and intellectually under-realized (pp. 65–66).

Up until this point, business management practice has largely been focused on optimizing employee productivity. That is, how do you get another person or group to achieve optimal performance and productivity at an undertaking that has, at its end, an agenda or objective they may know nothing about or care nothing for?

With these latest concepts, workers now needed to be individually and collectively understood, incentivized, and motivated to optimize their efficiency and productivity—in theory. This concept started to extend beyond workers to customers and engendered the phrase "markets of one" and the book by the same title (Gilmore & Pine 2000). Mass customization as a business management concept was 180-degrees removed from Henry Ford's vision, which he famously described by saying, "Any customer can have a car painted any colour that he wants so long as it is black" (Ford & Crowther 1922, p. 71).

Over time, as with previous approaches, the "individual" model showed its weaknesses as customers, employees, and investors became high-maintenance—all the time. Every employee has potentially different motivations, and customers also have fickle needs and wants. The variables at play started to become overwhelming, and the volume of management ideas, concepts, and tools exploded.

The individual as the nexus of business management also proved to be a fragile model over time—again, not because of inherent conceptual flaws but due to the constant evolution of needs and markets and the inability of companies to manage that degree of volatility. Today, companies certainly still want to satisfy individual customers; this has not changed. Employees and customers most definitely still expect to have their individual needs met, or exceeded. The business management concept of the individual, once again, brought too much variety and volatility into the management equation and proved difficult to execute upon over time.

Hindsight and History Need Each Other in Business

History is just that, what happened yesterday and the days before that. Hindsight is different, helping people understand why history unfolded the way that it did.

Time (and hindsight) is exposing the fatal flaw in history's approaches to business management—change. The historical integrity of each of these components—from the work, to the organization, and then to the individual— gets progressively weaker as the pace of change quickens. Rapidly changing behaviors, beliefs, and motivations all put these business concepts on a shaky foundation. The task of effectively executing the disparate management theories and practices espoused over the decades has become virtually impossible to accomplish efficiently.

Business management theory did not establish the corporation to be rapidly adaptable and constantly evolving—and for good reason. It didn't need to be while our worldwide economy grew up over the last century. Now that social technology is changing and amplifying human behavior daily, business finds itself flat-footed, unable to adapt, and unable to stay relevant.

Fortunately for all of us, the last hundred years hasn't been a total waste, and in fact much of the theoretical promise embedded in "early" thinking around business theory and practice hasn't been realizable—until now. The practice of management up until this point has been just that—practice that yielded partial answers to the challenges of companies and society at the time.

The irony of the entire hundred-year history of business management theory and practice is that employees are now unable to fulfill the very needs that they know they have as customers, because the artificial boundaries of the organization are in the way. Historical approaches to business management theory and practice amidst a landscape of shifting customer behaviors have created today's business crisis…and opportunity.

While Frederick Taylor (1911), Drucker (1993), Maslow (1943), McGregor (2006), and others may have envisioned much different results than have actually occurred, many of their core concepts remain very relevant and applicable.

I believe the tools to fully implement and realize their potential against a rapidly changing market environment, however, have lagged behind. Information and social technology has finally caught up to the management philosophy of the last century—today's social technology can fully enable and empower these visions, and others. The potential of the past and the possibility of the future can now be achieved through this next generation of social technology.

The Age of the Experience—Social Technology Shall Set You Free

A hundred years of business management history has taught that the practice of business is an evolutionary undertaking. People in business learn by studying, conceptualizing, and then by doing, although not always in that order. A new or next approach to business management is needed—because businesses, like humans, are evolutionary.

This next step is necessary because human behaviors are changing as a result of social technology. In addition, trust levels are low and sinking lower in governments and business institutions (Edelman Trust Barometer 2012, slide 7); people expect and want more. Finally, social technology tools offer the potential for massive workforce and intellectual productivity gains that cannot be ignored. Relevancy, satisfaction, and economic opportunity are drivers forcing business to continue to evolve its approach to management through these new tools.

Unique social technologies are enabling new types of engagement and making this next evolutionary step in business management both possible and necessary. The level of engagement and interaction now possible enables a Social Company to create and sustain a unique experience surrounding the interactions that anyone has with the company, its products, and its services.

The arrival of The Age of the Experience also has its roots in the past; specifically, with W. Edwards Deming. A professor of statistics before he became a world-famous management guru, Deming lived from 1900 to 1993 (The W. Edwards Deming Institute 2012a). Drucker lived from 1909 to 2005 (The Drucker Institute 2012), so both men saw and studied first-hand the entire progression of modern business management theory. (Unfortunately, both passed away before the advent of today's social technology developments, which most people date to Facebook and its founding in 2004.) Drucker's groundbreaking views of the organization in 1946 and his influence on the advancement of management as a practice and field of study are discussed in the Age of the Organization above. Comparatively, Deming was a late bloomer as a management consultant; his first management book, *Out of the Crisis* (1982), was published long after he became famous for his quality teachings and his impact on Japanese management practices (The W. Edwards Deming Institute 2012b).

Interestingly, both Drucker and Deming have significantly impacted the way that Japanese companies approach management and run their businesses, and are often credited with helping Japan emerge as a major economic power (Drucker 1993, p. 302). Deming is recognized as the man who taught the Japanese about quality (Aguayo 1990, p. 6), and the Deming Prize created by the Union of Japanese Scientists and Engineers (JUSE 2012) is testimony to his influence and impact.

Are the Japanese early adopters of leading business-management philosophy and practices? Toyota was an early adopter of both Drucker's and Deming's philosophies, (Drucker 1993, p. 302; Aguayo 1990, p. 6) and as Marc Benioff's earlier story illustrated, the company is also an early adopter of today's social technology.

Deming's thinking and teachings once again extended the business management philosophies and practices that came before; Deming's core philosophies are also the final link between the past and the present in understanding the next business management threshold of the Social Company. His core principles can be illustrated by highlighting one key point on which he disagreed with Drucker: Deming thought that merit systems, such as Drucker's Management By Objectives (MBO) were the single most destructive force in U.S. management (Aguayo 1990, p. 6).

Deming thought that MBO-type programs destroyed teamwork, and that individual performance is highly dependent on the overall system that exists in any one company. Deming's core philosophy therefore concerns the empowerment of the individual (Aguayo 1990, p. 243).

The Experience

Every company is an information and social technology company; most of them just haven't realized it yet. The experience that a company delivers in today's social technology-enabled world can claim its pedigree from the concept of "user experience" that has created the very social tools that have led us to this point.

The International Organization for Standardization (ISO) defines *user experience* as "[a] person's perceptions and responses resulting from the use and/or anticipated use of a product, system or service" (2010, p. 3).

Data, information, and knowledge are the backbone of every organization and today's social technology is the nervous system of the modern-day company. Companies are complex systems of policies, procedures, technology, programs, hierarchies, projects, people, data, information, knowledge, regulations, and so on. The system of the modern-day corporation now needs to evolve to compete based on the experience that it delivers (through today's social technology) to its users—its customers, employees, and investors.

"User experience" is a phrase and field well known in the IT community, particularly among website designers, and dates back to the mid- to late-1990s. In 2010, the ISO published *Ergonomics of Human–System Interaction—Part 210: Human-Centered Design for Interactive Systems*, which addresses "design principles and activities throughout the life cycle of computer-based interactive systems" (p. 1).

Today's Social Company is a computer-based interactive system. The experience that your company delivers to employees, customers, and investors with social technology is the next competitive threshold for your business.

The essence behind this new business management paradigm centers around you as a social technology-empowered consumer, employee, and investor. People—including you—are defining what it means for companies to be successful through social technology, in real time. These tools empower and liberate employees, customers, and investors in powerful new ways. Social technology is changing how people want to experience the world; it goes with each individual, bringing the world along for the ride as it changes how people interact with each other, and with their surroundings.

This next business management paradigm shift is the product of a supply-driven information explosion that is drastically changing human behavior—putting the individual and shared *experience* of being a customer, employee, or investor at the center of the *Social Inc.* business model. The experience that is delivered through social technology is about the enablement and empowerment of individuals and groups in new ways.

Today's social technology tools can create an interaction with anyone, or virtually anything. Consequently, the same concepts and principles that evolved from the emergence of user-centered design in the 1990s (Norman 1988) now need to be applied to the totality of business, so that companies can offer and deliver a unique experience to their markets based upon data and insight driven by these new tools.

Business management history has taught the basics and the role of the work, organization, and individual; businesses have mastered much in each of these domains, but those domains haven't been working all that well together as a system. The system that businesses have cobbled together lacks usability—this entire system is now the focus of the next chapter in business management.

How companies deliver the *experience* of doing business through today's social technology can redefine value propositions, markets, and the competitive landscape. It's a natural progression. First, people had to figure out how to get things done efficiently, and we did—we can now produce almost anything with precision and proficiency. Next came production at scale through organizing the people doing the work; this cooperative organizational approach is far from perfected, however. After that, business recognized that the true engine behind it all—the individual human—had to be motivated, engaged, and understood (as discussed above). Whether as customers, employees, or investors, reaching individuals became an important and vital part of the business management equation. Success in this arena has been elusive. It's a big guessing game and unfortunately employees, customers, and investors don't help the situation very much; our moods, motivations, and desires are a fickle riddle that most (if not all) companies struggle to understand.

To reach its potential, the global business environment needs some breakthroughs, entirely new ways of approaching problems that lead to more efficient and effective solutions. From governments to businesses, we need to—and we can—take an evolutionary leap forward. Today's social technology has provided the necessary tools. Rule 5 of *Social Inc.* focuses on the entire system that companies operate to create their users' experience through social technology.

Social Inc. Rule 5

The Social Company excels at delivering a unique experience.

Business success is now dependent on today's social technology, because customers, employees, and investors are using it, and they won't go back. The immediacy and intimacy of social technology enables relevancy like never before. If a company does not stay technologically relevant and keep up with users' advancing social technology sophistication, it will become increasingly irrelevant to them.

Will the majority of the world's population be online by 2020? The math largely works if historical internet adoption growth rates remain constant. The compound annual growth of internet adoption has been around 17% over the last decade (Internet World Stats 2012, World Internet Users and Population

Statistics). If it were possible for this growth rate to remain constant, and all else being equal, the total number of people online will converge with the total number of people on the planet sometime in 2020.

Growth in smartphone use and tablets will also drive adoption and help the planet get connected. Ericsson estimates that there will be almost 4 billion smartphone and mobile PC/tablet subscriptions in use by 2017 (Ericssson 2012, p. 9). Together with the fact that social networking is already the single most popular activity online for both PC users (20% of their time) and mobile users (30% of their time) (Nielsen 2012, p. 4), this trendline presents a clear, connected destiny. In the near future, the majority—if not all—of the world's population could be connected. Moreover, most online activity will center around interactions through social technology.

Rather than a slow-moving shift in tastes or a creeping demographic shift, humans are facing a present-day change in how people experience their worlds—their worlds of community, home, food, family, friends, sport, leisure, work, and so on. The elimination of space and time disruptions and inefficiencies between people, people and things, people and companies, things and things, companies and companies, markets and people, and things and companies changes the foundational rules of and about business.

Information technology has barely kept pace with the last hundred years of management theory and practice—it has now jumped ahead. Today's social technology is finally able to fully realize and reinvent the promise of one hundred years of business management theory and practice. The business management experiment is now focused on delivering a unique and rapidly evolving experience to customers, employees, and investors through social technology, and business management is now being open-sourced for everyone to help figure out. Deming (1982) believed that individual empowerment was the most important force in business management theory and practice, and the social technology tools to enable his thinking have finally arrived.

◂ All Companies Are Now Social Companies

Does the title of this section seem overly ambitious? The reality is that even if your company is not using social technology, social technology is still impacting your company. Many of your customers, employees, and investors are using these tools—this makes every company a Social Company, whether it faces that fact or not.

To understand how social and information technology are changing business as we know it, I look to Harvard, which introduced the world to the first MBA program in 1908 (Harvard Business School n.d., para. 1). (Moreover, a university dropout famously founded Facebook while attending Harvard in 2004 (Carter 2011).) In 2011, *Harvard Business School Working Knowledge* asked a collection of the university's leading thinkers to identify the most important management trends of the 21st century (Silverthorne 2011).

According to Business School Dean Nitin Nohria, "Globalization, enabled and accelerated by technology, has had a greater impact on business (and, indeed, on society) than any other development in the past decade" (Silverthorne 2011, para. 5). The school's Director of Research, Teresa Amabile added, "Over the last decade, nothing has had a more profound impact on business management than information technology" (para. 9).

Professor Carliss Y. Baldwin, Harvard's William L. White Professor of Business Administration, cited, "(1) the rise of business ecosystems caused by falling transaction costs; and (2) the empowerment of users caused by the global speed of communication technologies" (Silverthorne 2011, para. 14).

These Harvard thought leaders find that technology has—and is having— a big impact on business. (I revisit Professor Baldwin's comment about transaction costs in Part 5: Anarchy, One Connection at a Time, as this concept is a cornerstone behind social technology's disruption of traditional business practices.) If Harvard understands this truth, why is business so far behind and seemingly falling off the pace even further?

Sean Moffitt (2012), author of *WikiBrands*, thinks that consumers are three years ahead of companies in terms of engagement and collaboration, and that even the best companies are merely tied with consumers. This wasn't always the case. Over thirty years I've seen how the latest and greatest information technology used to get to people through the workplace—but not anymore, and never again.

Consumer technology has leapfrogged most corporate IT environments; employees and customers have voted with their feet and moved on to better software and devices. They've introduced their own devices into the workplace, and their technology choices as consumers have forced companies to react to try to stay relevant.

Business used to be the early IT adopter, as shown by the history of the landline telephone—and it took almost fifty years for the telephone to become adopted for "social" purposes. Today's social technology started with rampant consumer adoption, and new technologies are now being consumed and adopted for personal use in one year or less. Businesses now have to react to the rapid pace of adoption as well as understand what technologies consumers are using.

A few years ago, most corporate IT departments would have killed for an eager user group willing to try and adopt new information technologies; however, in my experience most IT groups have been forced through major cost rationalization over the last several years, due to the global recession (Goodwin 2012). The sunk costs of IT are an anchor around their necks. Employees, meanwhile, have liberated themselves from the corporate IT department—released themselves to improve things on their own, and to create chaos for legacy IT along the way.

This shift is presenting a real dilemma and competitive challenge to many companies, because if they cannot deliver a relevant or meaningful experience, someone else will. The door is now open to new market entrants who are not impaired by legacy technology, and new threats are posed by competitors who can execute on the tough choices to transform their businesses with social technology.

Social technology doesn't discriminate: The benefits behind these tools apply for small businesses, not-for-profits, and large multinationals alike. A primary driver behind these innovations and this democratization is cost. Because of developments like cloud computing and software-as-a-service (SaaS), the massive costs of development and the infrastructure to deliver social technology tools is being spread over a very large user group. Therefore, the per-unit costs of acquisition are lower, meaning that a one-person company can afford and access the same technology being used by some of the largest companies in the world.

Technology is finally at the forefront of what business needs to deliver in order to be relevant, which wasn't always the case. While technology has of course been present and been a part of the story, it was not the opening act like it is now. The business management experiment of the last century is now being enabled, driven, extended, and evolved through the power of social technology. Every business will achieve and stay market relevant through these tools, some more than others, but business dependency on technology has never been higher.

Thankfully, this development arrived just in time, as business hasn't exactly been hitting on all cylinders. The *2012 Edelman Trust Barometer* measures attitudes about the state of trust in business, government, NGOs, and media across 25 countries. Their survey of over 30,000 people from around the world shows just how large the gaps are between the public's expectations and actual company performance (Figure 3-3). In addition to the gaps in listening to customer needs and feedback, treating employees well, placing customers ahead of profits, and taking responsible actions shown in the figure, the survey addresses sizable gaps in using ethical business practices, practicing transparency and openness, communicating frequently, and being honest. In summary, the marketplace isn't happy with business—markets want more than what companies everywhere are delivering.

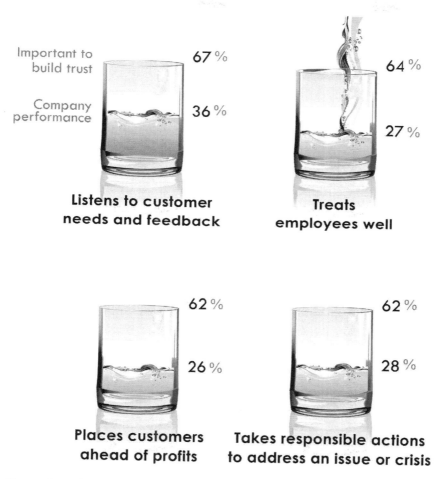

Important to build trust — 67%
Company performance — 36%

Listens to customer needs and feedback

64%
27%

Treats employees well

62%
26%

Places customers ahead of profits

62%
28%

Takes responsible actions to address an issue or crisis

Figure 3-3. The Business Expectations Gap.[11]

---

[11] Author's image; data from the *2012 Edelman Trust Barometer©* (slide 24):
- Questions 52–69: How important is each of the following actions to building your TRUST in a company? Respondents used a 9-point scale (a score of 1 meaning that action is "not at all important to building your trust" and 9 meaning it is "extremely important to building your trust" in a company). "Don't know" responses were excluded.
- Questions 103–118: Please rate [INSERT COMPANY] on how well you think they are performing on each of the following attributes. Respondents used a 9-point scale (a score of 1 meaning the company is performing "extremely poorly" and 9 meaning it is performing "extremely well").

Results in the figure represent the percentage of respondents choosing a score of 8 or 9 (the highest two ratings) for each set of questions, and include responses from the general population in their 25-country global total.

Because of the massive gaps in business trust all over the world, the potential for disruption is at hand. Couple rampant dissatisfaction with a disruptive new technology, and things are ripe for upheaval.

Every company needs to become a Social Company or suffer the consequences: Companies have no choice but to embrace this new social technology—market adoption and the economic benefits inherent in the tools dictate it. Historical business management theory and practices have delivered what they could, given what they had to work with up to this point. These new social technologies are something altogether different—not only will they release much of the unrealized promise trapped within your company, but they will also allow you to reinvent business to bring about the Age of the Experience.

❮ Is Everybody Smarter Than Anybody?

The research of James R. Flynn has documented the massive IQ gains of the last century. Flynn summarizes his work in his 2012 book, *Are We Getting Smarter?*, with the following question:

> Do we live in a time that poses a wider range of cognitive problems than our ancestors encountered, and have we developed new cognitive skills and the kind of brains that can deal with these problems? (p. 27)

His answer is an emphatic "yes" (p. 27).

The causes of these IQ gains remain open to analysis. Suggested causes have included being better at taking tests, better nutrition, better education, and environmental stimulation. In 2010, psychologist David Marks attributed these gains largely to increases in literacy.

Mark Cashman (1995) pondered the issue of whether information technology makes people smarter, and concluded that as a result of IT

> we are smarter, because we see more in a richer landscape of knowledge and we see farther because the number of shoulders we can stand upon is growing at least geometrically. We are solving real world problems as a result, and only as a result of these new tools. (p. 52)

However, Cashman's observation around geometric leverage didn't contemplate the exponential growth and capabilities of today's social technology tools to help people connect, communicate, collaborate, and create community.

All of this research and thinking, together with simple logic, seems to support the casual observation that humans are likely a lot smarter than we were a century ago. Moreover, information and social technology have played a role (either directly or indirectly) in advancing individual intellects.

From a business perspective, however, group intelligence is of more significance to the modern corporation. Are the groups of people working in a company as smart as the smartest person in the company, or as dumb as the dumbest? Or, is the collective brainpower of the group smarter than any one individual in the group? Is there the potential for the group to be much smarter than the smartest person?

Social technology has altered the way that we can engage with one another, undoubtedly. If prior iterations of social technology have made humans smarter and more productive, as I discussed in Part 2, how is today's social technology accomplishing the same in today's contexts?

I argue that harnessing and exploiting the collective brainpower of the people in your company (including customers, partners, and investors) is an untapped goldmine for creating and capturing new sources of value—both productive and creative value. Furthermore, I believe that Daniel Wegner would agree (Wegner, Giuliano, & Hertzel 1985; Wegner 1987).

Wegner first proposed the concept of *transactive memory* in the mid-1980s: "the study of transactive memory is concerned with the prediction of group (and individual) behavior through an understanding of the manner in which groups process and structure information" (1987, p. 185). Wegner explains that a transactive memory system is comprised of (a) the knowledge stored in the individual memory of each member of a group plus (b) metadata about each of the other group members' specific domains of expertise (Wegner, Giuliano, & Hertzel 1985, p. 256). He defines a *transactive memory system* as "a set of individual memory systems in combination with the communication that takes place between individuals" (Wegner 1987, p. 186).

So in other words, I know what I know and you know what you know, but if I also know generally what your expertise is, and vice versa, then together we can be more productive and creative. This "shared understanding of who knows what" (K. Lewis & Herndon 2011, p. 1255) is sometimes used to define transactive memory systems. However, it is not enough to just be connected and know what others know, as Lewis and Herndon explain. These key components also need to be present:

- differentiated knowledge among the members or the group
- encoding, storage and retrieval processes around how the group coordinates members learning and retrieval of knowledge in applying this to the tasks of the group
- dynamic functioning and interplay of the system (p. 1256).

So, while being connected is the starting point, it is also vital to have a well functioning system and processes to capture and leverage the diverse knowledge within a group or network. The capabilities of connecting, communicating, community, and collaborating all need to apply for the concept of transactive memory to achieve its promise. Imagine if employees could easily know what another person was expert in and interact with that individual without any friction, to solve a problem or perform a task—even from halfway around the world. What would the workplace look like and how would it perform if everyone were able to apply the collective knowledge of the entire workforce?

While research on transactive memory systems has grown since 2005 (K. Lewis & Herndon 2011, endnote 1), a full understanding is not yet available, but existing work shows this to be a very promising model for describing what social technology in the workplace can deliver. Lewis and Herndon summarize the body of research as follows:

> [transactive memory systems] are thought to improve performance in workgroups because they facilitate quick and coordinated access to specialized expertise, ensuring that a greater amount of high-quality

and task-relevant knowledge is brought to bear on collective tasks. (2011, p. 1254)

Dave Yarnold, ServiceMax[12] CEO and a pioneer and leader in social field service management, puts it this way:

> I love the fact that social collaboration allows every field tech to bring the collective expertise of the entire company on every service call. Anywhere, anytime—social allows that field tech, who's on a virtual island with the customer, to reach out to peers or experts within the company—without necessarily having to know who each of those experts are. (personal communication, 17 October 2012)

The benefits of transactive memory systems do not end with productivity, however; these systems can also enhance team creativity. Research conducted with product development teams showed that transactive memory systems (TMS) "improve team creativity" (Gino, Argote, Miron-Spektor, & Todorova 2010, p. 112). They conclude their study with a statement about creativity:

> Indeed, the development of TMS within teams allows team members to create a common knowledge base which combines information, perspectives, and expertise of the different team members—elements that are important antecedents of creativity. (p. 112)

I believe business is starting to unlock the potential of the conceptual model of transactive memory systems through today's social technology.

Although most people have never heard of transactive memory systems, such systems have existed in practice within every organization. Within any company, an individual's metadata knowledge of other people's expertise develops over time, slowly enabling a level of transactive memory capability. I've seen this in practice when organizations have long-term employees. In a social hub such as the mailroom, long-term employees both leveraged their network positions and built up their transactive memory system. The old-timers, through longevity and sustained interactions, then knew who knew what and how to get things done.

---

[12] ServiceMax offers a complete suite of "cloud-based, collaborative and mobile applications" (2012a, para. 1) in a SaaS (software-as-a-service) model for field service management.

Wegner et al.'s initial work (1985) was in fact based on the transactive memories that emerge when couples have been together for a prolonged period of time. Once again, given the time and stability, a transactive memory capability can emerge. But when time is of the essence, the parties to the system are constantly changing, and the demands on the system are volatile, something else is needed to enable the concept—a tool is needed to sustain the system.

Major constraints on transactive memory systems revolve around the costs inherent in the exchanges between the group's members (e.g., How do you figure out what other people know? What is their expertise? How do you leverage their knowledge efficiently?). Engagement costs hold back transactive memory systems, just as they do other exchanges between people. The bigger the group, the more inefficient it becomes.

Engagement costs have acted like a "tax" on the potential of transactive memory systems—until now. I believe that today's social technology can enable and release the power behind Wegner's concepts in a massive way within any organization that adopts and deploys these tools to become a Social Company. K. Lewis and Herndon contemplated technology's role in transactive memory system enablement:

> information technology has the potential to offer many of the benefits of a TMS [transactive memory system] (knowledge sharing, knowledge storage, access to specialized knowledge) across a large number of collocated or geographically distributed workers simultaneously. (2011, p. 1262)

The story of Dave Yarnold's field service technicians (personal communication, 17 October 2012) highlights the potentially huge economic advantages of enabling social knowledge sharing and leverage through a transactive memory system. Productivity rises the more often a tech gets things right the first time or reduces service time; cumulatively, this efficiency gain impacts the bottom line directly and indirectly in customer perceptions of the company. Dave's customers estimate that they may be able to reduce field service employee levels by 50% just through the productivity gains of these tools

(ServiceMax 2012b, video at 1:21). When the creativity benefits that will accrue over time are factored in, social technology tools offer companies a potentially game-changing capability.

The skills and competencies that an organization needs to exist and thrive are increasingly diverse, not to mention difficult and expensive to acquire, develop, maintain, and manage. These skills and competencies continually evolve, refresh, and develop—both in what combinations are needed and in how they need to be applied to move the organization forward.

In my consulting work with colleagues all over the world, we used to say, "If we only knew what we knew, we'd be amazing." This objective has always been the "holy grail" of business management.

With social technology, every company can now know what it knows *and* deploy that knowledge and more, effectively and efficiently. The concept of transactive memory systems explains why these tools make an organization greater than the sum of its component parts, and why being smarter is being enabled by today's social technology.

✂ Collaborating Is Not Cooperating—It's Much Better

The cooperative management model of the last hundred years of business divides up work to produce a desired output—goals and objectives are set by management based upon a read of market conditions, and then work is divvied up to accomplish that goal. Figuring out how to motivate people, supervise work, report on progress, and organize effort have all been tactics designed to enable this top-down cooperative model.

As history shows (see above), scale and volatile markets are the weak link of the cooperative model. Unfortunately, it's an approach founded upon a demand-driven, consumption economy and assembly-line perspectives. These days, not unlike the Model T and the Industrial Revolution principles it was built on, the cooperative model is a relic of another time.

Cooperation is subtly distinct from collaboration in definition, yet light years apart in approach and outcome as it applies to business. In a *cooperative* business model, work can be performed discretely, and it often is—in silo-ed functions or departments, in the assumption and hope that individual tasks and activities will add up to the desired outcome.

In *collaborative* environments, on the other hand, the outcome is shared because the solution is worked on together. Collaborative models enabled by social technology have the potential to yield breakthrough outputs by enabling transactive memory. This innovation-driven model is not based on assembly-line thinking or processes, but on leveraging the productive and creative power of the group.

Chatter, a salesforce.com product that creates a confidential Facebook-like environment for a company's employees to share, is starting to enable a massively efficient transactive memory system within the enterprise. Forget about email—it's been a big part of the problem. Email is about cooperation; Chatter is about collaboration. Exchanges within a system like Chatter are efficient, contextual, extremely low cost, and additive, enabling the individuals in the group to be smarter than they would be on their own.

In Chatter, each employee knows what others know, quickly. Work gets done faster, ideas flow more freely, teams get smarter, employees are more engaged and happier, and salesforce.com is a smarter and more efficient company.

Jim Steele, salesforce.com's Chief Customer Officer, shared this observation with me.

> Marc's [Marc Benioff, salesforce.com's Chairman and CEO] visibility into the business is better than it ever has been. There is less distortion as messages move up. Social accountability around messages in a social exchange has improved the quality of our discussions dramatically. (personal communication, 25 October 2012)

Jim then shared his views on why the quality of information flow is improving. He explained that one-to-one exchanges (e.g., an email) are different than one-to-many peer exchanges; people will say different things in an email than they will in a public environment. He added that people feel like they should know what they're talking about when they contribute to a peer exchange where many people will see the dialogue—group and social accountability come into play. So, the true experts on an issue weigh in, there's less fluff, and the quality of the collaborative communication improves noticeably. Salesforce.com gets things resolved more efficiently, and better. Leaders and others in the chain of authority get the unfiltered truth, for better and for worse.

As Marc Benioff noted in the Foreword to this book, collaboration platforms haven't been reimagined in decades. I think they are being reimagined right under our noses, and that tools like Chatter, Yammer, and Jive[13] are the first versions of these new social-collaboration platforms enabling the power of transactive memory.

Like most people, I've spent my entire career working in a team environment. Client teams, account teams, product teams, service teams, leadership teams, management teams, project teams, study teams, proposal teams, connectivity teams, recruiting teams, presentation teams, boards, coaching teams— nothing gets done in business without a joint effort. One person may have individual tasks and singular responsibilities but these are all part of a bigger system, and that larger environment is really a compilation of many, many individual systems.

Companies originally came into existence because of how efficiently and effectively they organized people to work together and stay together, but the need for large, monolithic organizations is ending. The rise of the Social Company will usher in a new, networked organizational model and design unencumbered by the transaction costs of the past. Fabio Rosati, the CEO of Elance, explains:

> Our global workforce is now on the threshold of a major transformation not witnessed since the Industrial Revolution. Through major advances in technology and the emergence of experts with

---

[13] Yammer (part of Microsoft) and Jive are software companies that provide private social networks for businesses to help employees and business partners connect, communicate, create communities, and collaborate.

highly demanded new skills in all regions of the world, labor markets have never been more fluid.

The result will be a leveling of the playing field for workers and companies alike. Professionals from anywhere will increasingly be able to compete for the best jobs, while businesses will have new freedom to hire the best online freelance teams for any given project. This revolution is only possible because of these shifting paradigms. It is the companies and workers who embrace these changes who will best succeed in tomorrow's exciting new economy. (personal communication, 15 October 2012)

So, I conclude that everybody *is* smarter than anybody—but only when social technology is a key component of the equation. As Wegner stated in his 1987 article, "The transactive memory system, in short, is more than its individual component systems" (p. 190). I believe the potential of transactive memory has finally been unlocked through today's social technology.

The effects that social technology has "captured and put to use" (Arthur 2009, p. 51) around the behaviors of connecting, communicating, collaborating, and community all facilitate the flow and exchange of information, the development of knowledge, and the ways companies deploy that knowledge. Finally, there is a technology that removes the friction and enables massive, collaborative information- and knowledge-exchange. The Social Company is not just incrementally smarter and better-informed because of this information flow—it is potentially orders of magnitude more productive and smarter. The innovation and creativity that will spawn from these environments has the potential to reinvent business, as social technology's 802,013 year journey continues.

✕ A Killer Future Forged through Social Technology

McKinsey has identified over a trillion dollars of economic value that can be released by business through social technology (Chui et al. 2012, p. 1), but this future is far from certain. The *2012 Edelman Trust Barometer* research shows that consumers around the world are extremely dissatisfied with business and governments (slides 24–25). Gallup adds that employees are grossly disengaged in their work (2010, p. 2). To make matters worse, U.S. economic growth is experiencing a considerable slowdown: Economics professor Robert J. Gordon even contemplates whether U.S. economic growth is essentially over and suggests it may decline to a rate below 0.5% per year for decades (2012, abstract). As the United States has been the "worldwide frontier of productivity and the standard of living…since the late 19th century" (p. 1), is the potential for a U.S. slowdown an ominous sign for the rest of the world?

How important is the issue of growth, and what is the role of social technology in driving it? Does the combination of consumer dissatisfaction, employee dissatisfaction, and stalling U.S. growth point toward a crisis for business in the United States and around the world? No matter how these questions play out, what the modern corporation has created needs to be improved upon because it is not working as well as it needs to be.

Being smarter and more productive are the cornerstones of social technology (see Part 2). Can the innovation and productivity gains delivered by these tools create new economic growth for companies and economies by making things more valuable? Can businesses use the current crisis to move to higher, more valuable ground? I believe they can, and to some extent already are. Stanford Economist Paul Romer has concluded, "Economic growth occurs whenever people take resources and rearrange them in ways that make them more valuable" (2008, para. 7); significantly, he also stated that "A crisis is a terrible thing to waste" (Rosenthal 2009, para. 2).

The global economic pie has been expanding for a very long time, although the rate of expansion has been slowing. The global average per-capita GDP was $467 in the year 1 C.E. and $7,614 at the end of 2008 (Maddison 2010, "PerCapita GDP" tab). In other words, even though the worldwide population expanded from 225 million 6.7 billion people over the last two millennia, there have been increasing economic returns for the human race; the economic pie has been expanding and the human standard of living along with it. The United States leads the world with a 2008 per capita GDP of $31,004; for comparison, the per capita GDP in China was $6,725 in that same year ("PerCapita GDP" tab). If China's per capita GDP growth were to rise toward

U.S. levels, that would reflect a very large upside for global economic growth—but it's not that simple.

The more recent, slower growth can be alarming, but can be interpreted differently when history is taken into account. Average per capita GDP growth in the United States between 1 C.E. and 2008 C.E. was about 0.2% —not a lot, but most of this growth occurred from the 1870s onward. The compound annual growth rate from 1876 (the year that Alexander Graham Bell invented the telephone) to 2008 has been almost 2% per year (figures based on Maddison 2010, "PerCapita GDP" tab). I highlight these numbers because that second, higher level of growth is what people in the United States and much of Western Europe have come to expect. The difference in the numbers is stark: It would take an economy 346 years to double at a 0.2% growth rate, whereas it would take a little over 35 years to double at a 2% growth rate, or about one generation. If economist Robert Gordon's (2012) prognostications come to fruition, a U.S. future driven by economic growth of less than 0.5% (abstract) will be a very different one than a future driven by 2% growth.

One might ask whether the economic pie would expand if the rest of the world were able to achieve the per capita output of the United States. However, Romer (2008) points out the problem with this assumption with his "simple metaphor from the kitchen" (para. 7):

> The cooking one can do is limited by the *supply* of ingredients, and most cooking in the economy produces undesirable side effects. If economic growth could be achieved only by doing more and more of the same kind of cooking, we would eventually run out of raw materials and suffer from unacceptable levels of pollution and nuisance. Human history teaches us, however, that economic growth springs from better recipes, not just from more cooking. New recipes generally produce fewer unpleasant side effects and generate more economic value per unit of raw material. (para. 7)

So, the growth challenge is one of both productivity and innovation for business. Companies and economies not only need to do more with less, but they also need to do things better—enabling Schumpeter's (2008) concept of industrial mutation driven by creative destruction.

The solution to sustainable growth and profit maximization can no longer be found solely by engineering costs. The *World Happiness Report* (Helliwell, Layard, & Sachs 2012) explains why by declaring that economic advancement, while important, is not the only human objective. Romer's (2008) kitchen example also helps to explain why: There are declining returns to scale for economic outputs if, in order to produce them, we destroy our health and environment, and create suffering for others along the way.

Companies need to focus not only on cost reduction as a means to economic success, but also on innovation—doing things better. The U.S. *Declaration of Independence* (1776) asserts that the "pursuit of Happiness" is an "unalienable Right" (para. 2). Rather than gross domestic product alone, Bhutan measures its progress as a country using a concept called Gross National Happiness or GNH (Ura, Alkire, Zangmo, & Wangdi 2012). This idea dates back to the unification of Bhutan: their 1729 legal code declared that "if the Government cannot create happiness (*dekid*) for its people, there is no purpose for the Government to exist" (p. 6).

The lesson here for business is that if your company doesn't make your customers, employees, partners, communities, and investors happy, there is no reason for your company to exist. Social technology and the billions of people using it are now an empowered judge and jury. In Part 3: Toyota Drives toward a Social Destiny, Marc Benioff tells the story of "Toyota Friend" and how Toyota is creating a unique experience for their customers and employees through social technology. What business offers to the world needs to evolve because the world has evolved.

Social technology is a key component of the changes taking place in the world; these new tools now have a leading role in shaping the future of business. There are very few definitive right answers in business—it's largely an iterative exercise to understand markets and provide them with the services, solutions, or products that satisfy their needs and wants. Customers and employees are not getting what they want, and economic growth is at risk. Social technology is already reinventing how people experience their world. The challenge and opportunity for businesses is to figure out how to focus on the experience of their customers, and this opportunity now unfolds in real time—actions, even inaction, have considerable weight.

Your company's job is to figure out how to use social technology to create a valuable experience that keeps your markets, employees, and investors happy. Happiness is a good thing, and as Toyota has already learned, happiness and economic success now go hand-in-hand.

Michael Porter
and
the Holy Grail

Companies achieve competitive advantage
through acts of innovation. They approach
innovation in its broadest sense, including both
new technologies and new ways of doing things.

–Michael Porter (1990, p. 1)

✦ Unique = Michael Porter + Social Technology

Social technology is a new competitive weapon for business and a way to change how companies do things and compete; it's not just a marketing or customer service tool. Those who have studied Michael Porter's thinking[14] already have a head start on understanding why social technology is such a game-changer.

Michael Porter is recognized as one of the greatest business management thinkers of our time. His breakthrough books *Competitive Strategy* (1980) and *Competitive Advantage* (1985) form the foundation of modern business management theory on these subjects. His "five forces" and "value chain" frameworks are the starting points for contemporary thinking around profitability and competition, and have been taught around the world.

Competitive strategy: what does it have to do with social technology, and why is it critically important? Porter provides us with the answer, in his own words.

> "I believe that many companies undermine their own strategies. Nobody does it to them. They do it to themselves. Their strategies fail from within." (as cited by Magretta 2012, p. 190)

Strategy is critical because the modern corporation has smothered it as well— suffocated it in same quagmire of institutional sludge that has drowned the rest of the organization.

What about competitive advantage—why does it matter? The social technology-empowered business collides with Porter's thinking through its ability to deliver something that is "unique." Competitive differentiation and value is now being driven, captured, and sustained by creating engagement and a unique experience through social technology, establishing a new playing field for business. Business management now centers on delivering

---

[14] Joan Magretta, Michael Porter's long-time editor at the *Harvard Business Review* wrote a fantastic book titled *Understanding Michael Porter: The Essential Guide to Competition and Strategy* (2012). This book offers a comprehensive look at Porter's body of work, and presents his thinking in a well-articulated compilation. If you are not familiar with Porter, Joan Magretta's book is a recommended read.

a differentiated experience to employees, investors, and customers through these tools.

Strategy is also impacted because social technology changes the balance of power between companies and their markets, which directly impacts the issue of profitability. Competitive advantage comes into play because the way value is created, sustained, and potentially captured is altered with this technology. Competing on innovation, rather than imitation, is now a market necessity.

Being unique is at the heart of Porter's thinking as it enables an organization to fully capitalize on the primary strategic mandate of every for-profit company—superior profitability (Magretta 2012, pp. 29, 71). This is easy to say, but difficult to achieve, of course; fortunately, Porter's thinking helps here, too. Magretta (2012) articulates Porter's influential thinking around competitive advantage succinctly:

> "[competitive advantage] means that compared with rivals, you operate at a lower cost, command a premium price, or both." (p. 64)

With this simple definition, a company has a competitive advantage if, on a relative basis, it commands a premium price or is operating more efficiently, or both. That's it. These two dimensions align with revenue and costs, which net to superior relative profitability. If your company does not have either one, you truly do not have a competitive advantage and your poor relative profitability will reflect it. If you have both, you have something really special—massive relative profits.

Porter's litmus test (above) identifies *when* a company has a competitive advantage, but what *is* a competitive advantage and where does it come from? Magretta (2012) explains:

> "For Porter, strategic competition means choosing a path different from that of others. Instead of competing to be the best, companies can—and should—compete to be unique." (p. 29)

Unique—what a great word and powerful concept. In our knockoff-enabled business world, being unique is difficult. Differences between discrete products and services have largely become a victim of the very business management practices that spawned them. Any new product or feature gets copied and brought to market almost immediately by all market competitors. In the end, competition is based on price and mediocrity reigns supreme.

Business has mastered the art of imitation; knock-off products, features, and services largely eliminate the ability of many companies to declare victory over Porter's concept of uniqueness as a driver of competitive advantage. If a company cannot differentiate along these lines, it cannot establish a competitive advantage, which means no superior profits. Where physical products or services become interchangeable parts, management focuses relentlessly on costs to maintain margins. A century of business management theory and practice focused on productivity has delivered business to this point.

Applying Porter's definition to modern companies, Apple has a strong competitive advantage. Apple commands a premium price for its products and has enormous profits—their strategy is working according to Porter's model. However, it hasn't always been that way. At the end of its 2003 fiscal year, Apple had slightly over $6 billion in revenue and had an operating loss that year (Apple 2003, p. 57). Less than a decade later, the company has over $150 billion in net sales and operating income margins north of 30% (Apple 2012b, p. 43). While Apple is a producer of some of the key tools enabling other companies to deliver a unique experience through social technology, they also excel at using these same tools to deliver their own, very Apple-esque experience.

Apple's strategy is interwoven with the *experience* that they strive to provide to their customers. The first line on page one of their 2012 *Annual Report* (Apple 2012b) under "Business Strategy," states that "The Company is committed to bringing the best user experience to its customers through its innovative hardware, software, peripherals, and services."

Social technology is an enabler of Porter's interpretations around strategy and competitive advantage, and is bringing out the value inherent in being unique.

Magretta summarizes this succinctly: "Competing to be the best feeds on imitation. Competing to be unique thrives on innovation" (2012, p. 31).

Innovation through social technology is the Holy Grail for the Social Company. While innovation is not a new mantra for business, understanding how social technology enables and delivers innovation certainly is.

As discussed in Part 2, history shows that social technology makes people smarter and more productive, which is inevitably good for business. Does being smarter help a company figure out ways to solve problems differently? Does it allow businesses to accomplish things more efficiently and effectively? Do these attributes help companies be more creative? Yes, yes, and yes. In addition, these attributes translate into helping a company figure out ways to establish and maintain premium prices, or to lower its cost base.

Leaders and managers have been overly focused on only one dimension of Porter's thinking: having the lowest relative cost base. Outsourcing, offshoring, downsizing, and mergers and acquisitions are all levers to achieve cost reductions through value redistribution. Anyone can cut costs, and anyone has. Achieving a premium price in the market by *creating* value has been a casualty of the incessant drone of cost-reduction initiatives. Business management history has been productivity-focused, and without the ability to achieve more output from productive assets (whether labor- or capital-based), the simpler way to raise productivity and preserve profitability has been to lower the cost of the company's inputs.

Creating value is a much different and more difficult undertaking, but the past has set up the social technology-enabled future for business. The history of business management theory and practice has been a roaring—albeit partial—success, accomplishing many things it was designed to do. As markets matured, however, the playing field leveled and businesses increasingly competed on price because their products and services were no longer unique (or were only fleetingly unique).

Focusing on "the experience" is a rational evolutionary next step in business management theory. This new avenue is built upon a thorough understanding and exploitation of the preceding business-management domains (the work, the organization, and the individual), the arrival of new social technologies, and the resulting changes in human behaviors that are occurring everywhere.

The stage is set for social technology-fueled innovation and transformation. Delivering on "the experience" requires creating something that is unique by using social technology—and achieving Michael Porter's strategic goal of superior profitability along the way.

The history of the word *experience* aligns closely with the concepts of "experiment," or to try and to test (Dictionary.com n.d., "experience"). A business management philosophy predicated on this concept compliments my earlier point that business management has been, and remains, an iterative activity. The experiment is now moving a lot faster than it has before, with a lot more people involved—the added dimensions of spatial and temporal relevancy are also new factors.

Porter says that technology is disruptive when it "would invalidate important competitive advantages" (Magretta 2012, p. 198). Both the arrival of social technology and its consumer-driven nature impact Porter's two points surrounding competitive advantage: premium price and lower cost. Social technology invalidates key competitive advantages directly and also by altering the structure around industry profitability and competitive rivalry.

Porter's thinking has been taught, dissected, and debated extensively, but his thoughts have never been more on-point than they are today. Social technology-enabled and -empowered businesses can exploit the promise of uniqueness to achieve the goal of superior profitability.

◂ A Sixth Force Collides with Porter's "Five Forces"

Porter's "five forces" model provides a framework for understanding industry structure and profitability, and his "value chain" model helps understand relative position within an industry (Magretta 2012, p. 65). Both are distinctively impacted by social technology.

Porter's five forces model starts by recognizing that firms in an industry have a rivalry directly with each other, as shown in the center of Figure 4-1. For example, McDonald's directly competes with Burger King, Dell with HP, and Starbucks with Peet's—or, in Southern California, the Coffee Bean & Tea Leaf (much of this book was written at Manhattan Beach store #22). The discrete actions of one firm directly impact the competitive environment between all of the firms.

Figure 4-1. Porter's Five Forces. Author's image; data from Porter (1985, p. 5).

This model also recognizes the other forces at play in the competitive environment: less overt but equally powerful agents competing for their own maximum advantage. Consumers (or buyers) want companies to lower prices, suppliers want to raise the prices they charge, and employees want raises— all so that they can have a bigger piece of the overall "pie."

In addition, new companies want to enter the market, and other companies want to introduce and substitute their products into the market. Burgers?

Have a Subway sandwich instead. PCs? Get an iPad. Another cup of coffee? 5-hour Energy is better. The direct forces competing for business are as powerful as the indirect forces trying to grab each revenue dollar.

These various dynamics create a constant state of volatility and risk, as well as a land of opportunity. As I explore in the rest of this section, social technology impacts the game distinctively along each of Porter's five forces and potentially increases the power of each. It changes industry dynamics and alters the competitive nature of direct rivalry by giving a company new tools to outperform its competitors in the never-ending battle for business.

Rivalry Between Firms

In head-to-head competition (i.e., a social technology leader vs. a laggard), the Social Company wins, hands-down, on the bottom line of superior profitability. First and foremost, social technology delivers worker productivity enhancements, which is a valuable advantage for early adopters. Because of this alone, the Social Company can deliver on this dimension of Porter's framework—lower relative costs—and thereby achieving superior profitability relative to others in the industry. Higher profitability translates into investor value.

However, social technology really stands out because of its effect on the business top line (revenue and sales). Social Companies are all about delivering a meaningful experience to their customers, employees, and investors through these tools. Leaders of Social Companies have a better understanding of their markets and can translate these insights into a more meaningful value proposition: Being smarter about customers, competitors, markets, and trends is very good for business. These companies then start to strengthen their bargaining power with their customers because they are delivering more value to their markets, which means they can support their prices more effectively. By delivering a unique experience, value is created, some of which will be captured by the firm that created it.

Employees who use today's social technologies are more engaged individually and more effective as a group, as the company's collective intelligence rises through better collaboration. As a result, problems are being solved more efficiently and effectively, productivity is rising, innovation is rising, and employee turnover is being favorably impacted. Information flows more effectively and transparency, and trust is going up. Employee engagement overall—a habitual problem in most organizations—also improves.

Enhanced employee engagement is a critical value driver for any company. Gallup's global survey on employee engagement[15] indicates that 89% of workers are either not engaged or are actively disengaged (2010, p. 1). Employees everywhere are "dialing it in." The business-management experiment of the last century is clearly not working for most employees around the world. Furthermore, Gallup's research[16] indicates that earnings-per-share for highly engaged groups were almost 350% higher than their less-engaged peers (p. 4).

Switching costs for customers are also rising as the overall experience with a company improves and takes hold. British Airways recently announced a program to use the social presence of their premium customers to identify them on sight in order to enhance their travel experience, starting with greeting them by name upon boarding (Hill 2012). That real-time approach to creating a unique experience through social technology is intended to enrich the experience offered to British Airways customers. This level of personalized engagement and service creates a strong dividing line between British Airways and other carriers that cannot or will not create this kind of overall experience. Experiences are comprised of a lot of little things that add up to one big thing: being unique. Every component part of the British Airways experience that their customers value, makes it that much harder for their customers to go elsewhere. Where value can be added, it can be captured.

Reinventing value propositions by delivering a unique experience with social technology and creating value in the process—this is the playing field of the future. The Social Company will compete on social technology-based innovation, not imitation. Commodity offerings will start to disappear from

---

[15] Gallup's 2010 survey included over 47,000 employees in 120 different countries.

[16] Gallup examined 54 companies from their 2010 overall survey; 14 of those 54 were included in the group of "exceptional employee engagement levels or engagement growth" (2010, p. 4).

the equation, and the race to the bottom through price-based competition will be relegated to the uninformed and the social technology-challenged.

Through social technology, competitive advantages are emerging that will sustain premium prices over time. Premium price, delivered more efficiently with social technology: the double Porter whammy for achieving superior profitability.

Disruption occurs most dramatically at the beginning of these cycles. Competitive intensity between rivals is rising as firms adopt and deploy social technologies, and as traditional business practices get disrupted and re-engineered. The costs and risks of morphing into a Social Company are not inconsequential, but the cost of *not* adopting this technology is far, far greater: irrelevancy.

Social Companies are starting to change industry structure and both the size and their share of the pie, much like Apple has done. When a Social Company creates new levels of value, or economic surplus, the opportunity to capture this value improves. Transition periods during the adoption and deployment of disruptive technologies are always volatile, and who ultimately gains is far from certain.

Buyer Power

Buyers benefit most from the shifting tides of power created through social technology, both in B2C and B2B markets. Socially empowered consumers create a permanent and unprecedented seismic shift in the balance of power because they have better information and the ability to collectively act as a result of this technology. Consumers can win a greater slice of the pie in the form of lower prices and better quality, service, availability, choice, and so on, through the power of social technology.

The ability of social consumers to collectively organize and act quickly and efficiently gives them advantages over every company around the world[17]; the

---

[17] A 14-year-old girl's change.org petition received support from 84,000 people and forced *Seventeen* to take a more truthful approach to the images of young women in their magazine (Huffington Post 2012); over 60,000 of these signatures were tallied in just 20 days (change.org 2012, News section).

fact that these consumers are significantly ahead of most companies in their use of social technology is a major risk for business. Massive boycotts and consumer demands are now possible on an unprecedented scale—imagine what a million consumers could accomplish through collective action!

Information asymmetries are closing for business because of social technology; all parties in Porter's model are potentially better informed than ever before. Implementation asymmetries will create advantages for the early adopters of these tools. Ultimately, though, significantly more power is in the hands of the socially enabled individual—this, in and of itself, is the ultimate trump card for Porter's five forces model.

When power skews so heavily toward one dimension, money follows. Social tools that enable mass organization and coordination potentially increase consumer power to quasi-monopolistic levels. Leadership and an understanding of this power amongst consumers is lacking so far, but that will change. We've seen collective action in a civil and social scenario[18] already— this power is coming to bear on the for-profit marketplace even as you read this book.

When supply catches up with demand and there are abundant market choices for undifferentiated offerings, the bargaining power of buyers increases. In late 2011 Amazon released its Price Check application for mobile phones, which scans the UPC barcode on a product and shows the consumer the same product through Amazon (see Amazon.com 2011). UPC codes date back to the mid-1970s, but this latest ability to exploit them is only now possible because of social technology. Amazon has successfully begun "showrooming": hijacking a competitor's customer at their competitor's point of sale, turning every competitor from Best Buy to Wal-Mart into a potential Amazon showroom. Customers browse, linger, look, touch, and feel—the facility costs for the store, staffing, transportation, marketing, and inventory are born by Amazon's competitors, but Amazon closes the sale. Price Check is a business model disruptor and an extremely powerful tool that increases the buyer's and

---

[18] See, e.g., Firger (2012), "Occupy 2.0: Protesters Go High-Tech"; Delany (2011), "How Social Media Accelerated Tunisia's Revolution: An Inside View."

Amazon's competitive power, and it is just one part of the entire Amazon experience that is changing the face of retail shopping.[19]

The dynamic shift in buyers' power offered by social technology skews Porter's model heavily in their favor. Buyers have never had more information, more leverage (individually or as a group), or more tools to get or give real-time feedback on a product or service. What has your company done about this permanent shift in the balance of power?

While social technology is a permanent win for buyers, companies are not defenseless. The Social Company counters with a social technology-enabled strategy, social engagement techniques, and a recognition that being unique is the best defense. Creating a unique experience can diffuse the collective power of buyers and actually leverage it in the company's favor.

Supplier Power

Suppliers also want the largest possible piece of the economic pie. For example, employees are an integral part of any company's supply chain. Unions are one traditional way that U.S. employees have collectively bargained and staked their claim to the pie. In Japan, the overt lifetime employment model and the labor laws supporting it ensure that employees get a larger piece of the pie than they otherwise would.

In business, every company is both a buyer and a seller—how does this dynamic counterbalance? I believe the pivotal issue is a subtle one, but it tips the scales heavily into the buyers' favor. Buyers always have the option of doing nothing, but sellers must always sell. Buyers hold the ultimate trump card; they can fire any company simply by taking their money elsewhere or by not spending it at all.

Sellers can fight back though, by developing a superior offer through social technology tools and techniques. That's the entire point of this new technology—changing the game to an experience increases the power of any seller in Porter's five forces model because of the ability to create a unique

---

[19] As with much disruptive technology, this application is not without controversy. See also Wohlsen (2012), Kain (2011), DesMarais (2011), S. Li (2011), and Weisenthal (2012).

and superior offer that buyers find irresistible. Social technology-enabled sellers can gain power through social technology because they are creating an experience that is driven by deep understanding and engagement with their markets. For example, Apple has a tremendous lock on its user base. From the iPhone to the App Store, iCloud, and Apple retail environment, an integrated symphony of experience occurs that is specific to Apple. Replicating the overall Apple experience is an enormous barrier to entry that Apple has built and is exploiting very effectively. Apple's buyers also pay a premium to opt into this one-of-a-kind experience.

This growth in supplier power occurs regardless of where a company is in the supply chain. The stronger a company's social technology presence and approach, relative to others in a market, the better-off the company will be.

Threat of Substitutes and Threat of New Entrants

Through these two forces, Porter's model addresses the fact that human tastes are fickle and fungible, and that there's always something better around the corner. Why fly when I can drive? Why own a car when I can use Zipcar? Why go to a restaurant when I can cook a nice steak at home? Why cook at all, when someone else can cook for me through Cookitfor.us? Why stay at a hotel, when I can find a nice room on Airbnb.com?

Substitute products and services are increasingly bountiful and directly and indirectly fight for the same dollar, euro, or yen in the mind of a buyer. Airbnb.com circumvents the traditional capital intensity of the hotel industry by eliminating the need to build rooms. Zipcar does the same for vehicle ownership and access, while Cookitfor.us lowers the capital barrier for food service by eliminating the need to build a restaurant. Each of these companies also connects with its marketplace in a location- and time-specific fashion, making its value proposition unique. Designed and built as natively social businesses, they've created new sources of value—where there were none before.

The fight for revenue has never been more intense or more unpredictable. Substitute products or services such as those mentioned above all have one thing in common: They are enabled and executed by information and social technologies. These services could not be delivered as efficiently or effectively, or at all, without these tools. Social technology changes the balance of power for substitute offerings and new entrants in the marketplace through its ability to reinvent value propositions, cost-effectively. If your company wasn't already worried enough about your existing competitors, it's time to realize that the potential for displacement from a new or non-traditional competitor has never been greater.

New entrants have the opportunity to leapfrog existing market participants with a social technology-enabled proposition, which raises the threat level that new entrants represent for any business or industry. These new entrants will deliver a social experience by design, and slow-moving incumbents will be disrupted before they know what hit them. As the examples above demonstrate, business and industry disruptions frequently come from the outside. Social technology is a competitive weapon that offers a powerful combination of business benefits around productivity and innovation. As social technology is understood further in terms of how it can be used for business, disruption will accelerate across many domains as new entrants learn how to change value propositions and industry dynamics in their favor.

Incumbents have enormous costs sunk into their legacy IT investments. The length of time needed for an incumbent to implement an enterprise-wide social technology strategy and move to the future is likely to create opportunities for new Social Company entrants. New entrants have an advantage when the barriers to market entry are lowered, and I believe that the traditional barriers to entry (capital requirements, cost advantages, switching costs, distribution access, and proprietary assets) are becoming less valuable to incumbents in the face of new entrants that can innovate with today's social technologies.

Changing the Balance of Power

Social technology, with its consumer-driven nature and usability, impacts Porter's constructs on industry profitability and rivalry. Breakthrough technology developments change competition by altering industry structure and by giving companies new ways to outperform their competitors. In short, they disrupt the status quo by changing the balance of power.

Social technology can potentially increase every one of Porter's forces, creating something like an arms race—a competition for supremacy where early adopters have a clear advantage in determining how industry structures and profits get redistributed. In the war for profits, social technologies actually get deployed, though; they are not merely a threat. As a result, the end state is guaranteed to be different than the beginning state because tools get adopted and deployed at different paces. There is an incredible opportunity for those companies that understand this dynamic and act on it.

Social technology presents companies and markets with both a new opportunity and new risks, changing the rules across every one of Porter's dimensions (most drastically with regard to buyer power, but significantly at every point in his model; see Table 4-1). That's why this is a game-changer for business—the big picture and macro dynamics are being altered by a new and disruptive technology. The social technology arms race is on.

◄ How Strong Are the Links in Porter's Value Chain?

Social technology not only changes the nature of industry dynamics, as we saw with Porter's (1980) five forces model, but also impacts his "value chain" model (1985). I've used Porter's value chain model, or derivatives of it, extensively throughout my career. This valuable tool helps managers visualize the totality of their business and understand how and why the collective whole is delivering those particular results. Figure 4-2 presents one possible value chain, representing the collection of activities that a business performs to achieve its strategy.

Joan Magretta explains that Porter would say that strategy should achieve "superior profitability" (2012, p. 20); the value chain is concerned with how a company arrives at superior profitability. She also concludes, "If your value chain looks like everybody else's, then you are engaged in competition to be the best" (p. 80). Porter, she goes on to explain, disdains "competition to be the best" (p. 21) as the path to mediocrity and instead promotes being "unique" as the path to creating value (p. 29).

Table 4-1: Social Technology's Impact on Porter's Five Forces

Porter's force	Δ	Outcome
Competitive intensity	Increases	Early adopters win over laggards; the productivity benefits delivered by social technology reduce costs and improve innovation.
Buyer power	Increases (the ultimate winner)	Social technology-enabled buyers are now in charge. Collective action, together with more and better information delivered quickly, means buyers win big. Information asymmetries are also diminishing and are in the markets' favor.
Supplier power	Increases	Suppliers can counter buyer power with the very same social tools. Social technology can deliver a unique experience that increases price and "stickiness" by increasing value. Early adopters will have an advantage—laggards will get annihilated.
Substitutes and new entrants	Increases	Power increases if competitors use social technology against incumbents. Markets want social offerings and incumbents have a handicap: their legacy IT environments and offerings. Market entry costs are lowered and innovation is occurring across many staid sectors.

Note. Author's table.

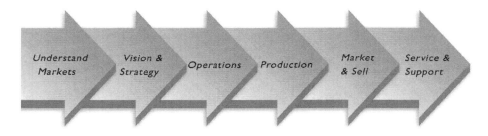

Figure 4-2. Porter's Value Chain. Author's image.

So far, companies have largely been focused on viewing social technology as a tool for marketing (getting a Facebook page, creating a Twitter feed, etc.; Bughin, Hung Byers, & Chui 2011, Exhibit 7); however, because social technology changes human behavior, it impacts every activity a company performs that involves employees, customers, investors, or partners. Today's companies are faced with the challenge of rethinking how social technology changes what it means to connect, communicate, collaborate, and create community across all of the activities in their business.

The activities along the value chain define how a firm achieves its profitability compared to its rivals. Differences in what these value chain activities are, how they are performed, how they sync, and what overall approach is taken can have material business model and performance implications.

Dell's famous approach was to sell before production, direct to the consumer, which changed their economic model and gave them other product advantages in a rapidly evolving market. Dell pioneered a different way to align these activities that let the company operate at a much lower cost-point, and also offer more value in its products (MaRS 2012).

Apple's model is very vertical and integrated with its design capability, software platforms, device platforms, retail distribution, and sales, but the component parts for its devices are largely manufactured and assembled by others. Apple controls the parts of its value chain that let the company own its distinctive experience.

The activities that a company chooses to perform, and how it does them, determine the firm's value chain, and that value chain drives the company's piece of the economic pie. The value chain is the essence of every company.

Understanding how these component parts come together is vital to being able to adopt and deploy a disruptive technology that is fundamentally about human behavior.

◀ Leveraging Porter to Become a Social Company

Getting started is always a challenge with large-scale transformations in any company—what comes first and where is the starting point? Porter's value chain is an effective way to deconstruct a business and then rebuild it against the 4 Cs of *Social Inc.* behavior. The 2x2 matrix in Figure 4-3 can be used to orient your ideas into a relative structure. These questions will start the conversation:

1. If we can bring time and spatial relevancy to our business, products, and services, how can we change what we do to create and capture more value?
2. How can we connect, communicate, collaborate, or create community with these tools to be more productive and also be smarter as a business and company?

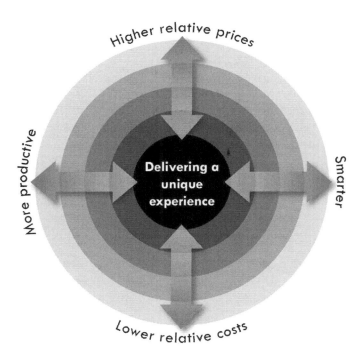

Figure 4-3. Where Porter and Social Technology Meet. Author's image.

Management practice, so far, has manifested itself in the commoditization of business, products, and services; management theory, especially as espoused by Michael Porter, has expected more. Business management doctrine to date has been wildly successful in teaching businesses how to drive costs down, but I believe that this one-sided approach is skewed and has contributed to the economic malaise of our time (e.g., deficits, stubborn unemployment levels, low- to no growth) and an economic pie that should be growing faster.

Business and individual consumers have seemingly "won" the battle by having vast options to purchase at lower and lower price points. However, I suggest we have won the battle but lost the war. Undifferentiated products and services abound. The quest for market share leans toward a monopolistic strategy that gives the monopolist a weapon against price reductions (i.e., the lack of choice).

I believe we have done a much better job on the cost dimension of Porter's thinking than we have on the other—and I believe more critical—aspect of innovating to be unique. The easy lifting in business management has been done and exploited; the heavy lifting is beginning with this latest version of social technology.

Porter's path to superior profitability derives from a value proposition that commands premium pricing and/or lower relative operating costs. However, the ability to command a premium price from markets has been relatively unreachable for most managers and their companies. Magretta summarizes Porter's view on the role of strategy: "What value will your organization create? And how will you capture some of that value for yourself?" (2012, p. 20). Delivering things less expensively can create value but value can also be created by *making things more valuable*.

It's time to focus on the hard stuff—creating value—and fortunately, social technology presents an opportunity to do just that. Historically, I argue, volatility in markets has exposed change, and particularly rapid change, as the weak link in traditional business-management theories (see Part 3). Change is now constant, rampant, and voracious, and the future will teach us that social technology is the right tool at the right time to take business management to its next monumental step—the Age of the Experience.

The *Social Inc.* model thrives in a changing environment and delivers on both value-creation and -capture. Competition based on delivering an experience requires a much better understanding of markets and an ability to execute that is markedly more nimble and agile than historical approaches. Social technology is the enabler, and is key to the overall equation; however, the entire approach to business must evolve to take full benefit of these tools. This is a technology-enabled opportunity, but every dimension of a company is impacted and will also need to evolve. Table 4-2 presents some of the key differences in the overall strategy and management approach required of the Social Company.

Table 4-2: *Social Inc.* versus Traditional Inc.

Management facet	Traditional company	*Social Company*
Strategy	Increasing market share	Achieving superior profits
Operational focus	Optimizing work, organizing at scale, motivating the individual	Creating and delivering a unique experience to employees, customers, investors, and partners
Delivery structure	Hierarchical	Heterarchical[20]
Organization model	Cooperative	Collaborative
Value source	Lowering costs	Innovation *and* productivity
Structure	Silo-ed, best practices, static processes, focus on preventing problems, reactive	Flat, unique practices, dynamic processes, focus on fixing problems, adaptive
Labor	Best company to work for	Best company to work with
Communications	Directive, top-down	Engaged, outside-in, bottom-up
Governance model	Oversight	Advisory
Decision model	Binary, research-driven, slow	Experimental, engagement-based, quick
Competitive ambition	Monopoly	Unique-opoly
Social mission	Support	Shape

Note. Author's table.

---

[20] *Heterarchical* describes a formal structure of connected nodes, without any single permanent uppermost node (Dictionary.com n.d., "heterarchy"), and is distinct from *hierarchical*, describing a group that is classified according to ability or to economic, social, or professional standing (Merriam Webster n.d., "hierarchy").

SOCIAL "INC-ONOMICS" AND THE Z-EFFECT

The Internet is the first thing that
humanity has built that
humanity doesn't understand,
the largest experiment in anarchy
that we have ever had.

–Eric Schmidt, CEO, Google
(Taylor 2010, para. 24)

⤴ Anarchy, One Connection at a Time

Economics is about people—how individuals choose, decide, and interact. Alfred Marshall said, "Economics is the study of men as they live and move and think in the ordinary business of life" (Marshall 1890, Book 1, Chapter 2, para. 1).

The first rule of *Social Inc.* is that social technology is about human behavior; when behavior changes, certain economic forces can also be altered. In this chapter I discuss social "Inc-onomics": a key economic factor influencing the Social Company.

The core economic impact of social technology has its roots in Nobel laureate Ronald Coase's work around transaction costs. His 1937 paper, "The Nature of the Firm," analyzed the question of why companies form at all. Essentially, tightly linking, organizing, and controlling people in an artificial structure such a company was much more efficient than the alternative of trying to organize and engage in the external market.

Larry Downes and Chunka Mui updated this concept for the internet and the digital revolution, in their book *Unleashing the Killer App* (1998). Building on Coase's work, Downes and Mui proposed a new law: the Law of the Diminishing Firm.

> As the market becomes more efficient, the size and organizational complexity of the modern industrial firm becomes uneconomic, since firms exist only to the extent that they reduce transaction costs more effectively. (p. 7)

They predicted, from 1998, that the new technology would lower transaction costs, and as a result, the size of the firm would decrease based on Coase's presumption.

While the practice of outsourcing exploded subsequent to Downes and Mui's work and downsizings have been the norm of late, the net effect is not definitive. The data does not show that firms have shrunk in size—yet.

I think Downes and Mui were right, and just how right is only becoming apparent now in 2013, almost fifteen years after they introduced their theory. Social technology is finally enabling what they proposed and changing Coase's conclusions from almost seventy-five years ago.

When transaction costs in the external market are markedly reduced because of information and social technology, as they are now, the corporation does not need to exist to wring transaction costs out of exchanges. The artificial structure and boundaries of the modern corporation, together with the handicaps that legacy IT imposes, have hobbled Coase's version of the company with massive inefficiencies.

Downes and Mui also proposed a Law of Disruption, which states, "Where social systems improve incrementally, technology improves exponentially" (1998, p. 9). The truth of this law has also been altered because of social technology—social systems have both exploded and imploded because of social technology tools. Rather than incremental, changes in social systems have been significant because of these tools. Changes in society and business now mirror the rapid pace of technology development.

Hindsight is always the best teacher. In 1937, I'm pretty certain that it was much cheaper to organize as a firm than to transact in the free market. The telephone was still in its relative infancy, travel was time-consuming, information exchange was paper-based, and transaction costs were everywhere. Markets were a lot less efficient than they are today.

As technology has advanced, humanity has now reached a tipping point for business and society. Social upheaval now happens quickly, and so does business disruption. The historical economic concept proposed by Coase, which led to the modern incarnation of "the firm," is now being disrupted by social technology.

"The firm" in its current incarnation is now the problem. The modern corporation is its own worst enemy in terms of getting things done—the bigger the company, the bigger the problem. Markets move faster than the speed at which modern firms can respond. The modern corporation or organization as it is conceptualized, organized, led, governed, and managed has become the weak link.

Managers exert tremendous effort trying to get employees to execute a certain set of behaviors, which it is assumed will achieve the goals that have been set for the company—that is, the goals that management has set for the company. As we now know, this model isn't delivering up to our expectations as customers or employees. Management is not to blame for this situation, however: the cooperative model and inherited business teachings of the past are. It has proven difficult to align the many management tools and techniques used up to this point and achieve the desired outcome. Information systems have also been a big part of the problem, forcing employees to work the way that their IT systems worked, as opposed to the most productive and effective way. Layer on volatile markets and the limitations become even more apparent.

Early in this century, the U.S. government passed the Enterprise Integration Act (EIA) of 2002. The goal of the EIA was "to work with major manufacturing industries on an initiative of standards development and implementation for electronic enterprise integration" (para. 1). The act intended to "increase efficiency and lower costs" (Section 2.6). Viewed as being in the national interest, the EIA resulted from research identifying massive inefficiencies in different industry ecosystems. Notably, the U.S. automotive industry was identified as having over $1 billion of waste per year attributable to inefficient information flows across its supply chain (Brunnermeier & Martin 1999, p. 6-1), making it less competitive with international car manufacturers. By 2005, McKinsey & Company research put this figure at $10 billion (Hensley & Knupfer 2005, para. 1).

Coase's (1937) theorems on transaction cost state that firms could be more efficient by controlling and internalizing exchanges—but in a time when information flowed at a much slower pace and smaller scale. Accelerating markets, massive amounts of information, and falling engagement and transaction costs have altered this premise. While the efforts of the EIA and

National Institute of Standards and Technology (NIST) never made headline news, the external markets have.

Massive changes have taken place with electronic information exchange since 2002. The internet, the cloud, and now social technology have presented new ways to manage and integrate supply chains—the EIA actually referred to the emergence of the "World Wide Web" (Section 2.3) but did not contemplate what would shortly occur and what is now possible through social technology. While the EIA was well-intentioned and needed at the time, free market innovations and social technology advancements have already addressed the problem it was designed to address.

The 4 Cs of *Social Inc.* sum up why Coase reached his conclusions in 1937 and demonstrate that in 2012, his perspective no longer holds. The artificial boundaries of the modern corporation now get in the way to create more barriers, not fewer, and legacy IT compounds the problem. The firm as it has been designed and implemented is now less efficient than engaging with the market—social technology has made this happen.

When discussing *transaction costs*, or the cost of an exchange between parties or things, I prefer a derivative term as it relates to social technology— *engagement costs*. This term refers to the costs of an interaction between people, or between things, or between people and things. Engagement costs are the economic backbone of social technology, or more accurately, the elimination of them is. Social networking tools like LinkedIn have reduced— and indeed almost eliminated—any real costs of engagement between people. Finding and connecting with people has never been easier or more inexpensive.

Staying connected is now possible—the sustainability of networks through social technology is a powerful weapon for individuals and businesses. The historical approach to locating people through the telephone, directory assistance, and even the phone book were inefficient and laborious. Once a person was located, connecting with them was another challenge altogether. Today, the costs of searching, connecting, and engaging have virtually been eliminated between people, and are decreasing between people and things, and things and things. Social technology makes it nearly free to interact, directly or at scale—with millions, even billions of people. These costs might seem trivial on the surface, but when considered at scale, they are gigantic.

The end result is that the costs of information exchange have been reduced to virtually zero. The fire, printed word, and telephone all dramatically reduced such costs, but social technology drops information exchange costs to the very bottom, as low as they have ever been.

Mathematics, and specifically Metcalfe's Law (Gilder 1993), can illuminate the engagement costs inherent between everything. The inventor of the Ethernet, Metcalfe proposed that while the cost of expanding a telecommunications network is a linear function (a fixed cost for each added node or user), the *value* of the network (V) goes up much faster, proportional with the number of users (n) squared (G. Li 2008, p. 1):

$$V \sim n^2$$

Although Metcalfe's original observation focused on value as it related to connections between devices, not people, "[a]t its core [the law] captures the concept that value increases as the number of users increases, because the potential links increase for *every* user as a new person joins" (emphasis added; Hendler & Golbeck 2008, p. 1).

Social technology has leveraged this concept across people already, but an explosion in device-to-device and device-to-people connectivity is now at our doorstep. For a network with n people, there are: $n * (n - 1) / 2$ possible unique connections.[21] For example, if you had 5 people at a party including yourself, you'd need to make 10 introductions for everyone to meet each other. Scaling up, there are 124,750 connections between 500 people, or between 500 things. You would be very busy at that party to try to get everyone introduced....

---

[21] Each person in a group of size n can make $n - 1$ connections, so the total number of connections possible is $n * (n - 1)$. However, for the number of *unique* connections among the group, we want to count a John–Mary connection once, not once for John–Mary and once for Mary–John. So, divide the total number of connections by 2, resulting in the formula above: $n * (n - 1) / 2$.

These numbers reflect the first phenomenon of the 4 Cs of *Social Inc.* in action: connecting. Facebook, Twitter, and LinkedIn have all tapped into connecting people efficiently. More importantly, those who are connected stay connected for as long as they want to. While previous iterations of social technology allowed people to connect (e.g., by telephoning a colleague in Germany or having a conference call with a team 5,000 miles away), the scale was much, much smaller and less efficient. In other words, the costs of engagement were much higher. With today's social technology, a major step forward has been made in the reduction of engagement costs.

I believe a new law is emerging to reflect the fact that engagement costs are now approaching zero within the context of social technology: the *Z-effect* or *Zero-effect*. This rule centers around engagement costs, stating that when engagement costs approach zero, disruptive potential is maximized (Figure 5-1). The Z-effect derives from the observation that the level of engagement

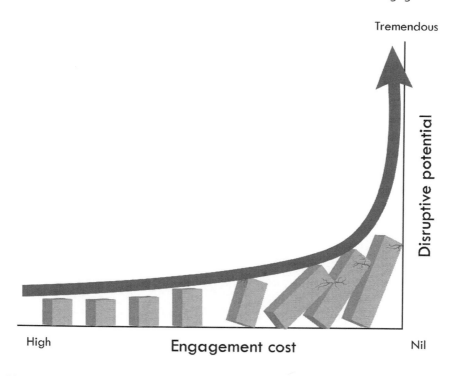

Figure 5-1. The Z-Effect. Author's image.

goes up exponentially when engagement costs approach zero. Consequently, new forms of engagement occur that would not have otherwise, and these newly created interactions have the potential to drive massive change, disruption, and innovation.

The sheer scale of participation and interaction that occurs when there are no engagement costs contributes to this disruptive capacity. The multiple benefits of social technology (making people smarter and more productive) get exploited in different ways, the more people and things interact. We simply figure things out better, faster, and cheaper. Lower engagement costs work to improve workplace productivity and also enable Daniel Wegner's theories on transactive memory (Wegner et al. 1985; Wegner 1987). Eliminating engagement costs and releasing the full potential of these concepts drive the potential for maximum disruption—to enable the Z-effect.

"The internet of things" is also starting to emerge as a reality as advancements in wireless connectivity allow the efficient connection of objects through the internet and social technology. As data starts to flow between things and people, "engagement" will take on an entirely new meaning. A new human–machine interface will start to emerge, changing the experience of working with a company and its products or services in wildly unpredictable ways.

According to Dave Yarnold, CEO of ServiceMax,

> The idea of extending the social construct out to your equipment on the customer's site—so your equipment can "talk" to you, is amazing. For starters, I can see big-time savings in solving problems and getting customers up and running faster. (personal communication, 17 October 2012)

While the social technology learning curve is creating some distractions and disruptions for the early adopters, their understanding of what's possible is growing considerably. These early Social Companies will establish and write the new rules of engagement and define what it means to offer an experience that others will need to react to and live by. The early adopters will survive and thrive because both the technology and the behaviors are changing, and when behavior changes, it rarely reverts back.

◄ Tropicana Turns Oranges into Lemons, and Back Again

Even if businesses try to ignore social technology tools, these tools will definitely not ignore businesses and will still influence their future. Whether or not a company has committed to social technology as a powerful new competitive force, its markets already have.

In February 2009, Tropicana's long-standing product packaging was replaced by a new design in a traditional repackaging move. One month later, amid public outcry, negative publicity amplified through social technology, and the declining sales that resulted, Tropicana decided to go back to the old packaging (Elliott 2009). Leo J. Shapiro & Associates (LSJ) studied the impact of social media on the Tropicana product launch and recall of 2009 with some enlightening findings.

For starters, only a minority of consumers—approximately 20%—even noticed the new packaging (proprietary LSJ analysis, used with permission). Opinions among the 20% who did notice were markedly mixed (Figure 5-2). With a relatively balanced (or even slightly favorable) reaction from the market, how did the campaign go sour?

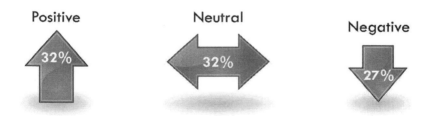

Figure 5-2. Feedback on Tropicana's New Packaging.[22]

Owen J. Shapiro, a Partner at LSJ explains, "Part of the story is the relatively small percentage (1%) of consumers who knew of the issues and broadcast messages, generally negative, about the new packaging through social media"

---

[22] Data from Leo J. Shapiro & Associates; the survey did not receive responses from 9% of those asked.

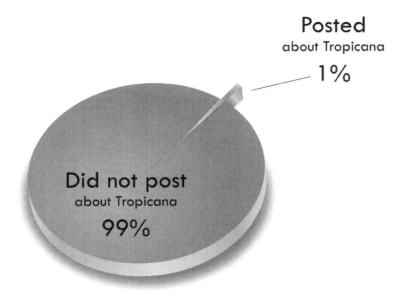

Figure 5-3. Distribution of Social Media Attention Among Those Aware of the Packaging Change.[23]

(personal communication, 1 October 2012). A small group of socially enabled consumers were upset (Figure 5-3), and social technology gave them a way to vent their frustrations.

This story illustrates the first lesson that has been learned with these tools: With social technology, customers no longer suffer in silence. Even in a situation where there is a favorable majority, social technology has incredible power to amplify a minority message and affect a company's behavior. NM Incite, a joint venture between Nielsen and McKinsey & Company, quantified this amplification at 500%. That is, a single negative comment has as much impact as five positive comments, on average (2012, p. 2).

As events unfolded with Tropicana, consumers started to get confused. Prior to the new launch, social media comments about price and ingredients dominated internet conversations about premium OJ. During and after the

---

[23] Graph reproduced with permission from Leo J. Shapiro & Associates.

launch, the online conversation changed to every business's nightmare—confusion at the point-of-purchase, in the store (Owen J. Shapiro, personal communication, 1 October 2012).

The numbers are quite interesting. Only 20% of customers noticed the switch in packaging, and of these, 1% posted comments on social media. So, that's actually 1% of the 20%. For every 10,000 customers, only 2,000 noticed the packaging change; of these 2,000, only 20 went online and said something negative.[24]

A socially engaged and vocal customer base equivalent to 20 people out of every 10,000 created enough "negative noise" to cause Tropicana to revert back to their old packaging—in about a month. *The New York Times* reported at the time:

> It was not the volume of the outcries that led to the corporate change of heart, Mr. [Neil] Campbell [President of Tropicana North America] said, because "it was a fraction of a percent of the people who buy the product." Rather, the criticism is being heeded because it came, Mr. Campbell said in a telephone interview on Friday, from some of "our most loyal consumers." (Elliott 2009, para. 17)

If Tropicana had ignored the very vocal minority, what would have occurred? While the 1% of customers who posted online did negatively impact sales, would sales have rebounded? Did the real-time and iterative nature of Tropicana's approach save the company from a much bigger calamity that could have materially impacted their business? Possibly, though it might have blown over on its own. At a minimum, by monitoring and reacting quickly, Tropicana certainly avoided spending an inordinate amount of time and other resources fighting what could have been a losing battle, or a no-win struggle.

Did they reinforce the strength of their relationship with the market by listening and responding so quickly? Tropicana demonstrated that it was monitoring the social media conversation—which is a leading practice. The next lesson here is for companies to act quickly. A singular voice amplified

---

[24] Data from Leo J. Shapiro & Associates.

through social technology can influence thousands or even millions of others; Tropicana's leadership understood this, and then engaged and acted.

When these events occurred, there was no blueprint or guide for what to do in such a circumstance. Brands like Tropicana were figuring this new medium out as they went along. Tropicana leadership set an example and listened to their markets, in real time.

Since 2009, Tropicana's story has been reenacted by other companies and brands who have been getting up-to-speed with social technology tools (Fiegerman 2012). However, these early social media mishaps have proved far from fatal, despite the amount of press they've received. Tropicana may have even reinforced their brand and the experience they provide to their customers by showing that the company is listening and engaged with what customers are saying. Tropicana's customers know that their opinions matter—what a great experience that always is.

One of the key findings of the InSites Consulting *Social Media Around The World 2012* survey is that 80% of internet users would be willing to help a company co-create its products or services. In return, however, they expect feedback on what the company does with their input (Van Belleghem, Dieter, & De Ruyck 2012, slide 20). In China, nearly 100% of consumers are willing to help a brand they like. Australia is at the low end of the scale, but still at almost 70% (slide 91). Consumers want to be engaged, they want to help, and they'll work for free…what are companies waiting for?

✺ Zappos Delivers Big Bucks through Social Sharing

Zappos is an online retailer that was bought by Amazon in 2009 and is famous for its culture and exceptional approach to customer service. I've been a Zappos customer for a long time as they have a phenomenal selection of large-size shoes; I wear a size 16. To this day, I cannot walk into a shoe store and walk out with 16s—Zappos is my salvation. But what am I to Zappos? Is there value for Zappos in me and my online network beyond the pair of size 16 Asics I just bought? You bet there is, a ton of value…and a ton of revenue.

Zappos was an early adopter of social technology, and CEO Tony Hsieh was one of the early CEO users of Twitter (@zappos). Zappos Labs[25] is trying to understand the value Zappos is deriving from social engagement and translate this into the experience that Zappos is delivering with these tools and techniques.

In a recent article, Zappos shared some of their initial data on the value of social technology for its revenue growth (Kucera 2012). When customers share a purchase with their online networks, revenue "pop" circles back to Zappos from the traffic and related commerce that the network produces. Zappos buyers Tweet their purchases much less often than they share them on Facebook, and are most likely to pin an order on Pinterest (para. 8). However, so far, value is inversely related to this behavior, with a Tweet generating the most income for Zappos and a pinned order the least, as shown in Figure 5-4. While this data is emergent, and so far not definitive, it is important that Zappos tracks the traffic and business resulting when someone "shares" their purchase through each of these respective channels.

Even after adjusting for sharing an order through the different networks, based upon this initial analysis Twitter is still hands down the winner, with a Twitter share worth 245% more to Zappos than Pinterest and 102% more than Facebook. This is real money, flowing back to Zappos from their customers' online order-sharing and these numbers do not even reflect the second- or third-degree activity that takes place. It's not difficult to see how an individual's network could be more important and even more valuable than the individual consumer.

So how do these facts influence Zappos's marketing and customer-acquisition strategy? Does Zappos cultivate social consumers as an active strategy? Is the Twitter button more conspicuous? Increasingly, companies need to pay attention to and understand more about customers with an engaged and active social network. Obviously choice of network also matters, as not all

---

[25] Zappos Labs, a San Francisco-based unit of Zappos that is now a part of Amazon, has a mission of "disrupting online retail" (Ha 2012, para. 3).

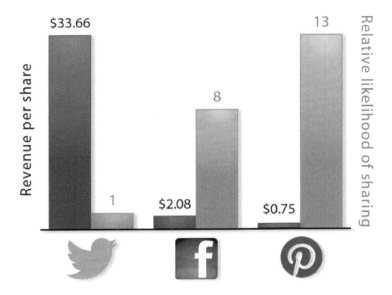

Figure 5-4. Social Networking's Value to Zappos. Author's image; data from Kucera 2012, para. 8.

tools or networks are created equally. Does Zappos now encourage more active sharing online?

The answers to these questions are not trivial. This investigation for Zappos is no doubt an ongoing experiment, which captures the next important rule of *Social Inc.*: Because social technology centers around human behaviors, the only way to figure it out is by using it (Rule 6). Experimenting and iterating in real time are needed to succeed with these tools.

Social Inc. Rule 6

Social technology is experiential.

Understanding how consumer behavior is changing as a result of social technology and identifying the value and business impact of the tools is a journey of discovery—a journey that Zappos has no choice but to be on, because their customers have put them on it. Zappos is using these tools to deliver a unique experience with social technology as an integral part of their strategy.

In this experiential approach, Zappos is creating value for their customers who want to share and learn from their networks, and also capturing some of this value for themselves. Networks matter—a lot. The *Social Commerce IQ: Retail* survey of 1,800 U.S. Facebook users found that 43% of respondents have asked their Facebook friends for advice before making a purchase (Kubo & Smith 2012, p. 27), 70% prefer their friends to share about specific products rather than general brand preferences (p. 27), and 65% have themselves shared a product on a social network (p. 28).

This report also calls out two trends that I discuss in depth: context, and the inevitability of social tools and techniques to specialize (see Part 7: In Business, Context Is King, and Part 2: *Homo Erectus* and the First Social Technology). The report remarks on a refocusing of social commerce to "Interest Graphs" (Kubo & Smith 2012, p. 3) such as Pinterest, where people connect based on their interests instead of their friendships. The report also raises a point about deeper business process integration: "[I]nnovative retailers have begun deeply integrating social shopping into their websites rather than relying on social network websites for engagement" (p. 3).

These two points relate to the value of context around social engagement, and to the deeper integration of the social experience into all business processes. Both drive value for companies from social tools and techniques, and demonstrate the value inherent in social technology as a competitive tool for businesses.

It's not difficult to imagine users experiencing networking overload and difficulty in culling through the volume and velocity of information passed around on an external network like Facebook. Within a business, though, context starts to bring more relevancy to the information exchanges and flow—it is easier to see which information is useful, what to comment on, and who to connect with. The ability to sift through the data offered by this information explosion will be a critical part of making these tools work effectively, and context is the key that is driving tremendous value for business.

How Social Companies Create Value…Lots of It

Any corporate initiative, technology-driven or not, boils down to business impact and therefore to financial impact or P&L (profit and loss). Being smarter and more productive sounds good, but until these capabilities are translated into financial statement impact, business doesn't usually budge.

Fortunately, some metrics are starting to emerge and what's striking is that they are not incremental in nature. Compelling numbers are being reported by early social technology adopters and researchers (see below), with the realized benefits starting to get a lot of attention.

The business impact behind social technology is more than Facebook or broadcasting a marketing message into a social channel. Understanding the many economic and financial implications behind these tools and creating a business case for social technology across an entire business is a complex undertaking.

McKinsey & Company has published an annual survey since 2007, looking at the ways in which organizations use social tools and technologies.[26] Their research provides not only results but also a trend line to learn from. Their 2011 summary of over 4,200 global executives reports:

> When adopted at scale across an emerging type of networked enterprise and integrated into the work processes of employees, social technologies can boost a company's financial performance and market share. (Bughin et al. 2011, para. 1)

They also show increases in the number of respondents reporting benefits from prior years across many categories, which may reflect the experiential

---

[26] "The online survey included 4,261 respondents across sectors, geographies, company sizes, tenures, and functional specialties…The survey covers the adoption and usage of technologies, their benefits, and corporate performance" (Bughin et al. 2011, footnote 1).

nature of social technology. The more people use it, the more they understand how to get business value out of it.

Highlights of their 2011 survey results include the following.

- 74% of respondents reported at least one measureable benefit to increasing the speed of their internal knowledge access.
- 58% of respondents reported at least one measureable benefit to reducing internal communication costs.
- 69% of respondents reported at least one measureable benefit to increasing the effectiveness of customer marketing.
- 43% of respondents reported at least one measureable benefit to reducing customer marketing costs.
- 61% of respondents reported at least one measureable benefit to reducing communication costs with external partners, suppliers, and others (Bughin et al. 2011, Exhibit 3).

These results support my overall premise that Social Companies are getting smarter and more productive. The following additional data points illustrate the range of observations and results being reported around the business impact of social technology. The Allstate Heartland Monitor XIII survey[27] conducted in 2012 illustrates several key points around social influence and trust:

- 79% of social media users are likely to seek the opinions of others before buying goods or services, and 64% have changed their minds because of those opinions (Heartland Monitor Poll 2012, p. 1).
- 86% of social media users trust information from friends and family members a great deal or somewhat, compared to only 42% trusting information to the same degree from leaders of major corporations (FTI Consulting 2012, p. 4).
- 59% of social media users say a company's social media activities make the company appear "accessible and responsive" (Heartland Monitor Poll 2012, p. 3).

---

[27] Heartland Monitor surveyed one thousand U.S. adults to examine "how [their] views of government and major corporations are shaped by the information they receive and by their use of social media" (FTI Consulting 2012, p. 1).

In summary, people are less trusting of what corporate leaders tell them than they are of their own network, who are extremely influential to people's opinions and purchase decisions. With social technology, customers are more than just individuals—as the example of Zappos illustrates, the "best customers" may be defined differently when their influence and networks are factored in. Not only does business need to continue to focus on the individual, but companies need to start to consider and understand how each individual's network comes into play.

A Deloitte survey in 2012[28] provided some curious data points around how far businesses still need to go to enable social technology effectively, and also identified a massive gap between leaders and their staff on the use of social media to build what I term a Social Company.

- 45% of executives say social media has a positive impact on workplace culture, while only 27% employees agree.
- 41% of executives, but only 21% of employees, believe that social networking helps to build and maintain workplace culture.
- As it relates to management visibility, 38% of executives think social media allows increased transparency, while only 17% of employees agree. (Deloitte 2012, 3rd bolded results section)

The authors conclude by calling out executives for faking it:

> Executives may be using social media as a crutch to build culture and seem accessible—but good leadership can't be dialed-in. Norms for building an exceptional culture and organization have not changed. (3rd bolded results section)

Accountability is both the Beauty and the Beast of social technology. The collective voices of employees and customers will no longer tolerate platitudinous efforts.

---

[28] Harris Interactive surveyed 1,005 U.S. adults (aged 18+, employed full-time in a company with 100+ employees) and 303 corporate executives on a number of questions related to culture in the workplace (see Deloitte 2012).

Social Media Examiner's *2012 Social Media Marketing Industry Report*[29] identifies the following benefits from marketing into external channels (Stelzner 2012, p. 14):

- 85% of respondents indicated increased exposure,
- 69% identified increased traffic,
- 65% indicated that social media marketing provided marketplace insight,
- 58% said it generated leads,
- 58% said it developed loyal fans,
- 55% said it improved search rankings,
- 51% said it grew business partnerships,
- 46% said it reduced marketing expenses, and
- 40% said it improved sales.

Visibility, market intelligence, stronger customer connections, business development, and finally, cost reduction and improved revenue—not a bad mix of marketing outcomes for a large percentage of users. Imagine extending these benefits across your entire business.

A Telligent 2012 survey of social technology in the UK workplace[30] identified latent demand for these tools in the workplace.

- 74% of people surveyed said a social platform would improve their job performance, yet
- only 21% of workplaces provide social tools to employees (Telligent 2012, para. 2).

Employees want social technology and they know that it works—companies that are social laggards need to pick up the pace or be left behind. A 2012 joint MIT/Deloitte survey[31] on the expanding footprint of Social Companies indicates trend lines pointing to the unavoidable destiny of social technology and its impact on business (Kiron, Palmer, Nguyen Phillips, & Krushwitz 2012).

---

[29] This study surveyed over 3,800 marketers with the goal of understanding how they are using social media to grow and promote their businesses (see Stelzner 2012).

[30] Telligent surveyed 1,000 UK employees to gain their views on workplace communication and remote working.

[31] This global survey included almost 3,500 "business executives, managers, and analysts" (Kiron et al. 2012, p. 21) from 115 countries, 24 industries, and both large and small organizations (p. 21).

- "A majority of respondents (52%)…believe that social business is important or somewhat important to their business today. Fully 86% of managers believe social business will be important or somewhat important in three years" (p. 3).
- "Leadership and a clear vision are cited most frequently as critical to the adoption of social software. Lack of management support is cited most frequently as the biggest barrier to adoption" (p. 3).
- "Leaders most responsible for the strategic direction of an organization—CEOs, presidents and managing directors—are almost twice as likely as CIOs and CFOs to say that social business is important to their organization" (p. 3).

Leaders, particularly those with a strategic orientation, generally see social technology as an issue rising in importance. Moreover, implementing social technology cannot be done without leadership: Getting the board of directors and CEO on board is job #1 for a Social Company.

The use of social technology by your markets will feed changing expectations around what is viewed as acceptable levels of treatment and engagement. These tools are changing service and support expectations. A survey by the social media customer service company Conversocial (2012)[32] found that, when contacting a company via social media, approximately

- 30% of clients expect a response in the same business day (at worst) with 30% expecting a response within hours;
- 13% expect a response in less than 1 hour; and
- 16% expect a response in *less than 10 minutes* (p. 4).

In Part 1, I started with the McKinsey Global Institute declaration that social technology is a business opportunity with a price tag of well over $1 trillion. The final point of their key findings section provides this assessment and warning:

---

[32] Conversocial (2012) surveyed "589 American adults. These adults were approached exclusively online through social networking sites, forums and dedicated emails. There was a quota sampling technique applied so that it guaranteed the sample was reflective of the American population, with an average age of 39" (p. 3).

> The benefits of social technologies will likely outweigh the risks for most companies. Organizations that fail to invest in understanding social technologies will be at greater risk of having their business models disrupted by social technologies. (Chui et al. 2012, p. 4)

Are there other trillion-dollar business ideas out there? I'm not aware of any. Social technology is the business management opportunity of the next decade. The status quo for business—customer mistrust, lack of employee engagement, and slowing economic growth—needs a different answer. This is a leadership moment for business, and boards and CEOs need to take up the challenge.

CEOs, Boards, and Some Social Sobriety

The customer is the person who pays everyone's salary and who decides whether a business is going to succeed or fail. In fact, the customer can fire everybody in the company from the chairman on down, and he can do it simply by spending his money somewhere else.

–Sam M. Walton
(Wal-Mart Annual Report 1988, p. 4)

◄ The Scary State of Social Governance

This is a frightening time for boards: The roll call of companies who have found themselves on the wrong end of social technology's wrath is impressive, with new members seemingly added daily. The press barrage of social missteps and disasters from McDonald's to Macy's (Fiegerman 2012) has created fear and angst throughout most boards around the risks that surround the social technology "monster." Misunderstood and maligned, social technology continues to be perceived by many board members as frightening and out of control.

Board members are right, though, and they should be afraid. The truth is that social technology is to be feared because it is out of control—out of the board's control. Ignoring it won't make it go away. Social technology is a beast with a mind of its own, and it demands a proactive approach from boards and CEOs to manage its risks—and opportunities.

Even if your company has not done anything with social technology, it will find you—it already has. Fay Feeney is CEO (@FayFeeney) of Risk for Good, which helps directors navigate the disruption of their business in a social and mobile world. She shared this summary of the situation with me:

> I regularly tell board chairmen, "Just because you're not on a social network like Twitter, doesn't mean we're not talking about you, your board, your CEO, your business, and your competitors." Each year companies will see their customers' social capital rising and their voices getting louder. (personal conversation, November 15, 2012)

According to Fay, the Social CEO is adapting by building a culture that listens and engages in the conversations taking place on social media. The board needs to be listening to and understanding what its markets are telling them—good advice.

The use of social technology by customers, suppliers, and employees outside the boundaries of every organization is a fact. An uncomfortable fact, perhaps, but one that still requires board members to understand social technology so that they can perform the role expected and required of them. CEOs and board members who are unprepared will find themselves in a panic over events that are beyond their control—and their reactions can compound the problem exponentially.

One of the early lessons of social technology is that the response to an issue matters. A poorly handled response, or no response at all, can inflame a relatively benign occurrence. The right approach views every single customer interaction, good and bad, as an opportunity to reinforce the company's values, culture, and customer experience.

Operationally, social media command centers are emerging as a way to monitor and address the real-time conversations taking place. Salesforce.com's Marketing Cloud product[33] powers many of these command centers (A. Nelson 2012). The focus of these efforts is to monitor in real time what is happening on the social channels in the broader marketplace and to engage with that conversation. At present, these centers are primarily being used for marketing, customer care, and service or risk identification. As a leading practice, a social media center is an always on, always listening and engaging model that supports the key objectives of creating a unique experience around dealing with your company.

This monitoring will eventually extend into all domains including competitive intelligence, investor sentiment, employee engagement, and enterprise risk. While management has the responsibility for the tactical management of these channels, boards have the added responsibility of understanding and governing the overall IT and social technology environment.

◄ Learning from the IT Governance Hangover

Just as social technology is more than information technology (IT), social technology governance is different than IT governance. Although the scope of social technology certainly involves an IT component, it's much broader because of the behavioral implications of social technology. However, to

---

[33] Marketing Cloud is a desktop application to scale social media engagement across an organization; it "helps companies listen, engage, and measure their outreach across teams and departments" (Salesforce.com Marketing Cloud 2012, para. 2).

achieve better social technology governance, the IT governance problem also needs to be addressed.

For board members and CEOs, social technology is a brand new ballgame relative to information technology (IT) governance—and boards weren't exactly winning the old game of IT governance. The historical track record of IT project performance is impressively bad.

In what they claim is the largest global study done of IT change initiatives, Brent Flyvbjerg and Alexander Budzier focused on the magnitude of IT project ineptitude. In their examination of 1,471 U.S. and European projects with an average cost of $167 million, the average project "overrun" was 27% (2011, para. 4). Startlingly, they go on to identify that "one in six of the projects…was a black swan, with a cost overrun of 200%, on average, and a schedule overrun of almost 70%" (para. 4).

As these statistics reflect, IT is a governance and management challenge for many companies and organizations. Flyvbjerg and Budzier (2011) recommend that to manage IT initiatives appropriately, leaders should determine if the company can absorb a budget that runs over by 400% or more and plan for only 25% to 50% of the project's benefits being realized (para. 8). A National Association of Corporate Directors/Oliver Wyman analysis indicated that the world's top 500 companies lose more than $14 billion each year because of failed IT projects (Cohn & Robson 2011, p. 2).

I've witnessed this terrible performance record firsthand over the last 30 years, countless times. In many cases, my teams have been called in to fix these problems, which is never cheap—or easy.

Given this poor track record, and the current and unmistakable social technology-fueled disruption that's all around us, what are boards doing? Ed Merino is CEO of Office of the Chairman, which provides coaching to board chairmen, board members, CEOs, and their direct reports; he thinks this situation sounds eerily like the financial reforms forced onto U.S. companies due to Sarbanes Oxley.[34] In his words, "The financial failures of the 1990s resulted in SOX [Sarbanes Oxley] and a financial expert in the boardroom. Are we one social or cybersecurity crisis away from a mandated IT expert in the boardroom?" (personal conversation, November 7, 2012). If boards cannot address these shortcomings on their own, regulators may do it for them.

With this track record and number of dollars wasted—let alone the dependency on IT for business continuity—IT governance should be a really hot topic. While IT is being discussed, however, the conversation is not at the level it needs to be. Boards simply do not know what they don't know. Only 6% of boards have a technology subcommittee, according to Spencer Stuart (2011, p. 28)—the only logical conclusion to make about the poor performance is that the IT governance skillset has not had a seat at the boardroom table. The right oversight and conversations have not been taking place, plain and simple.

Board members do believe, nearly unanimously (99% of 204 surveyed), that "IT will have a significant impact on their organizations in the next five years" (Cohn & Robson 2011, p. 2). In this survey, a full 30% felt that IT would be a "competitive advantage for their company," with another 19% indicating it would "transform their company" (p. 2).

However, while board members recognize IT as a huge part of their future, they don't have the ability to do anything about it. Boards are insufficiently skilled to provide oversight on IT and social technology risks and opportunities. Only 16% of NACD respondents reported "having been a CIO or senior IT executive earlier in their career" (Cohn & Robson 2011, p. 2); consequently, 47% of surveyed board members were "dissatisfied with their board's ability to provide IT risk oversight" (p. 2).

Couple poor IT project-performance with little-to-no IT skill or competency at the board level, and sprinkle in the disruptive development of social

---

[34] The Sarbanes-Oxley Act of 2002 was a federal law enacted to "protect investors by improving the accuracy and reliability of corporate disclosures" (para. 1). Among the law's provisions were greater management accountability for the accuracy of corporate reports, increased penalties for fraud, and creation of a federal oversight board.

technology and it's no wonder that social technology mishaps occur almost daily for businesses in a variety of industries. It's a perfect storm— a convergence of opportunity and ineptitude that almost guarantees social and information technology-related problems will continue and even proliferate.

Fortunately, fixing this problem is not too difficult, and it starts with getting the right IT and social technology skillsets into the boardroom. Information and social technology-led change initiatives have room for improvement in both execution and governance. Fix the governance pieces, and better IT execution will naturally follow.

In addition to adding IT and social technology skills, boards need to develop a much more proactive approach not only to IT governance, but also to risk and opportunity management given these new social tools. One necessary and major shift will be a more structured approach to social crisis response and management. Fixing problems needs to become a stronger core competency, because preventing them is increasingly unlikely due to the unpredictability of social technology.

Companies that learn to solve problems effectively will have an opportunity to enhance the unique experience of doing business with them, which will create value in the process. I've always thought problems were an opportunity for companies. Perhaps I have more frequently seen their positive side as I was the fixer and watched the benefits emerge without having to deal with the calamity on the front end.

Regardless, within every problem there is an opportunity. Customers don't expect perfection, but they expect issues to be resolved promptly and to their satisfaction when issues inevitably occur. Being good at solving problems, in real time, will reinforce a company's brand and the user experience it offers. Preventing every problem is a fool's errand; it cannot be done in a social technology-enabled world. *Social Inc.* Rule 7 reflects this point: "Social technology is controls-resistant." Resolving problems will become a new differentiator in the eyes of the socially empowered market.

Social Inc. Rule 7

Social technology is controls-resistant.

There is no shortage of frameworks that can be applied to IT governance—the failure has been a lack of leadership, and boards no longer have the luxury of ignoring the issue. Boards certainly see the business opportunity of IT and understand their companies' increasing dependence on IT (Cohn & Robson 2011, p. 2). They are also aware of the social technology risks; there's too much press coverage not to be.

So why are boards moving so slowly in adapting to social technology and its risks? Demographic trends illuminate the ongoing, underlying problem. There are three primary trends working against a board's ability to provide adequate information and social technology governance and oversight:

- **There's a lack of new blood**—There has been a 25% drop in independent directors elected to U.S. boards since 2006 (Spencer Stuart 2011, p. 5).
- **The board is getting older**—The average age of independent directors is 62.4 years, up from 60.2 years a decade ago (p. 5).
- **Boards are adding the wrong skills**—Only 3% of new board candidate searches are focused on getting new directors with digital or social media skills (p. 13).

Herein lies the opportunity for Social Companies—adding IT and social technology skills to the board goes a long way toward enabling a successful social future and immediately reducing risk. For success as a Social Company, you must have a Social CEO as well as a social board. Where can you find qualified director candidates? In several groups that have not traditionally been called upon for board governance duties—based on my work, there are executives who are able and want to serve in this capacity in the boardroom.

Because the social component of this issue is a relatively new one, boards may need to look a little harder for the right executives to fill this role. I recommend starting with the following three groups or networks:

1. **Former or current CIOs** are a natural starting point. This role has sometimes attracted a range of executives from varied backgrounds, and the right executive will understand the business ramifications of social and information technologies and have deep experience in managing technology-driven change.

2. **Management/IT consultants** may be your biggest resource pool. The right consulting executive has been implementing information or social technology projects for many different companies across multiple industries. These consultants often come in to fix problems around failed projects, and are very strong in understanding enterprise risk around varied information or social technology projects. They are also adept at bridging the translation gap between business and IT, and are often on the leading edge of new disruptive technologies.

3. **Social or information technology professionals** can bring a deep understanding of the technologies that they have worked with and the capabilities of specific tools. However, they may be limited in their implementation experience with a broad set of tools and also may not have deep knowledge of the risk arena. Another caveat is that marketing has dominated the social space up until this point, so social executives may have a deep level of understanding in this functional area only.

Individuals may offer experience across several or all of these domains, as there is liquidity in the market between these roles and industries. The bottom line is that these executives exist and are willing and able to serve in the boardroom. Given the strategic importance of social and information technology for every business, addressing this gap in the boardroom is a critical first step for board chairs and nominating committees.

◄ Hotels.com Fumbles a Super Bowl Reservation

The unpredictability of social technology is one of its hallmarks, and that frightens boards. As *Social Inc.* Rule 7 warns, social technology is a very controls-resistant tool: Smart governance practices revolve around fixing problems quickly, not trying to prevent them from occurring.

In this section, I offer a perfect example that compares the traditional customer service response (to email and chat) with what I would call *social customer care* (through Twitter). While the example illustrates the extreme disparity between the two channels, it also showcases the sad state of the traditional customer service approach and philosophy. Some companies seem to have devolved customer service into an exercise designed to wear customers down in the hopes that they'll just go away.

Companies are paying attention to social technology differently than to other media. As people become increasingly socially enabled and empowered, we can only hope that this higher standard becomes the norm and displaces these other more ineffective practices. The following communications are the actual ones I exchanged with the parties involved.

My story begins on January 14, 2012, when I booked a hotel for the 2013 Super Bowl in New Orleans through Hotels.com (Figure 6-1). I had used Hotels.com before and had made heavier use of its parent corporation, Expedia.com, and so was not a novice to online travel planning. I had my reservation; so far, so good.

I was pretty pleased with myself for finding what looked like a great place and booking a year in advance for the Super Bowl—in New Orleans! This was going to be a special trip, as my wife and I had eloped to New Orleans in 1983. We had been back only once since then, and were looking forward to our first trip in 25 years to the city where we married.

Sadly, everything then started to go horribly wrong. The hotel billed my credit card in February 2012 for a no-show. Their records indicated that the reservation was for 2012, not 2013. Less than thirty days into my reservation, I was billed for a room I didn't use, for a 2012 reservation I didn't make, and moreover, I no longer had a 2013 reservation.

Hotels.com

Dear Valued Customer,

Your reservation is now confirmed. Payment will be taken by the hotel.

Your Hotels.com Confirmation Number is: 76558767. Thank you for booking with Hotels.com

 View or cancel your reservation online

 Print this page

 Download Hotels.com for mobile

 View and print a receipt

 Customer Service and FAQs

 Book this hotel again

Reservation details

SONIAT HOUSE

★★★★☆ | **4.5** ⬛⬛⬛⬛◻ from 4 guest ratings

1133 Chartres Street
New Orleans, Louisiana 70116
United States

Reservation

Check-in:	Friday, February 1, 2013
Check-out:	Tuesday, February 5, 2013
Number of nights:	4 Night(s)
Room type:	ONE BEDROOM SUITE, 450SQFT, KING BED, - LIVING ROOM, AC, WIFI
Number of rooms:	1 Room(s)

Room 1:

Guest(s):	Bob Zukis 2 Adults
Preferences*:	Non-Smoking

*Please note: Preferences and requests cannot be guaranteed. Special requests are subject to availability upon check-in and may incur additional charges

Figure 6-1. The Original Reservation. Author's image.

Three months of back-and-forth communication ensued, including the involvement of my bank. Neither the hotel nor the booking site would acknowledge fault, and I kept getting passed back and forth between Soniat House and Hotels.com. After a few phone calls and live chats on the Hotels.com site, I decided to write the Hotels.com help email (Figure 6-2) to try to escalate the matter.

BIG RESERVATION PROBLEM 76558767

FROM: Bob Zukis   Thursday, February 23, 2012 11:21 AM

TO: help@hotels.com

I've talked to your customer service twice, thought we resolved this the first time when hotel agreed to reverse, but now the problem is back and hotel is not being cooperative.

As you'll see this reservation was clearly made for Feb 1, 2013–Feb 5, 2013. Hotel charged me for a no show thinking it was for 2012. They are blaming you.

They have two charges they've stuck me with:

2/6 - 1,816.65
1/17 - $605.55

HELP!

Bob

Figure 6-2. A Call for Help. Author's image.

More back-and-forth ensued, with no one seemingly able to figure out what happened or to acknowledge that I was caught in the middle of some sort of error between Hotels.com and Soniat House. My patience was wearing thin by mid-March, along with the courteous tone of my communication (Figures 6-3 and 6-4).

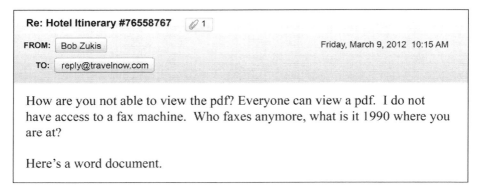

Figure 6-3. My Patience Is Running Out. Author's image.

Figure 6-4. My Anger Is Building. Author's image.

The run-around continued, and all Hotels.com did in their response (Figure 6-5) was to refer me back to Soniat House, again. Back and forth, back and forth.

Hotel Itinerary #76558767

FROM: reply@travelnow.com   Thursday, March 22, 2012 7:07 AM

TO: bzukis@yahoo.com

Dear Bob Zukis,

Thank you for taking the time to contact us and we apologize for the delay in re-spoonse.

We are not the billing party for this reservation, and upon checking our notes the hotel will refund you the amount charged to your account. We strongly advise you to call SONIAT HOUSE at 1-504-5220570 and your financial institution if a credit has been posted to your account.

Thank you for using http://www.hotels.com.

[name withheld for privacy]
Please include itinerary # 76558767 when replying.

Figure 6-5. Stuck In Customer Service Hell. Author's image.

By this time my bank had refunded the charges and then cancelled the refund twice. The hotel, which was the billing party, kept refuting my cancellation of the charge.

Hotel Itinerary #76558767

FROM: reply@travelnow.com   Friday, April 20, 2012 10:03 AM

TO: bzukis@yahoo.com

Dear Bob Zukis,

Thank you for taking the time to contact us and we apologize for the delay in re-spoonse.

We are not the billing party for this reservation, and upon checking our notes the hotel will refund you the amount charged to your account. We strongly advise you to call SONIAT HOUSE at 1-504-5220570 and your financial institution if a credit has been posted to your account.

Thank you for using http://www.hotels.com.

[name withheld for privacy]
Please include itinerary # 76558767 when replying.

Figure 6-6. Still Stuck In Customer Service Hell. Author's image.

Is there an echo in here? I felt like I was stuck in some kind of scripted response hell. These Hotels.com emails (Figures 6-5 and 6-6) are almost a month apart, but are otherwise identical.

I was getting nowhere. Up to this point there had been over twenty emails and about a dozen faxes and phone calls, each. (What was up with the faxes?) I was about to jump out the window—this "resolution process" was going absolutely nowhere.

Then it dawned on me that I'm a social technology guy. I thought, "Go onto Twitter and take this bad boy viral. See what happens." If nothing else, I'd be able to get some justice in the court of social accountability. I began my new campaign with an email (Figure 6-7).

Then another question occurred to me, about what kind of reaction the threat of a socially enabled action might have. I wondered if I could launch a kind of social technology cold war, where the threat of the nuke (or tweet) is as powerful as, or even more powerful than, the actual act.

Re: Hotel Itinerary #7558767 **LEGAL ACTION**

FROM: Bob Zukis   Friday, April 20, 2012 10:50 AM

TO: reply@travelnow.com

Here is how I plan to move this forward. I am getting the run around from you, and the run around from Soniat House. Here are the facts:

-I made a reservation through hotels.com for February 1-5, 2013 for a stay at Soniat House
   -I have the documentation that supports this
-Soniat House charged me the full cost of the stay for a no show, because they had the reservation for February 1-5, 2012 in their systems.
   -They have told me that their documentation from you is for February 1-5, 2012
-After repeated communications with you, you continually refer me back to Soniat House
-After repeated communications with Soniat House, they continually refer me back to you
-My bank is also engaged, and is also getting the run around from you both

Clearly the both of you refuse to deal with a problem that is between your two organizations.

I will be taking the following actions, unless this is resolved to my satisfaction this week:

-Online reviews of your hotel with details of this situation, which I consider fraudulent, through all applicable social media sites
-Submission to Conde Naste Travel Ombudsman
-Legal recourse

Kind regards, Bob Zukis

Figure 6-7. It's War! Author's image.

Net result...nothing. Whoever receives their email didn't seem to care about the threat of legal action or even my threat to use "all applicable social media sites." I sent the same email to Soniat House, and they didn't react either.

Enter Twitter. On June 4th I went straight to the Hotels.com Twitter account—
surely this avenue would escalate my problem to a higher service level. It did.
Here's my tweet (Figure 6-8), and boy were they responsive! Kudos to the
Hotels.com Twitter team for their decent turnaround time to respond to me:
within 24 hours.

Figure 6-8. Twitter to the Rescue. Author's image.

Alright! It felt like I might be getting this issue resolved at last. On June 8th, they got back to me (Figure 6-9)…with instructions to go back to the hotel!

Hotel Itinerary #76558767

FROM: CustomerServiceTier3@expedia.com   Friday, June 8, 2012 7:33 PM

TO: bzukis@yahoo.com

Dear Mr. Zukis,

Thank you for contacting Hotels.com and giving us an opportunity to address your concerns. We received your feedback provided through Twitter and have researched your records in order to assist you.

On January 14, 2012 you made a reservation...When the hotel received the reservation they believed it to be for check in on February 1, 2012...

On February 2, 2012 you contacted us regarding the charges. We contacted the hotel on your behalf...At that time the hotel advised that they would refund the charges back to you.

You contacted us again regarding the charges on March 9, 2012. The hotel is the billing party, not Hotels.com...

On March 22, and April 20, 2012, we received more correspondence from you in regards to the charges made by the hotel...We replied to you and advised that you should contact Soniat House directly at 1-504-522-0570; as they are the billing party, Hotels.com will not be able to affect any changes to the charges. You may also wish to contact your financial institution to verify if the charges have been refunded.

We thank you for booking with Hotels.com and look forward to assisting you in the future. If you have any further questions, please contact our Customer Service Department at 800-246-8357. Our agents are available 24 hours a day seven days a week.

Sincerely,

[name withheld for privacy]
Senior Specialist

Figure 6-9. A Road to Nowhere. Author's image.

I was now officially at the end of my rope. I sent a very annoyed email (Figure 6-10) to the Hotels.com Tier 3 customer rep, who was monitoring their Twitter site. I was a lot more explicit regarding my intent to take my experience to Twitter, and also threw around some of my LinkedIn clout.

Re: Requested Email: Hotel Billing and Refunds - Itin: 76558767 - Case ID : [REQ:O-29704]

FROM: Bob Zukis   Friday, June 8, 2012 11:15 PM

TO: CustomerServiceTier3@expedia.com

This is totally inadequate. The hotel keeps telling me this is your mistake and you keep telling me it's theirs. I keep getting the run around. You as their agent seem to be unable to work with them to resolve this. I am launching a public campaign on twitter and other social media sites about this issue in one week if you both cannot come together and resolve the problem you have amongst yourselves. I suggest you communicate this directly to them and copy them and get me out of the middle of both of your entirely unacceptable customer service approaches. I will never use hotels.com again nor this hotel. My social influence reaches over 12m people through LinkedIn and I look forward to highlighting this in an upcoming article I am publishing if you do not resolve it this week. It's a great case study for how not to do things.

@bobzukis

Figure 6-10. Game Over: Executing the Nuclear Option. Author's image.

"My social influence reaches over 12m people through LinkedIn," I wrote. That number is actually the number of third-degree connections I have through the 800+ first-degree contacts I have on LinkedIn. It's a big number, and I assumed their social media rep would understand the implications of it.

Finally, finally, I got some traction. Between their email on June 8th and their final response on June 20th (Figure 6-11), Hotels.com decided that they would resolve the matter by refunding me the hotel charges.

Figure 6-11. A Social Technology Victory! Author's image.

I never did receive a definitive story about where the problem originated, but it was likely somewhere in the handoff between their information systems. I did, finally, get my money back, because I was obviously knowledgeable about social media, not a happy camper, and was giving them a chance to resolve it before taking it viral. Unfortunately, I no longer have a room for the Super Bowl.

Table 6-1 shows the final tally comparing the traditional channels of email, chat, phone, and fax with my experience using Twitter. This has been a fun story to write about but far from an enjoyable one to experience. The lessons for companies are simple: Listen and engage in real time through these social technology tools.

This tale of two drastically different experiences illustrates the respect that companies are giving to the social technology channel. Business knows the power that sits in the hands of consumers because of this technology, and smart firms are devoting their top resources to it and changing their strategy and approach.

Table 6-1: My Customer Service Experience

Event	Customer Service Channel	
	Email, chat, phone, fax	Twitter
First Communication	February 8, 2012	June 4, 2012
Discrete communication events	50+	5
Resolution	June 20, 2012	June 20, 2012
Elapsed time	134 days	16 days
Role in resolving	Inconsequential	Pivotal
My experience	Terrible	Nice job!

Note. Author's table.

⤳ The Liberation of the Truth

Whether you are a customer, employee, or investor, you now own the truth. Board members, CEOs, and management team members no longer have a monopoly on the truth or on their company's brand—the markets now own both. Your brand is a real-time collection of social opinion, conversation, and banter owned by the collective of your employees, customers, and investors. Scary—or not, depending on how your stakeholder community is led in this new world.

Governments have already found this out; a country's official leader is no longer the keeper of the truth, despite government censorship that is often implemented in the name of protecting the citizenry. The truth has been set free by the elimination of space and time distortions in communications around the world. People no longer get news filtered by others, unless they want it that way. People learn of things when they happen, not after the fact in accounts distorted by censors, time, or geographic distance.

Do you have any idea how difficult it is to say something relevant and meaningful in 140 characters, that can actually make sense to people?

You do now—that sentence was exactly 140 characters long—the maximum length of a Twitter post. Information now arrives in staccato bursts that reach people instantly.

Twitter and other social networking media get credit for playing a major role in many of the social upheavals of 2011 and 2012.[35] Real-time social communication media and corporate tools like Yammer, Chatter, and Jive are the champions when it comes to eliminating time lags around people's awareness of events anywhere in the world. These are powerful productivity enhancers for business to do things better and more effectively, and for a team or company to be collectively smarter than each individual within it.

Twitter as a communication and engagement medium for business is just a small part of the entire social technology story. Business is still figuring out the implications around this style of communication brevity, velocity, and volume, but it's an important part of the ongoing experiment.

Back in Gutenberg's day, information flowed in much bigger chunks. While individual pieces of communication are now much smaller, the overall volume of information is much, much bigger and there are many more people involved in the conversation. Whether it's Chatter or Twitter as the communication channel, these behavioral changes in how people exchange information and the removal of temporal and spatial parameters are as foundational a development to humanity's future as the printed word, telephone, or even fire.

Social technology brings a new level of accountability around truth, trust, and transparency for business and organizations of any kind. True accountability in business belongs to the people who choose to engage with any company—the employees, customers, and investors who self-select into its value proposition.

The ultimate point of accountability for every business comes down to this: the collective will of a social technology-enabled customer, employee, or

---

[35] See, e.g., Srinivasan (2012), Lam (2012), and O'Donnell (2012).

investor base. Through that collective power, the socially empowered world will now judge what your business has to offer and how you offer it.

A convergence of events has set the stage for this next chapter in business management history, making this an exciting time. I spent thirty years in the middle of large corporate changes or disruptions, and I'm as excited as I have ever been about what lies ahead. We are all now a part of this shared and collaborative destiny. Here's what CEOs and boards can start doing about it.

◄ Springboks to the Rescue with an IT Governance Model

The ability of an individual to hold corporations accountable adds a new dimension to corporate governance—an area that is already fraught with challenges. While there is some common ground around the role and responsibility of the board (e.g., CEO selection, performance and pay, risk-monitoring, investor value, and fiduciary obligation), the application of practices to achieve these means varies wildly from board to board. The overall framework of laws, regulations, guidelines, and best practices coupled with the competing interests of investors, management, stakeholders, markets, governments, and employees makes corporate governance an extremely convoluted and dynamic undertaking—both within a particular governance jurisdiction and across the world. It's not a one-size-fits-all model.

Boards have a very difficult role to play, and the scope and breadth of their universe is constantly expanding and changing. Employees can create social technology-driven problems for CEOs and boards, regardless of whether they were using technology that the company itself put into place. A board's ability to stay up-to-speed with what social technology can do is daunting enough, let alone understanding the implications that technology presents to the business and overall risk environment.

Given the velocity with which issues can now run amok, boards are struggling like never before. It's a governance crisis—board members are ill-prepared to govern IT and social technology, and the potential for something unexpected occurring has increased considerably along with the potential impact of such an event.

Historically, the U.S. Audit Committee has often had oversight for information technology, due to the role that enterprise resource planning (ERP) systems have played in financial reporting. Many ERP systems were initially established to support the automation of finance and accounting functions and they played a key role in reporting. As a result, the Audit Committee was the proxy for IT governance. A different approach is now needed, as demonstrated by the track record of IT project failures over the last decade (Flyvbjerg & Budzier 2011).

From what I've seen, audit committees were often overburdened with financial reporting issues, or perhaps lacked the IT background to provide the necessary oversight (or both). Adding on the rapidly evolving social technology- and IT-governance agenda not only reduces their focus on financial reporting but also does no justice to the strategic value or risks around today's information and social technologies. The good news is that there is a clean slate to work with because boards historically haven't done a lot with IT governance anyway, much less social technology governance.

Fortunately, there is help readily available to immediately improve IT governance. Of the frameworks that exist, I like the South African model for its strategic emphasis.

The *King Report on Corporate Governance* (*King I*) was originally developed in 1994 by the King Committee led by retired Supreme Court Judge Mervyn E. King (Institute of Directors in Southern Africa [IDSA] 2009). Revisions were undertaken with *King II* (IDSA 2002) and *King III* (IDSA 2009), when the IT governance framework was added.

Compliance with the *King Reports* is only required for companies listed on the Johannesburg Stock Exchange, but they provide a useful model for companies anywhere. Cited as the "most effective summary of international best practices in corporate governance" (Banhegyi 2007, p. 317), *King III* addresses IT governance in considerable detail, which the South African Institute of Chartered Accountants (SAICA) then condensed into its summary report (Figure 6-12).

SAICA Summary of Report on Governance for South Africa – 2009 (King III)

The Board should ensure that IT is aligned with business objectives and sustainability.

- Information technology is essential to manage the transactions information and knowledge necessary to initiate and sustain economic and social activities. Accordingly, it is necessary to manage the risks and constraints of IT and to identify the strategic importance of IT.

- It is recommended that IT governance be placed on the Board Agenda.

- IT governance is essential to the achievement of corporate objectives and information resources, such as people, funding and information.

- IT governance should focus on four key areas, namely:
  - strategic alignment with the business and sustainability
  - optimising expenses and improving the value of IT
  - addressing the safeguarding of IT assets, to ensure disaster recovery and continuity of operations
  - resource management: optimising knowledge and IT infrastructure

- As IT governance is the responsibility of the Board:
  - Board members should be active in IT strategy and governance
  - the CEO should provide organisational structures to support the implementation of IT strategy
  - Chief Information Officers should provide a bridge between IT and the business
  - All executives should become involved in IT Steering Committees

- It is important that business and IT plans are linked.

- The overall objective of IT governance is to understand the issues and strategic importance of IT.

- The importance of IT in driving and supporting the company's objectives is emphasised.

- The Board should take ownership of IT governance. This could be done by:
  - placing IT on the Board Agenda
  - challenging management's activities with regard to IT
  - aligning IT initiatives with real business needs
  - insisting that IT performance is measured and reported on
  - establishing an IT strategy committee
  - insisting that there be a management framework for IT governance

- The importance of IT security is emphasised. This includes the components of confidentiality, integrity and availability.

[previous page] Figure 6-12. South Africa's Approach to Corporate IT Governance; data from SAICA 2009, pp. 34–50.

As stated in the summary above, "The overall objective of IT governance is to understand the issues and strategic importance of IT" (SAICA 2009, p. 35). As an objective for or definition of IT and social technology governance, I think this works well; as a major development in IT, social technology demands priority attention by the board.

There are other standards and frameworks that boards can deploy around IT governance. For example, the Standards Australia *Corporate Governance of Information and Communication Technology (ICT)* was published in January 2005 and defines *corporate governance of ICT* as:

> the system by which the current and future use of ICT is directed and controlled. It involves evaluating and directing the plans for the use of ICT to support the organization and monitoring this use to achieve plans. It includes the strategy and policies for using ICT within an organization. (p. 1)

The point is to not to get caught up in debating which framework is better than the others; they can all be effective. What is essential is to add IT and social technology skills to the boardroom, have a structured approach to governance over both, and make the understanding of these disruptive tools a core board capability. Improving information and social technology governance will support both the creation and preservation of corporate value—and social technology will become a less frightening issue for board members and CEOs.

Mocha Choca Lattes and Social Governance Sobriety

Fortunately, some boards are emerging as leaders on this issue—leaders who recognize that IT and social technology governance are a required part of the overall governance and management equation. Here's one story of a social governance leader: Starbucks.

In December 2011, Starbucks appointed 29-year-old Clara Shih to its board. Clara is the author of *The Facebook Era* (2009) and the CEO of Hearsay Social, which she founded to help companies leverage the power of social technology. The media raved about the news of her appointment.

> Hearsay Social CEO Clara Shih has been elected to the Starbucks board of directors, the coffee chain announced in a statement. Shih has been named one of *FORTUNE'S* Most Powerful Women Entrepreneurs of 2011, and has held technology, product and marketing positions at Google, Microsoft and Salesforce.com. She is author of *The New York Times* bestseller "The Facebook Era: Tapping Social Networks to Market, Sell, and Innovate." "Clara is a true technology leader and will bring fresh insight to our strong and forward-thinking Board," said Howard Schultz, chairman and CEO of Starbucks. "We could not be more thrilled about the social-media expertise and ideas Clara will bring to our business as we continue to amplify the online experience and interactions Starbucks has with our customers, partners and communities." (Directorship 2012, para. 29)

As Starbucks demonstrates, Step 1 to fixing this issue is addressing the technology skills gap in the boardroom.

❤ The Boardroom Social Technology Calendar

Boards already have a full calendar, but are about to get even busier. Once a company has accomplished Step 1 and closed its boardroom IT and social technology skills gap, Step 2 is to create a board agenda with an IT and social technology governance framework—and calendar.

Boards need a plan for social technology, and Table 6-2 presents a list of the tasks that should be included. This calendar doesn't just look at Twitter activity and Facebook "likes," but also integrates a comprehensive strategic and risk-based approach to the impact that social technology will have across the entire business. From strategy to tactical operational issues, social technology will touch every part of the company.

My recommendation is that an IT subcommittee take responsibility for this calendar. I do not recommend it being integrated into an audit committee, as discussed above.

Table 6-2: Social Strategy and Technology Board Calendar

Activity	Objective	Frequency
1. Review and appraise overall social strategy covering media, networking, and technology plans.	Strategic	Annual
2. Review and critique criteria for monitoring social activity for crisis. Assess incident response plan including resources for response.	Risk	Annual
3. Understand and assess applicable social regulatory environment.	Risk	Annual
4. Review market trends and developments around social technology.	Strategic	Semi-annual
5. Engage outside experts to provide insight into social enterprise and technology strategy and risks.	Strategic	Semi-annual
6. Review and critique employee policies and training on social technology and risk management.	Risk	Annual
7. Hold private sessions with leaders of operations, marketing, and IT (i.e., COO, CMO, and CIO).	Strategic/ risk	Annual
8. Review and critique investor relations, social strategy, and communications plan.	Risk	Annual
9. Review social media monitoring outputs and internal/external metrics, activities, and compliance.	Risk	Quarterly
10. Review competitor social activity and trends.	Strategic/ risk	Quarterly
11. Receive updates on social technology projects.	Risk	Quarterly
12. Review and assess social information security strategy and plan with information security leader (i.e., CISO).	Risk	Annual
13. Receive update on social information security risk monitoring and issues from CISO.	Risk	Quarterly
14. Review social information risk findings with audit committee.	Risk	As-needed
15. Monitor CEO's social engagement and communications.	Risk	Quarterly

Note. Author's table.

≺ Ten "Beyond Facebook" Social Questions Boards Should Be Asking

Board members need to broaden and deepen the conversation with their management teams around social technology. To end this chapter, I share a series of ten questions to get the conversation started (Figure 6-13).

Board of Directors Management Questionnaire for Social Companies

These ten questions will extend your social technology conversation beyond Facebook and marketing. Board members should ask the following ten questions of their management teams to assess the relative understanding and maturity of the company's overall approach.

1. Is there a point of view for what social technology is now, and in the future?

2. How do social technology, media, networking, and the ability of these tools to change or amplify behavior impact the company on the following dimensions:
    • strategically,
    • competitively,
    • financially,
    • operationally, and
    • from a risk perspective?

3. Do we have a view for how social technology impacts each of our functional areas (e.g., human resources, finance & accounting, research & development, customer service, supply chain, marketing, sales)?

4. How do we think social technology impacts each of our key stakeholder groups (e.g., customers, employees, investors, communities, partners)?

5. What regulations and compliance requirements are impacted by social technology across our business?

6. What is our approach to monitoring what is happening inside and outside the company on the social platforms and media that exist today?

7. How does our social incident response and business-continuity approach categorize risk, escalate issues, and resolve them?

8. How are we staying current on emerging and disruptive social technologies and their impact for our business?

9. What key performance indicators are we tracking and monitoring around social technology, inside and outside the company?

10. What are the main concerns around how these tools will impact our culture and values as a business?

[Previous page] Figure 6-13. Social Questions Your Board of Directors Should Be Asking. Author's image.

A management team will likely need some time to formulate their responses to these questions, so this questionnaire is designed as a working tool. Through the conversations that result, the emergent Social Company can start to address and understand the scope and implications of this disruptive new technology for their business.

Taking Your Company from Social Misfit to Social Butterfly

Science discovers,
genius invents,
industry applies,
and man adapts himself to,
or is molded by, new things.

–Chicago World's Fair 1933
"A Century of Progress" (p. 11)

⤳ Business Makes the Future

Eighty years ago, Chicago hosted the 1933 World's Fair with their 150-day exposition, A Century of Progress, dedicated to the theme of "science." The organizers invited the world to Chicago's shores to celebrate global technological progress, "the victories of a glorious past and the promise of a more glorious future" (p. 10). The Fair's guidebook described the theme as follows:

> Science, patient and painstaking, digs into the ground, reaches up to the stars, takes from the water and the air, and industry accepts its findings, then fashions and weaves, and fabricates and manipulates them to the usages of man. Man uses, and it effects [sic] his environment, changes his whole habit of thought and of living. (p. 11)

The story of the 1933 Chicago World's Fair wove humanity's great science and technology achievements up until that point together with the potential of the future. It was not merely a showcase, however—the organizers wanted to show the effects of these advancements. In their words, they wanted to "show you how Man has come up from the caves of half a hundred thousand years ago, adapting himself to, being molded by, his environments, responding to each new thing discovered and developed" (p. 12).

What the organizers of the 1933 Chicago World's Fair understood was that the unrelenting advancement of technology-fueled change, driven by business, plays a significant role in pushing the world forward. Human evolution is inextricably linked to the tools and technologies we invent and use in our daily lives. Every company's evolution, including yours, is tied to the social technology of today and tomorrow. How your company adapts and moves forward from this point in time will determine its future.

⤳ Context Is King

Social technology releases innate desires that compel people to use these tools. The triggered behaviors manifest themselves in every share, like, friend, post, or comment made using social technology—and use is only rising.

Nielsen reports that social networking continues to be the most popular activity online in the United States, accounting for 20% of all time on PCs and 30% of time spent on mobile devices (2012, p. 4). Users spent 121 billion minutes on social media—more than 200,000 person-years—in July 2012 alone through all devices (pp. 4, 6). Time spent on social media sites grew 37% from the year before, which amounts to around 32 minutes per user per day (figures based on data from Nielsen 2012, pp. 5–6).

Within a company though, one other very powerful element comes into play: context. Business is inherently contextual. While a person's conversations or reasons for connecting on Facebook can be entirely random and very diverse, the use of such tools within a business has natural meaning.

Context creates and supports meaning, and the workplace is naturally contextual. As social technology makes its way into a company, it takes hold because there is context to the connections, communications, collaboration, and community that social technology supports and enables; the interactions that take place in a work environment among employees, customers, and partners are inherently more meaningful. While Facebook created a public place to initially exploit these phenomena, the workplace is where they will truly excel—because of context.

I frequently hear executives talk about social technology as a novelty or a toy because the conversations, announcements, and declarations can be trivial—and many of them are, in fact, given the personal use of the medium. However, that personal use is the dividing line for business: When people use these tools in the context of work, the conversation, declarations, and announcements are serving the purpose of the business.

Adding social technology tools into the workplace means eight hours a day of interaction, engagement, and relevance within the context of people getting their jobs done. The Pew survey reported that people like to interact with social technology because it's fun (Madden & Zickuhr 2011, p. 7); Nielsen found that 76% of users have a positive feeling after participating in social networking, with the words "connected," "informed," "amused," "energized," and "excited" describing their feelings more specifically (2012, p. 12). In the shift from using social technologies for an average of 32 minutes per day personally (minutes based on data from Nielsen 2012, pp. 5–6) to potentially using them 480 minutes a day in the workplace, what people do with the tools will be reinvented all over again.

Any company would be hard pressed to be competitive without telephones, the printed word, or even the primitive tool of fire. Today's social technology is as fundamental to the survival and success of your company as these other social technologies have been.

◄ The Predictable Path to Social Technology Diffusion

Ten years from now, social technology will be intertwined into people's daily existence and will no longer be a separate category unto itself, much like the way fire exists all around us but its visibility is obscured by our ability to manipulate and control it. By 2023, most IT will be inherently social in its design and functionality and in how it supports human needs. Many "things" will become social in nature. These outcomes are a natural expression of how people want to experience the world and get things done—to connect, communicate, collaborate, and create community.

Understanding how other social technology stages have played out in history can predict how this new social technology will evolve for business. It is impossible to foresee all of the incredible derivative tools and applications that will emerge and the particular ways they will change our world, but the development path toward these innovations is already established. Rule 8 of *Social Inc.* captures the pattern behind how these technologies have evolved.

Social Inc. Rule 8
Social technology adoption follows a pattern.

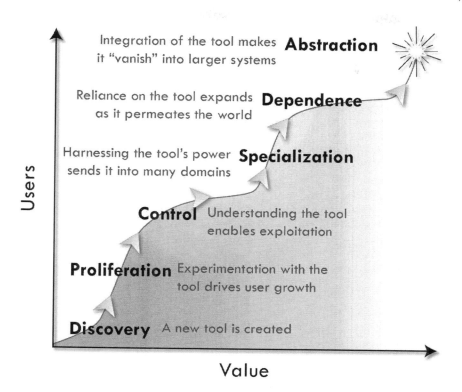

Figure 7-1. Major Social Technology Stages. Author's image.

I argue that social technologies go through six major stages in their adoption and diffusion across human societies (Figure 7-1). Each of these major stages has key lessons that can help people understand how today's social technology will evolve and impact business.

Discovery

Fire was not invented—it was discovered as a natural occurrence—and I argue that today's social technology has also been largely stumbled upon or discovered. There was no grand plan; instead, several key technology developments evolved simultaneously in a complimentary fashion. The acceptance and adoption of social technology grew significantly in 2011 and seemingly caught most people by surprise.

Adoption and engagement continue to spread at unprecedented rates (e.g., Pinterest; Constine 2012, para. 1). Social technology is not just a U.S. phenomenon either; in fact, engagement with these tools in countries like Russia, Turkey, and Venezuela exceeds that in the United States (comScore 2011, graphic). Given these trends, the social future may very well be invented outside of the United States.

Back in 2004 (Facebook) and 2006 (Twitter), it was difficult to understand the purpose of every social technology or what phenomenon they were addressing. Even today there continue to be skeptics: those who see the activities enabled by social technology as inconsequential.

While Facebook and Twitter are not naturally occurring forces, they do allow people to express behaviors that are forces of human nature. The point isn't that these particular technologies *are* the future of social technology—for business, they are only a small part of the overall opportunity. The critical task is to understand the essence behind what these tools enable, and to figure out what the changes in human behavior mean for business; that's the key point that makes social tools sustainable. Humans have discovered new ways to connect, communicate, collaborate, and create community—what the technology allows people and businesses to do is the game-changer.

Discovery cycles are iterative and painful. As discussed in Part 2, major technology advancements can be chaotic; in addition, social media disasters for businesses are often in the news (e.g., Fiegerman 2012). While today's social technology is a major evolutionary step forward, it's still early in its cycle. Humans have just discovered these tools—what they can be used for is still evolving, particularly for business.

Proliferation

Discovery and proliferation are close cousins. In my experience, people often use new tools and devices without really knowing what can be done with them, experimenting with them simply because others are and because they are new. As tools proliferate, new discoveries fuel further use and adoption.

Proliferation around social technology is occurring at different rates across different user groups, but the overall trend engages nearly all demographics and most geographies. Billions of individuals have adopted this technology, and corporate adoption has been lagging but is catching up.

This level of proliferation signals that the new social technology taps into an innate human need or desire—like fire, the printed word, and the telephone in the past. The important things that today's social technology can do are not yet known in their entirety, but as users of these tools, we know we want to figure them out.

Control

Proliferation leads to control, both actual control of the new technology through deeper understanding and attempts to control it based on fear of change. Control signals an important milestone in a social technology's development: People are starting to understand the impact the new tools can have, for better and for worse.

Control results from understanding the forces at work, and can lead to an incredible wave of innovation, and/or to repression. Fire, the printed word, and the telephone were often tightly controlled by the authority structures of the time. Once more people could harness their powers through a deeper understanding, an incredible period of advancement and innovation followed as the phenomena that the social technology "captured and put to use" (Arthur 2009, p. 51) were exploited in many dramatic ways.

Management wants to control what goes on in a corporate context; but can social technology be controlled? Even if it can, should it be? Control of today's social universe eludes most organizations. Fear is rampant in the boardroom and among CEOs about the things that could—and do—seem to go wrong with social technology. Individuals are experimenting and discovering what's possible, new behavior is emerging, and business is trying to figure it all out.

Forms of control include regulatory oversight on the one hand, and people's ability to harness, manage, and manipulate social technology on the other. Regulation is emerging from many governments and agencies, as is the ability of individuals and companies to innovate with these tools—both of these elements are vital to the adoption cycle. Regulatory oversight can be useful in and of itself, but also breeds a different kind of innovation: Those who refuse to be subjected to its control figure out how to work around it.

Efforts to control are a good sign. Regulation and censorship signal that the new development is real and valuable, and that major disruption is around the corner.

Specialization

Once there is a deep understanding of the new social technology in place, specialization starts to occur. People begin to apply the technology to other domains, and the new behaviors start to embed themselves into niche domains. Once humans controlled fire, it was applied to many industrial functions, changing the nature of agriculture and materially impacting everything it touched (see Part 2: *Homo Erectus* and the First Social Technology).

These social technologies are tools. We figure out how to use their core features and functions to change our world through them. The first generation of these latest tools have taught us the basics, we will now lift and shift these principles into specific uses. When business takes over a social tool or technology, a lot of creative things can start to happen.

This is where we are today with the progression of today's social technology tools—at the beginning of the most disruptive stage of diffusion. Say goodbye to the status quo.

Dependence

As a social technology permeates human existence, we grow increasingly dependent upon it. People find themselves hard pressed to imagine how we got anything done without it—imagine society without fire, the printed word, or the telephone.

As the technology becomes baked into its many niche applications, it becomes part of the fabric of our existence. Although not everyone adopts a new social technology at the same pace and some resist it entirely, critical mass around its use changes the world, usually for the better.

Abstraction

The final evolutionary step makes the social technology disappear—like magic. The new tools become abstracted and integrated so finely into other, larger systems that their discrete nature disappears. Fire is all around in light bulbs, automobiles, and kitchens, but only as a component part of other systems. Humans can effect these changes through our ability to control these tools (almost) absolutely, while our dependence on them forces them into many different domains.

The "internet of things" will become abstracted like this over the next decade as people and things, and things and things seamlessly interact and engage. Will the big community hubs like Facebook and Twitter still exist? History suggests that they will not, at least not in their current forms; the approaches and techniques they taught around social engagement will morph and fragment as deeper applications develop. I predict a decade-long cycle of disruption beginning now—most of the opportunity, and the potential pain and suffering, is yet to come for business.

Death to Change Management—Long Live Engagement Management

Want to see an executive's eyes glaze over? Start a conversation with, "Let's talk about change management." Throughout my career, I've never seen a single positive reaction to the term. As a management consulting buzzword and concept, *change management* attempts to deploy tools and techniques to get people to do things differently—whether they want to, or not. Unfortunately, because of that last part, it's usually ineffective. Change management thus becomes an unnatural act associated with large, disruptive corporate occurrences. Implementing enterprise resource planning? You need change management. Merger or acquisition happening? Here comes change management. New strategy? Change management time.

In theory, change management should work because it concerns human behavior, communication, and learning. However, it is not usually well received by those it is intended to change. Take one part communication, add one part training, throw in some incentives (i.e., carrots and sticks), and change management is intended to move people from Point A to Point B. Change management treats people like unthinking cogs in a great big machine—à la Frederick Taylor (1911) over 100 years ago. Change the cogs, and the machine will move in a different direction—theoretically. Unfortunately, the problem has not historically been with the cogs, but with the machine.

The machine that the historical approach to business management has created is like an oil tanker that takes miles to change direction. Once set upon management's course, that's where the machine is heading—regardless. Businesses, and especially large ones, were not designed to be nimble or to change course quickly.

Traditional change management techniques attempt to retrain the oil tanker crew to tack, like a sailboat. However, knowing how to tack like a sailboat does nothing when the crew is still on the oil tanker. The foundational structure of business from its command and control management, hierarchies, and matrix organizational structures to its rigid job descriptions prevents the very change that management seeks to implement.

These top-down initiatives are excruciating to implement, often fail to yield the desired benefits, and more often than not are doomed to failure right out of the gate. Change management initiatives regularly crash upon the rocky shores of passive resistance and cynicism.

Because of this track record, I hereby declare: "Death to change management." There is a better way—one that is only possible because of social technology. So, not only does social technology provide the tools to transform business, these same tools will also make that transformation happen.

With social technology, engagement takes the place of change management. *Engagement management* is a bottom-up approach to the rapid, agile, and iterative evolution of your business. Those who know the most about the new social tools—employees—lead. Rather than top-down coercion, engagement management is about bottom-up empowerment. With engagement management, change management dies and is reborn altogether through social technology.

I do not subscribe to the belief that humans are averse to change; I believe that humans are averse to *senseless* change in which they have no vested interest. Human instinct is to adapt, to grow, and to learn. I know that people voluntarily seek out and try new ways of doing things, or buy new products or services when they see there are clear benefits—sometimes even when they don't yet understand the benefits. People like to experiment.

From my experience, I know that people most often have (or want to have) pride in their jobs and their company. While this pride may wane over the years as the institutional sludge of their organization destroys their enthusiasm, there's still an ember there that can be relit.

As a management consultant, I have frequently been called on to cut through the sludge inherent in most organizations. I often liked to say that we were market makers in knowledge transference: We took business knowledge from one domain (i.e., one company) and spread it around to other companies. In other words, we made the business market for knowledge-acquisition efficient. After 29 years of doing this, I noticed all too frequently that most companies, or at least the employees in the company, already knew the solution to whatever problem we were called in to fix but could not wade through institutional barriers to get it fixed. We heard a lot of "It is what it is," which means, "We know this doesn't work, but we also know we're powerless to fix it."

In contrast, the Social Company is self-healing. Social technology is an antiseptic that cures all manner of corporate dysfunction. Remember, change management concerns human behavior, communicating, and learning. Rule 1 of *Social Inc.* states, "Social technology is about human behavior." Successful Social Companies have discovered a new, more powerful, and effective approach to enabling their future—by enabling and engaging their workforce with the social technology on which their future depends.

The future is social technology-enabled, and it's already here. Let the early adopters of this technology be your guide—they want to help and they are your existing employees and customers.

⌁ The *Social Inc.* Maturity Model

Integrating a disruptive technology into a business impacts all aspects of the company—from strategy to operations to governance. A maturity model is an effective tool for establishing context around large-scale business initiatives—maturity models help assess where the company is relative to where it wants or needs to be. Rule 9 of *Social Inc.* reflects the inevitability of this journey: Markets are already using social technology, which means your company has no choice but to adopt these tools as well.

Social Inc. Rule 9
Social disruption will happen with or without you.

The *Social Inc.* Maturity Model describes a company's evolution through five stages of social technology adoption and integration, with specific strategic and tactical behaviors for each stage (Table 7-1). This high-level framework will help your company conduct an initial assessment of its use and understanding of social technology, as well as assisting with initial board-level discussions.

While the model is purposely simplistic, the journey is not. Reimagining and executing how things get done with social technology tools is a difficult undertaking. However, since you now understand the forces at play, your journey has already started.

Ferdinand Magellan conclusively demonstrated that the world was round, and it's inconceivable today that there was ever anything other than this fundamental truth. At some point in the future, people will wonder how there was ever anything other than a social technology-driven model of leading, managing, and running a business.

Table 7-1: Strategic and Tactical Behaviors of the Social Inc. Maturity Model

Maturity stage	Strategic and tactical behaviors	
1. Nowhere	- Board and CEO are silent on social technology - IT is not a strategic presence - Social technology viewed as a distraction - Employee cynicism or frustration with IT	- Access to social technology sites blocked for employees - No social presence on public channels (e.g., Facebook) - Social technology conversation ignored - Fearful of social technology
2. Dabbling	- Wait-and-see mindset - Passive leadership toward social technology - Company has a social technology presence - Silo-ed approach to social technology internally - Social technology plan is marketing-driven	- No monitoring of social activity mentioning company - Employee engagement is ad hoc - IT focused on security around social technology - Reactive approach to social technology engagement
3. We get it	- Articulated social technology vision in place - Active board and CEO sponsorship - Regular Social CEO engagement - Social technology viewed as a strategic weapon - Initial social technology metrics tracked	- Proactive market engagement - Cross-functional involvement with social technology plan - Internal social technology tools in place - 24/7 monitoring of social technology activity - Sense of urgency about social technology approach and plan
4. All in	- IT/social technology skills added to board - Risks are understood - Sense of excitement is high - Openness, transparency, and trust abound - Multiple stakeholders engaged	- Social and IT enterprise architecture in place - Enterprise-wide engagement - A unique social technology experience is emerging - Analytics are raising understanding and corporate IQ
5. *Social Inc.* leader	- Social technology is a standing part of the board calendar - Social CEO sets the example - Risks are managed - Sense of satisfaction is high - Agile business approach has emerged - Products and services are unique	- Processes are social technology-based in design and execution - Market propositions revolve around the experience - All stakeholders are socially engaged - Revenue and profitability gains are being realized

Note. Author's table.

◄ Ten Practical Implementation Steps

I close this chapter by providing some tactical recommendations and a high-level roadmap for CEOs and board members to launch—and manage—their company's social technology journey around. These ten steps will help plot the initial course, but you'll no doubt be "tacking like a sailboat" along the way.

These steps also reflect the tenth and final Rule of *Social Inc.*—this technology is about you. Because of the power inherent in being connected and empowered on a global scale, in real time, you are now in charge.

Social Inc. Rule 10
Social technology is about *you*!

Step #1—Improve the Board's Social Company IQ

Conduct a social briefing for your board of directors and CEO, and then get some social technology skills onto the board. Social technology has both strategic and operational implications, including new risks. Active governance is needed to understand and capitalize on this next chapter in business management history. Social technology impacts every company—whether you want it to or not. It is vital to approach these developments from a top-down *and* a bottom-up perspective to properly capitalize on them. From both perspectives, board understanding and engagement are prerequisites to success.

Step #2—Make Your CEO a Social CEO

Your CEO should lead by social example. Engagement cannot be faked. Social technology tools are where an increasing number of your employees and customers are spending their time. Whether your company uses Twitter or an internal communication tool like Chatter, Yammer, or Jive, CEO participation in the conversation is a necessary part of the experience your company offers.

Of course, your CEO will need training before joining the conversation, and your company should also have a social communication policy in place. Your employees will reward this show of openness and transparency, and so will your customers. Some mistakes will undoubtedly be made, but they will probably not be fatal. The "tone at the top" will be established and an example will be set for all employees to follow (and, I suspect, you'll have some laughs along the way).

Step #3—Make Being a Social Company Core to Your Mission

Get a cross-functional, cross-geographic, cross-business, cross-hierarchical launch team organized to help you understand how social technology impacts and changes your world. This group of 15-20 internal champions and advisors can represent the core of your business but should also be generationally, cognitively, and gender/identity diverse. Becoming a Social Company is a large-scale enterprise undertaking, and it's a very creative process. I suspect your people will volunteer *en masse* to participate—they want to use this technology and to help fix what they know is broken.

Start at a manageable scale, and then expand to the entire organization. Get external help to understand the technology landscape or to facilitate your team. The advisory team needs to move fast—give them a 30-day mandate to recommend a social technology-enabled strategy and a prioritization of specific actions to enable it. Executive sponsor? Your newly minted Social CEO. There cannot be a Social Company without a Social CEO, and this is a sizeable business technology and market disruption with strategic, operational, risk, and financial implications. Experimentation and adaptability are core skills for this journey.

Step #4—Open-Source Innovation with Social Technology

Being unique is an innovation-driven model. Being a Social Company is about innovating with social technology tools and creating a unique experience in your markets (PricewaterhouseCoopers 2010, p. 1). By engaging your employees and markets to get the pump primed for continuous improvement and innovation, you signal to your employees that business-as-usual is not going to cut it. Hopefully your core launch team will make this recommendation on its own, but if not, add it to their plan.

Priming the conversation also engages your customer base, and launching the conversation with them will provide more feedback than your company will know what to do with. Some of it will be surprising, and not all of it will be positive—but that's the point. Being part of the conversation and being engaged are cornerstones to your success and the experience that your company offers. This step starts to craft an overall experience of working for, and with, your company.

Step #5—Raze Your IT Shantytown

When Cortés set out to conquer the Aztecs in 1519, he famously told his troops to scuttle their ships (R. Marks 1993, p. 85). Now is the time to take a fresh look at your entire IT environment and figure out what needs to be scuttled.

Unfortunately you're still sailing to your destination, unlike Cortés, and your existing IT environment needs to continue to support your business day-to-day. Nonetheless, without this vital step, your legacy IT will continue to slow you down.

You must rebuild and re-architect your IT around social technology—you don't have a choice. Social Companies will have different economic advantages, and yours will not be able to compete over time if you do not address the economic and operational disadvantages of your existing IT environment.

Step #6—Start Real-Time Social Monitoring, Keep Score, and Engage

Establish a social technology command center as your company's "ear to the ground." Listen, observe, learn, and engage. Do you know which social metrics are important for your business? They are more nuanced than just the number of "followers" or "likes," but that's a starting point. You need to figure this out and start tracking those numbers.

Social technology monitoring tools are evolving quickly. The challenge in this environment is the volume and velocity of the information that you are monitoring. Start to think beyond just the connections that are getting established, and work on understanding the underlying economics behind communication, collaboration and community.

Step #7—Train for Quickness and Speed

Being quick is different than being fast. *Quickness* describes a company's reaction time to external stimuli and is a measure of time. How quickly do you respond to the almost instantaneous feedback that permeates social technology? Being *fast* is a measure of speed and is also important to becoming a Social Company. Unfortunately, neither has been a hallmark of most business models, historically.

As discussed in Part 3: The 100-Year Business Management Experiment, history shows that rapid market changes are the Achilles' heel of traditional business management theory and practice. In contrast, a Social Company welcomes and embraces market volatility, and indeed thrives on it.

Step #8—Become Great at Fixing Problems

Fixing problems needs to become a core competency at every level of the organization. Most companies focus an inordinate amount of resources on trying to prevent problems. With social technology, you need to be good at detecting and then fixing problems quickly, and to accept that preventing them is increasingly a losing battle.

A discriminative focus on prevention handicaps an organization's ability to resolve the problems that do arise—and they inevitably do, especially with social technology. Being able to identify issues in the marketplace with real-time monitoring, and then acting on this knowledge, is a new core competency of Social Companies.

Step #9—Trust Your Most Valuable Asset

A culture that truly allows employees to be empowered and that embraces the iterative nature of business is your secret weapon with social technology.

Business leaders have been saying that employees are their most important asset for years, and now is the time to prove it.

Openness, transparency, trust, engagement, and the experience that your company creates are the hallmarks of the Social Company. Achieving this vision requires a shift in how you've thought about many aspects of your organization and business, but it will unleash the power that is your workforce in ways that you have never imagined.

Your future has never looked brighter.

Step #10—Expand the Pie

Business is naturally social. Using social technology to create value for customers, employees, investors, and communities will create vibrant ecosystems that have never been more intertwined and interdependent. Business success will always be primarily defined by profit and loss, but success will be increasingly dependent upon the ability to deliver something that the entire stakeholder community finds meaningful and relevant. Many companies have supported their communities, but the expectation is to now play a meaningful role in shaping communities as well.

People want more from business—and business has the potential to deliver more. Value-creation is the cornerstone of this next generation of business management theory and practice, and social technology provides the tools to achieve that value. Employee engagement can be better, customer trust in business needs to improve, and economic growth can be stronger. The future is one of innovation for business. Business has mastered the "lower cost" part of competing as expressed by Michael Porter (see Part 4: Michael Porter and the Holy Grail). It's time to now master the innovation enabled and delivered through social technology.

Remember, social technology is not new—only this latest iteration is. People have changed the world before through social technology. Our new and collective future is in all of our hands now.

What will we do with this incredible opportunity?

A 2020 Future
Brought to You
by Social Technology

People ask me to predict the future,
when all I want to do is prevent it. Better yet,
build it. Predicting the future is much too easy,
anyway. You look at the people around you,
the street you stand on, the visible air you breathe,
and predict more of the same.
To hell with more. I want better.

–Ray Bradbury (1982, p. 155)

◄ Pulling the Future into Place

Marshall Poe (2012, pp. 7–9) and many others believe that demand "pulls" new media into use. Supply then emerges to fulfill this need and "[pushes] societies and ideas in new directions" (p. 11). I believe that the changes in the world today are being driven by a wave of demand—and pull—with unprecedented size and might. People want things to be better, and they know they can be. What companies now do with these social technology tools will determine the future that business pushes into being.

The following observations are made throughout *Social Inc.* and describe the forces coming to bear on our collective, social technology-enabled future.

- **New behaviors**—Changes in human behavior are disrupting the business status-quo.
- **Market dissatisfaction**—There are enormous trust and engagement gaps between what markets and employees want and what business is delivering.
- **Economic maturation**—Many global economies are maturing, and the global recovery and future economic growth are on shaky ground.
- **New knowledge frontiers**—An explosion in information supply is flooding us with new data and information that will yield new knowledge.
- **Mastery over a new environment**—Advancements in social technology have removed most information distortions attributable to space and time, making immediate relevancy an important part of any value proposition.
- **New means of engagement**—Collaboration tools and social technology are changing how people interact with their world and accomplish things.
- **Shifts in power**—Individuals and groups now have much greater power and can collectively act on a massive scale.
- **Economic revival**—Economic forces are being altered through new social technologies.
- **New competitive plateaus**—The social technology "arms race" is creating competitive intensity, redefining value, and enabling new levels of intellectual and labor productivity.

The *Social Inc.* Rules That Will Push Business Forward

The ten rules of *Social Inc.* (Figure 8-1) have been presented in detail in previous chapters. These rules are pushing the future into place for business.

Business is at a pivot point. People know companies can do better, we want them to do better, and we now have tools to make them better. In Part 3,

1. Social technology is about human behavior.

2. Social technology makes people smarter and more productive.

3. You can learn from social technology's history.

4. Changes in human behavior disrupt the business status quo.

5. The Social Company excels at delivering a unique experience.

6. Social technology is experiential.

7. Social technology is controls-resistent.

8. Social technology adoption follows a pattern.

9. Social disruption will happen with or without you.

10. Social technology is about you.

Figure 8-1. The 10 Rules of *Social Inc.* Author's image.

I declared the next chapter of business management history to be a revolution focused on delivering an experience (see The Age of the Experience—Social Technology Shall Set You Free). The Age of the Experience is a revolution enabled by today's social technology and by the customers, employees, business leaders, and investors who want something better.

◄ Ten Predictions for a *Social Inc.* 2020

The last eight years have brought rapid, large-scale, social technology-driven changes on multiple fronts. Here are my 2020 predictions for the next eight years for business and beyond.

2020 Prediction #10—The Rise of Information Poverty

Widespread corporate adoption of social technology will create and contribute to inequality and disadvantage for those who cannot engage or transact through these media. Lack of online access for all citizens of Earth will become a major political and economic issue around the world by 2020. Increasingly, the information have-nots will be economically and socially disadvantaged, individually and as communities, cities, and nations.

The information haves and have-nots will increasingly align with economic haves and have-nots. Higher economic prosperity for early adopters of social technology will continue, like in Gutenberg's day (see Part 2: Gutenberg Prints Up 385% Faster Economic Growth), and the gaps will become more severe. Rampant corporate adoption of social technology will expose this issue and bring it to the forefront.

Affordable access to the online, global social communities will be a necessity for everything in business from applying for jobs to getting paid, being informed, learning, doing a job, and being gainfully self-employed. Once people fully transition to this new world, the economic disadvantages of not being connected will become apparent. Those who are social technology-connected and -enabled will increasingly interact only with others who also share these domains, essentially discriminating against those who are not a part of these networks and ecosystems.

Business will push this issue onto the political and economic policy agenda by 2020, and governments will experiment with different solutions to close this growing "info-nomic" divide. Governments and businesses who work together and lead on this issue will alter the global balance of power economically and socially for decades to come, in their favor.

2020 Prediction #9—Education Gets Socially Re-Educated

Many education systems around the world are underperforming in dramatic fashion, and are not improving.[36] UNESCO reported in 2012 that progress toward the goals set by the Education For All (EFA) initiative by 164 countries in 2000 is slowing and that "most EFA goals are unlikely to be met" by the agreed-upon 2015 deadline (2012b, p. 1).

Being smart is a good thing for business and humanity. Social technology—especially the printed book—improved literacy rates and contributed to raising IQs and driving economic prosperity (see Part 2). UNESCO (2012b) describes the leverage achieved through education spending: "for every US$1 spent on education, as much as US$10 to US$15 can be generated in economic growth" (p. 18)—more than a 1,000% return on investment. UNESCO (2012c) is also interested in leveraging the availability of mobile devices to support the spread of education.

I think social technology can have a significant, direct and indirect influence on major education reforms from preschool to K-12, post-secondary education (college), adult, and vocational learning. The inherent behaviors leveraged through social technology—connecting, communicating, collaborating, and creating and sustaining community—all can positively contribute to education objectives and learning outcomes at every level of education.

There is an enormous opportunity to reengineer the entire approach to education through social technology. Technology makes markets efficient, and social technology is driving transaction or engagement costs to virtually

---

[36] This underperformance is less widely discussed for early childhood education, but I see some very interesting developments at that level (Dilawar 2011; Early Connections: Technology in Childhood Education n.d.; Swanson 2012).

zero across many domains (see Part 5: Anarchy, One Connection at a Time). The advent of the printed word showed that lowering the costs of reading in turn lowered barriers to learning how to read (see Part 2: Gutenberg Prints Up 385% Faster Growth).

"Social education" through today's tools will improve the world. All the pieces are in place: Mobile technology reaches over 85% of the world and this number is growing (Ericsson 2012, p. 5), literacy correlates with higher IQs (D. Marks 2010), and economic growth went hand-in-hand with the social technology of the printing press (Dittmar 2011)—to say nothing of the economic impact of fire or the benefits of the telephone.

Corporate learning will lead the way because such efforts need to be fast and effective; it's more profitable that way. Companies want their employees to learn quickly and deploy their new knowledge as soon as possible. As businesses diffuse today's social technology, they will directly and indirectly improve the individual and collective intelligence of their workforce.

Rising demand for educated workers will put pressure on the education system to respond. Georgetown University's Center on Education and the Workforce forecasts that by 2018, 63% of U.S. job openings will require workers with at least some college education (Carnevale, Smith, & Strohl 2010, p. 13). The education industry will rethink and reengineer how education is delivered and validated using social technology to enable this transformation, following the lead of business.

Lessons learned in business will fuel a grassroots reform effort from corporate leaders and employees who take these insights back into their education systems to force reform. Innovators like Khan Academy, Stanford, and the MIT/Harvard joint venture will continue to change the way knowledge is gathered, distributed, and validated.

In 2012, Harvard and MIT announced their joint venture around online education, edX (Harvard Magazine 2012; MIT News 2012). Stanford's early work with their online courses has proven wildly popular (Baker 2012; NPR 2012). People want to learn, and a technology-leveraged approach is now available for this latent demand. Organizations like Coursera are making learning markets efficient and accessible.

Smart businesses and societies will own the future, because they will be inventing it. Collectively, we can be much smarter than we are individually. Being smarter as a business is one of the foundational powers behind the disruption and transformation of business through social technology. Using these tools and reforming the malfunctioning education system at every level to achieve this transformation may very well be the ultimate "secret sauce" in social technology.

2020 Prediction #8—Internet "Eclipses" Create a Global Crisis of Connectivity

Blackouts, extended outages, limited bandwidth, and general downtime will create a crisis of connectivity over the next eight years. To some extent, these eclipses are already starting to occur. University of Southern California researchers reported that Hurricane Sandy in October 2012 created twice the level of network outages than historical baseline levels (Heidemann, Quan, & Pradkin 2012, p. 2). The digital infrastructure is already vulnerable to the weight of explosive adoption and use.

While infrastructure resiliency issues are a logical growing pain as use continues to skyrocket, there will be some unintended consequences. Infrastructure failure will reinforce the importance of people's reliance and dependency on these technologies at a national and global level. National security, the economic system, and global communications are all highly dependent on this infrastructure—national policy and resources will be shifted to the information infrastructure to shore up its resiliency.

A coordinated global effort will take shape with the goal of ensuring the basic right of connectivity for all communities and citizens on Earth. The resulting coordinated approach will be the first truly united approach to governing and connecting this part of our global community. The realization of our interdependencies will finally enter the conversation around human destiny. This achievement will be a monumental step forward for humanity, or it will be a total disaster—I'm betting on the former.

With social technology, the power is with the people—customers, employees, investors, and citizens. This power transference is a threat to the status quo and those who benefit from controlling it today. Shutting down the mechanism that enables collective action removes the threat, but is not a good outcome for anyone. It is undeniable that some governments and politicians do not trust the empowerment of the people. The power of social technology can be used for destructive means as easily as for constructive purposes.

Social technology-infused and -enabled "social sabotage" will rise as a major risk to any and all authority frameworks—from schools to companies, the press, and governments. The only way to completely eliminate this risk will be to shut down the infrastructure that enables it. George Orwell (1949) was a man ahead of his time, but time has caught up with him—welcome to Oceania,[37] brought to you by social technology.

This is the "disaster" scenario: governments and power structures trying to hang on to the past. For a while, the internet will regularly go dark—a victim of its own success and of acts of nature, intentional mischief, malfeasance, reliability issues, or government regulation. The battle for the soul of our social technology-enabled destiny will unfold over the next eight years.

I predict we'll rise to this challenge together. Multilateral government responses to the issue of the internet—and related social technology— resiliency will be unprecedented and a positive step forward for humanity.

2020 Prediction #7—Social Searching Reinvents an Industry

The internet search is searching for its next incarnation. The massively expanding digital haystack of big data makes it increasingly difficult to search for and find a digital needle. Data sharing totaled 65 billion gigabytes

---

[37] George Orwell brought his fictitious community Oceania to life in 1949 in his book *1984*. HIs dystopian society is characterized by constant government surveillance from "Big Brother" and the suppression and prosecution of individualism and thought crimes in the name of the supposed greater good by the ruling "elite."

worldwide in 2007 alone—"the equivalent of every person in the world communicating the content of six newspapers every day" (S. Wu 2011, para. 10).

Siri, Google voice, and Dragon Search are making voice-based search a reality, and an increasingly effective step up from typing a query, but these apps are still just searching, wading through a sea of information. The quantity of available, searchable data is growing exponentially, as demonstrated by the more than doubling of computing capacity every two years for the last decades (58% per year 1986–2007; S. Wu 2011, para. 12).

Would you rather get an answer or recommendation from your personal or professional network or from an algorithm that creates an index and presents links to what it thinks is most relevant, with a bunch of sponsored ads mixed in? Recent search statistics show that ads are basically just noise on the screen. In 2012, SEO Peace released research that shows low levels of sponsored click-through and irrelevancy beyond page one of the algorithmic search result. Specifically, their research reports the following:

- …79% of search engine users say they "always/frequently" click on the natural search results (organic).
- …80% of search engine users say they "occasionally/rarely/never" click on the sponsored search results.
- …75% of search engine users never scroll past the first page of search results. (infographic, top section, bullets 1–3)

If people today don't bother to wade through an index of results that is 4,267,826 items long, they certainly won't go through the 10,654,201 results generated two years from now. Search in its current form is tapped out, delivering all the relevancy it is capable of.

What I term *social searching* promises to deliver an answer, not an index. As business starts to engage in much more meaningful ways with its markets, the social graph will become the search, answer, and find engine of the future. Influence and push will bring users what we need when we need it, including advice, recommendations, and answers that are relevant to our location at that moment in time. We will no longer want or need to access or actively look for things online—they'll find us. Business will lead with tools and techniques that anticipate people's needs and deliver content, information, knowledge, and engagement when individuals want or need it, creating tremendous value from spatial and temporal relevance. Even when people don't know they need that information, it could be "pushed" to them anyway. Notwithstanding the Orwellian connotations, this will be a welcome development for many people.

A person's social graph will be able to deliver a near-instantaneous answer, comment, suggestion, or recommendation to a specific question or query, or will recognize a latent need and respond proactively. The relevancy of spatial and temporal context will make it possible to know what information or interaction to deliver and when.

People don't want an index—they want contextual information, or knowledge. Increasingly, predictive, pushed content will reach us. Walking by a cupcake store, you'll get a note that 27 of your friends love the cinnamon bacon cupcakes. In you go, and 12 cinnamon bacon cupcakes later, you de-friend these people. A simplistic example, but when time and space distortions are virtually eliminated, the quality of content or engagement that can be pushed directly to individuals rises dramatically.

By 2020, getting answers from one's social graph will be more meaningful, relevant, and increasingly more efficient than searching, because of each person's relative social "footprint." The "needle" will find its way to you, because it knows where you are, what you do, what you know, who you know, how you behave, and why you do the things you do. Millions of people have been sharing these things voluntarily for almost a decade, on Facebook and other social networking sites. Privacy and security issues notwithstanding, interactions and experiences will become seamless between people and things. Humans have been abstracting complexity out of systems since the beginning of time, and social engagement will be no different.

Social search will reinvent the very concept of search, threatening the search status quo and reducing at least one former search high-flyer, and possibly the entire category, to a shadow of its former self. Data, information, and knowledge will find and reach us through our social footprint by 2020. (Those who do not have a social graph will be increasingly disadvantaged; see Prediction #10.)

2020 Prediction #6—The Social CEO Reboots Political Leadership

Why doesn't the U.S. government work more effectively and efficiently? How can the monopoly of the United States Post Office be essentially bankrupt? Why is there such rampant dysfunction in so many government services? Dictators are being taken down with some frequency (O'Donnell 2012), it seems—political incompetence, ineffectiveness, and impotence will be next.

By 2020, politics will get a much-needed makeover, and it will start because business takes a leading role in transforming the future. The leadership and execution problems faced by governments worldwide have created an opportunity for new leaders to emerge. In the 2020 U.S. presidential election, candidates will emerge who have established themselves as trusted leaders in business through the use of social technology. The unprecedented levels of engagement, visibility, and trust that these candidates establish through their business engagement as Social CEOs will propel them into the political stratosphere.

Through social technology, these future government leaders will also be supported and promoted by a socially enabled citizenry; these events could occur in the United States or in any country, given the near-universal adoption of social technology worldwide. Citizens across the world will exert their social influence by bringing at least one business leader to political power through a collective social voice. This leader will be thrust into the conversation through the power of the people and a reputation built upon social engagement, leadership, and trust.

The Social Company will reveal a new class of business and community leader, so this person may or may not be a relative unknown today. This new leader will be a social technology champion, visionary, and evangelist, and will truly believe in the constructive empowerment and engagement of citizens to effectively govern and lead. For too long, authority has been masquerading as leadership, but not anymore—this new leader will understand that authority and leadership are different. This individual doesn't need to control in order to lead.

In the United States, this presidential candidate will have been born in the 1970s or 1980s and grown up with information technology and social technology. Older candidates will be seen as irrelevant and out of touch, because they will be late adopters or neglectors of these tools. In a social technology-driven world, the socially abstinent will be at a dramatic disadvantage. Engaged and reaching and inspiring hundreds of millions on a regular basis through the platform of their business, this leader will be a welcome respite from the mediocrity and bedlam of the current U.S. political system.

John F. Kennedy was 43 when he was elected to office in 1961—a 2020 U.S. presidential candidate could be younger than this. On a historical note, Teddy Roosevelt was the youngest U.S. president at age 42, assuming the office after William McKinley's assassination; Obama and Clinton were not far behind at ages 47 and 46, respectively (White House n.d.).

2020 Prediction #5—Social Self-Employment Becomes the New Jobs Act

The U.S. workforce has changed considerably over the last century. Workers moved from rural self-employment on farms to urban wage-earners in professional, technical, and service industries (Fisk 2003, para. 4; Social Security Administration 2012, para. 33). Almost 78% of all workers were in service industries by 1999, compared with 31% at the start of the century (para. 4).

A broad range of technology advancements in the workplace, home, and economy are cited as direct and indirect contributing factors to the evolution of work and the worker. From communications, electricity, air conditioning, and the microwave oven to the automobile and computers, human technological evolution changed how, why, what, where, and who got things done (Fisk 2003, para. 18).

Why would today's social technology be any different as an agent of change? Big companies thrive on improving productivity, because the system is designed to reward them for it, but massive, technology-driven worker productivity improvements are generally negative factors on unemployment rates. Social technology makes people more productive; big companies will exploit this increase in workforce productivity, by eliminating (or at least not adding) jobs. Many employees may have already felt the pain of downsizing and outsourcing, which is why innovation and creativity must be pursued hand-in-hand with productivity.

As social technology creates a new plateau around enterprise productivity, these tools also have the potential to solve the very labor problem that they exacerbate. As MIT Professor Erik Brynjolfsson and MIT Center for Digital Business coauthor Andrew McAfee discuss, while the "Great Restructuring" facing business today can destroy jobs, it can also paradoxically fuel growth at the same time (2011, pp. 9, 28).

Social technology will usher in a new distributed and agile work model that will drive self-employment and entrepreneurism as an economic growth strategy for smart economies. Big business will cause this disruption because companies won't be hiring as many workers, but government intervention will also incentivize a shift to a new model. This model will enable a return to greater worker self-sufficiency through self-employment and entrepreneurship.

A recent *Kaufman Fellows Report* article describes how Israel is innovating in this regard and already implementing this new model of government-supported worker independence. The report concludes with the statement:

> As the pace of disruptive invention seems sure to accelerate, regions and companies that have access to a well-prepared and agile technical workforce will magnify their edge in competitive advantage in creating advanced societies and value. (Brady-Estevez & Stirgwolt 2012, p. 41)

I believe the transformation of business management to create and deliver an experience will be a positive factor in economic growth, which I refer to as *expanding the pie.* Even as the human population has exploded over time, the average size of the economic pie per person has increased more than 15-fold (see Part 3: A Killer Future Forged Through Social Technology).

There is money on the table with social technology (see Chui et al.'s 2012 research for the McKinsey Global Institute; Maddison 2010). Companies who create—and deliver—an experience through social technology will increase the economic pie by improving productivity while also innovating at new levels with creative destruction. Tightly integrated industry ecosystems and an explosion in the self-employed and small- and medium-sized businesses connected to those ecosystems will drive future employment growth. By 2020, the United States will see a return to worker self-sufficiency through self-employment and entrepreneurism because of the low engagement costs afforded by social technology and the ability to efficiently couple and decouple as a contingent, contract, or self-employed workforce.

Large corporations will migrate to a larger contingent workforce to help manage market volatility and the public relations backlash associated with firing large parts of their workforce. The socially connected self-employed will tap into the power of their network to be gainfully and sustainably engaged across their social graph, making self-employment a work-creation juggernaut. In a massively contingent workforce, companies will easily source and integrate socially self-employed workers into their socially designed enterprise.[38]

By 2020, governments will realize (or finally admit) that long-term high unemployment rates are increasingly driven by permanent and technology-led productivity improvements. Companies and economies simply no longer need the same relative employment base that they traditionally retained. Governments will start to implement policies that encourage and incentivize the self-employed and small business initiation.

---

[38] One barrier to this model in the United States is the lack of a national healthcare initiative, which makes people dependent on employment for healthcare benefits. "Obamacare" (i.e., the Patient Protection and Affordable Care Act) is a step toward a solution, but will need to go further for this future to become a reality.

The free market for labor, goods, and services will be much more efficient on a global scale, allowing those with desirable skills to freely and effectively sell their services to buyers all over the world. The extended organization and social ecosystems will engage many more workers (including contingent ones), than employees.

However, workers will have much more personal responsibility for the relevancy of their skill-set, which will cause some major transitional problems. Governments will need to incentivize lifelong skills development, rather than providing jobs that are quasi-welfare systems for irrelevant skills. (This transformation of the workforce will also contribute to the transformation of the global education system; see Prediction #9.)

Government programs that support and encourage entrepreneurship will be a required part of the equation. The U.S. Jumpstart Our Business Startups (JOBS) Act that passed into law in 2012 is a good example. For the first time, equity crowd funding is now legal in the United States, which should make it easier for entrepreneurs to find funding for their ventures (Colao 2012, para. 4). With this policy change, a regular person can invest $100 in a startup such as the next Facebook as an angel investor, where only official, accredited investors could have invested before. I expect these changes to increase the number of new U.S. companies launched every year.

Policy will shift to skills redevelopment, priming the small business pump, and innovation as the backbone of the successful society of 2020. Those countries who will not—or cannot—deliver will suffer major economic and political upheaval.

2020 Prediction #4—"Inc-onomics" Redefine Business Success

The workplace and intellectual productivity advantages behind social technology will drive economic growth, massive corporate profitability, and meaningful shifts in the broader role of business in society. A virtual cycle of economic advantages will emerge, in what I refer to as "Inc-onomics," for companies that deliver on Drucker's words in 1946 about the role of the corporation in society (see Part 1).

The "Great Recession" that started in 2007 (Sum et al. 2009) will be a distant memory eight years from now. Social Companies will be designed to natively deliver broader and deeper levels of social relevancy as part of their value proposition. Fulfilling a broader social obligation will be a required part of the experience that a Social Company delivers to its markets, and the company will in turn be rewarded for that experience by its customers, employees, and investors.

The next major business management revolution is the Age of the Experience; business management theory has evolved through and past the Ages of the Work, the Organization, and the Individual. Social technology lets leaders build on the successes of the last century and fix the flaws in these prior models. Profitability and investor value will not go away as the primary metrics of capitalist success or failure, but profitability and consequential social engagement will increasingly go hand-in-hand.

Social CEOs know that their communities are an important part of their stakeholder group and that being responsible to those communities is good for business. This broader vision creates a vibrant ecosystem that renews and nourishes itself. Healthy customers, communities, and environments are a requirement for sustainable success in business.

The economic advantage that surrounds social technology is compelling. Companies will experience massive productivity gains, and innovation and collaboration will drive breakthroughs across many different fields and endeavors. Interaction and engagement are reinventing everything—making things better so that business success involves more than just lowering costs to produce more of the same.

This growth will flow across society and has the potential to create economic prosperity, rejuvenation, and a renaissance that is long overdue. I believe that Social Company early-adopters will post outsized gains, redefine profitability in their industries, and reinvent what it's like to do business with them through these technologies. The future is about expanding the pie for everyone.

2020 Prediction #3—Social Networking Will Disappear, But Social Engagement Will Be Everywhere

Social technology history teaches that new tools and techniques get abstracted into larger systems, and become muted over time until they merge into the background of human lives. By 2020, consumers will no longer log on to a discrete site to join the conversation, share, pin, like, or tweet. Today's social networking experience will be wrapped into our day-to-day existence, integrated in ways we have yet to imagine—and through this integration, abstracted into the background.

Why are devices so important to Apple, Google, and Microsoft? The device is critical because the tool subsumes discrete functions over time; they get integrated into the interface. The need to deliver an experience—the focus of this latest evolution in business management history—naturally demands stronger points of integration. The discrete layers of information management start to merge and "mash up." They can still exist as individual elements, but are now also a component of an integrated and more complex system.

Business will only succeed in this effort if it can avoid or abstract the complexity of the overall system, so that the complexity is removed from the user's experience and blends into the background. The automobile is a perfect example. Today's driving experience is radically evolved from where it started. Cars are simpler to drive, but much more complicated systems to operate. Variable ratio power steering, Xenon adaptive headlights with dynamic auto-leveling, rain-sensing windshield wipers, park distance control, dynamic stability control, tire pressure monitor, remote keyless entry, 20-way power seats, brake energy regeneration—I don't know what half of this means but these are features of the BMW I drive regularly.

All of these elements have improved the overall experience of driving without sacrificing the ease of operating a car. Cars that drive themselves? (see, e.g., Fountain 2012; Kelly 2012; Wood 2012). That will be an even simpler driving experience, but a much more complicated system. None of my neighbors work on their own cars anymore, but we all used to—new cars are too complicated for novices to tinker around with. Cars are easier to drive and maintain, until they break. The car's evolution has been focused on delivering a better driving experience without making the car more difficult to drive. Devices are critical to technology leaders because when you build a device yourself, the overall user experience can be controlled and advanced further with tighter integration.

By 2020, people, things, brands, and engagement will move into contextually rich, niche social tools and applications. Social technologies embed themselves into niche applications (see Part 2), which then have deep context and relevance in both our day-to-day existence and to getting specific things done. Facebook taught the tools and techniques of social engagement, and by 2020 these techniques will be "specialized" and integrated into many subdomains, seamlessly. Discrete portals will become less relevant, or vanish altogether.

The social technology of the community fire, 800,000 years ago, has fragmented into hundreds of little fires that remain all around us, integrated into the fabric of our lives but abstracted from conscious view. Similarly, today's social technology will be everywhere—taken for granted while people wonder how they ever got things done without it.

2020 Prediction #2—Brand Hijacking Will Hold Corporate Leaders Accountable in the Court of Social Governance

Confidence levels are at all-time lows across almost every major company, group, institution, and political environment around the world (Edelman Trust Barometer 2012, slide 7). Because of social technology, you as an individual can now do something about this situation—and you will, in a big way. Governments struggle to function effectively and efficiently, and business has been largely unable to live up to expectations, creating a sizeable opportunity for disruption. Do something bad enough, for long enough, and someone will come along with a better way: Business has invited this revolution to its doorstep.

A major brand will be hijacked and occupied by dissatisfied customers—not a thousand people, but more like a million. Customers will rally, boycott, or defect *en masse*, causing major financial distress for the company and pushing it toward ruin. The court of social accountability and governance is now in session, and it will be swift and merciless. Mass customer and investor activism will take down brands on a regular basis, holding leadership to an unprecedented level of accountability. Millions will organize and rally to hold a major organization, its CEO, or its board accountable for a real (or perceived) act deemed inappropriate, unjust, incorrect, or irresponsible. There will be collateral damage and unintended consequences of these mass actions, including CEO and board disruption for the companies impacted; the first victim could be a U.S. multinational, although my gut feeling is that the first mass action will happen outside of the United States. These events will likely cause a chain reaction in other companies as they witness what is now possible.

As a result, companies will realize that they no longer own their brands. The market does—and even worse, a single individual will be able to hijack a corporate reputation in an instant. Even as some companies ride social technology to tremendous heights of success and profit, others will be pushed to the brink of financial or brand collapse, both at a scale and pace never before seen.

The idea of corporate governance will finally have some "teeth." In areas where boards, regulators, and investors have historically failed, they will now be held accountable by the collective action of the most powerful governance body for every company around the world: their customers.

Dealing with human behavior is inherently unpredictable. The unintended consequences of social technology will be good, bad, and ugly. The good will outweigh, by far, the bad and ugly—but only over time, and not for every company or every individual. Everyone from factory workers to customer service reps to CEOs will be impacted by the disruption that is coming. The bad and ugly will get massive amounts of press, but the good will win out over time.

As consumers realize the magnitude of the power they wield, "business baiting" could become almost a kind of sport, with social hunters preying on the weak and infirm. External forces now have the technology to effect bottom-up or outside-in change. The "hacktivist" group Anonymous has already staked a claim in this respect (Norton 2011); dissatisfied (or just destructive) consumer groups will be the next to act. New meaning will be given to the idea of fighting for the consumer, as mass customer exodus will also create opportunities for mass customer acquisition.

Therefore, crisis management and being able to remediate "black swan" events is an important risk-management competency for the social technology future. Part 6 of *Social Inc.* addresses the corporate governance issues around unpredictable events and highlights the need for boards and companies to get better at fixing problems, because preventing them will become increasingly difficult.

Social technology is about companies enabling a unique experience, which is a fragile promise and a very difficult thing to deliver consistently over time. Risks will go up, but so will the opportunity for those firms agile and adept enough to meet this challenge. Transparency, honesty, and integrity—all traits of the Social Company—will provide corporate leaders with the ability to weather the storms of change. "Dinosaurs" only paying lip-service to these qualities will be taken down. By 2020, a new group of corporate innovators and leaders will emerge: those who can and will continually fulfill and even exceed market expectations through these new tools.

2020 Prediction #1—Social Innovation Will Deliver a Major Breakthrough

By 2020, business will achieve a major breakthrough on a major societal or human problem, using the power of social technology to bring together and optimize our collective human intelligence. The potential of "transactive memory" will be fully realized against the bulk of the planet's population, which will solve at least one—if not several—of the greatest riddles and challenges of our time: the cure for or elimination of a disease, a major environmental breakthrough, a political or social problem, or some other breakthrough touching most of humanity.

Because groups collectively encode, store, and retrieve knowledge better through these tools, everyone *is* much smarter than anyone (see Part 3: Is Everybody Smarter Than Anybody?). The social technologies of fire, the printed word, and the telephone, along with their derivative impacts, all contributed to and enabled "transactive memory systems" at some level.

The collective intelligence of the planet, for the first time, can now be exploited efficiently and effectively with today's social technology. The ability to harness, cultivate, and curate cognitive diversity at scale will yield this achievement.

Conclusion

Gloria Steinem, famed U.S. writer and social justice activist is widely quoted as saying, "The truth will set you free. But first, it will piss you off." Humans are entering our first period of truly global interconnectedness. What will we do with it? What will this information-fueled social renaissance foster? The competitive landscape is changing for business around a new set of social tools and technology. As businesses everywhere leverage social technology to become smarter and more productive, trillions of dollars of value will be released and created.

The future of business is now what each of us makes it in The Age of the Experience—our new set of social technology tools will forge a better future, everywhere on the planet. For millennia, humans have invented new tools and found creative ways to use them that have raised our standards of living. Now we need to do it again—but this time, the future is being open-sourced. We all can be, and need to be, an active and engaged part of the ongoing business experiment.

It's time to go social, and set your future free.

Works Cited

Aguayo, Rafael, 1990. *Dr. Deming: The American Who Taught The Japanese About Quality*. Seacaucus, Lyle Stuart.

Alperson-Afil, Nira and Naama Goren-Inbar. 2010. *The Acheulian Site of Gesher Benot Ya'aqov Volume II: Ancient Flames and Controlled Use of Fire*. New York, Springer.

Amazon.com. 2011. "Price Check." http://www.amazon.com/Amazon-com-Price-Check/dp/B005QTZSRA/ref=sr_1_2?ie=UTF8&qid=1355516023&sr=8-2&keywords=price+check.

American Library Association. 2012. "100 Most Frequently Challenged Books: 1990–1999." http://www.ala.org/advocacy/banned/frequentlychallenged/challengedbydecade/1990_1999.

America's Library. n.d. "The First Telephone Call." http://www.americaslibrary.gov/jb/recon/jb_recon_telephone_1.html.

Anderson, Chris. 2012. "About Chris Anderson." *The Long Tail blog*. http://www.longtail.com/the_long_tail/about.html (accessed 10 November 2012).

Apple, Inc. 2003. *Form 10-K: Annual Report*. http://files.shareholder.com/downloads/AAPL/2232666740x0xS1047469%2D03%2D41604/320193/filing.pdf.

Apple. 2012a. *Apple Reinvents Textbooks with iBooks 2 for iPad* [press release], 19 January. http://www.apple.com/pr/library/2012/01/19Apple-Reinvents-Textbooks-with-iBooks-2-for-iPad.html.

Apple, Inc. 2012b. *Form 10-K: Annual Report*. http://files.shareholder.com/downloads/AAPL/2232666740x0xS1193125%2D12%2D444068/320193/filing.pdf.

Arthur, W. Brian. 2009. *The Nature of Technology: What It Is and How It Evolves*. New York, Free Press.

Ashton, Kevin. 2009. "That 'Internet of Things' Thing." *RFID Journal*, 22 June. http://www.rfidjournal.com/article/view/4986.

Associated Press. 1989. "Reagan Urges 'Risk' on Gorbachev: Soviet Leader May Be Only Hope for Change, He Says." *Los Angeles Times*, 13 June. http://articles.latimes.com/1989-06-13/news/mn-2300_1_soviets-arms-control-iron-curtain.

Automatic Electric Co. 1916. "What American Business Thinks of the Automatic Telephone" [advertisement]. *Literary Digest 52*(14–26), 1870. http://books.google.com/books?id=TbdZAAAAYAAJ&pg=PA1875&dq=literary+digest+1916+june+24&hl=en&sa=X&ei=kDDAUPL_DOKsjALBzYD4Aw&ved=0CDAQ6AEwAA#v=onepage&q=american%20business%20thinks&f=false.

Bailey, Bob. 2000. "Human Interaction Speeds." *UI Design Update Newsletter*, August. http://www.humanfactors.com/downloads/aug002.htm.

Baker, Celia. 2012. "Disruptive Innovation: Open Online Courses Are Changing Education Forever." *Desert News*, 16 December. http://www.deseretnews.com/article/765618020/Disruptive-innovation-Open-online-courses-are-changing-education-forever.html.

Baldassarro, R. Wolf. 2011. "Banned Books Awareness: Alice in Wonderland." *Banned Books Awareness*, 1 August. http://bannedbooks.world.edu/2011/08/01/banned-books-awareness-alice-wonderland/.

Baldwin, Clare and Alina Selyukh. 2011. "LinkedIn Share Price More Than Doubles in NYSE Debut." *Reuters*, 19 May. http://www.reuters.com/article/2011/05/19/us-linkedin-ipo-risks-idUSTRE74H0TL20110519.

Banhegyi, Steve. 2007. *Management: Fresh Perspectives*. Cape Town, Pearson Education South Africa.

Baten, Joerg and Jan Luiten van Zanden. 2008. "Book Production and the Onset of Modern Economic Growth." *The Journal of Economic Growth 13*(3), 217–235.

Benioff, Marc. 2011. "Welcome to Dreamforce 2011." Keynote address, San Francisco, 31 August. http://www.youtube.com/watch?v=reNYRQNTwPk.

Benioff, Marc and Karen Southwick. 2004. *Compassionate Capitalism: How Corporations Can Make Doing Good an Integral Part of Doing Well*. Pompton Plains, Career Press.

Blanchard, Kenneth H. and Spencer Johnson. 1981. *The One Minute Manager*. New York, William Morrow.

Blodget, Henry. 2012. "The inside story of Facebook's IPO." *MSNBC*, 23 May. http://www.msnbc.msn.com/id/47538876/ns/business-us_business/t/inside-story-facebooks-ipo/#.UKfR2KWikt0.

BloombergBusinessweek Magazine. 2003. "Mark Benioff, Salesforce.com." 28 September. http://www.businessweek.com/stories/2003-09-28/mark-benioff-salesforce-dot-com.

Blum, Jonathan. 2012. "Apple's Big Pay Raise Makes Stock a Big 'Buy.'" *CNBC Stock blog*, 3 July. http://www.cnbc.com/id/48059102/Apple_s_Big_Pay_Raise_Makes_Stock_a_Big_Buy (accessed 7 November 2012).

Bosman, Julie. 2011. "Publishing Gives Hints of Revival, Data Show." *The New York Times*, 9 August. http://www.nytimes.com/2011/08/09/books/survey-shows-publishing-expanded-since-2008.html.

Bradbury, Ray. 1982. "Beyond 1984: The People Machines." In *Yestermorrow: Obvious Answers to Impossible Futures*. Santa Barbara, Capra Press. 1991.

Brady-Estevez, Anna and Hazel Stirgwolt. 2012. "The Startup Generation: Building The Next Generation Workforce from the Holy Land." *Kauffman Fellows Report 4*(Fall/Winter), 32–41.

Brox, Jane. 2010. *Brilliant: The Evolution of Artificial Light*. New York, Houghton Mifflin Company.

Brunnermeier, Smita and Sheila Martin. 1999. *Interoperability Cost Analysis of the U.S. Automotive Supply Chain*. Research Triangle Institute (RTI) Project Number 7007-03. http://www.rti.org/pubs/US_Automotive.pdf.

Brynjolfsson, Erik, and Andrew McAfee. 2011. *Race Against the Machine: How the Digital Revolution is Accelerating Innovation, Driving Productivity, and Irreversibly Transforming Employment and the Economy*. Lexington, MA, Digital Frontier Press.

Bughin, Jacques, Angela Hung Byers, and Michael Chui. 2011. "How Social Technologies Are Extending the Organization." *McKinsey Quarterly*, November. http://www.mckinseyquarterly.com/How_social_technologies_are_extending_the_or ganization_2888.

Buringh, Eltjo and Jan Luiten van Zanden. 2009. "Charting the 'Rise of the West': Manuscripts and Printed Books in Europe, A Long-Term Perspective from the Sixth through Eighteenth Centuries." *The Journal of Economic History 69*(2), 409–445. doi: 10.1017/S0022050709000837.

Burton, Francis D. 2009. *Fire: The Spark That Ignited Human Evolution*. University of New Mexico Press.

Butler, Chris. 2007. "FC74: The Invention of the Printing Press and Its Effects." *The Flow of History*. http://www.flowofhistory.com/units/west/11/FC74 (accessed 13 November 2012).

Byrne, John and Lindsey Gerdes. 2005. "The Man Who Invented Management." *Bloomberg Businessweek Magazine*, 27 November. http://www.businessweek.com/stories/2005-11-27/the-man-who-invented-management.

Carnevale, Anthony P., Nicole Smith, and Jeff Strohl. 2010. *Help Wanted: Projections of Jobs and Education Requirements Through 2018*. Georgetown University Center on Education and the Workforce. http://www9.georgetown.edu/grad/gppi/hpi/ cew/pdfs/FullReport.pdf.

Carr, Nicholas. n.d. "The Big Switch." *Nicholas G. Carr*. http://www.nicholasgcarr.com/ bigswitch/ (accessed 3 November 2012).

Carroll, Lewis. 1865. *Alice's Adventures in Wonderland*. London, Macmillan.

Carter, Beth. 2011. "Dropout Zuckerberg Welcomed Back to Harvard." *Wired Magazine*, 8 November. http://www.wired.com/business/2011/11/dropout-mark-zuckerberg-welcomed-back-to-harvard/.

Cashman, Mark. 1995. "Does Information Technology Make Us Smarter? If So, How; If Not, Why Not?" *ACM [Association for Computing Machinery] SIGCHI Bulletin 27*(2), 52–53. doi: 10.1145/202511.570125.

Change.org. 2012. "Seventeen Magazine: Give Girls Images of Real Girls!" http://www.change.org/petitions/seventeen-magazine-give-girls-images-of-real-girls.

Chicago World's Fair. 1933. *Official Guide Book of the Fair 1933*. Chicago, A Century of Progress. http://ia600200.us.archive.org/21/items/ officialguideboo00centrich/officialguideboo00centrich.pdf.

Christensen, Clayton M. 1997. *The Innovator's Dilemma: When New Technologies Cause Great Firms to Fail*. Boston, Harvard Business School Press.

Chui, Michael, James Manyika, Jacques Bughin, Richard Dobbs, Charles Roxburgh, Hugo Sarrazin...Magdalena Westergren. 2012. *The Social Economy: Unlocking Value and Productivity Through Social Technologies*. McKinsey Global Institute. http://www.mckinsey.com/~/media/McKinsey/dotcom/Insights%20and%20pubs/MGI /Research/Technology%20and%20Innovation/The%20social%20economy/MGI_The_s ocial_economy_Full_report.ashx.

Coase, Ronald H. 1937. "The Nature of the Firm." *Economica, New Series 4*(16), 386–405. doi: 10.1111/j.1468-0335.1937.tb00002.x.

Cohn, Jonathan and Mark Robson. 2011. *Taming Information Technology Risk: A New Framework for Boards of Directors*. Oliver Wyman and the National Association of Corporate Directors. http://www.oliverwyman.com/media/OW_EN_GRC_2011_PUBL_Taming_IT_Risk.pdf.

Colao, J. J. 2012. "Breaking Down the JOBS Act: Inside the Bill that Would Transform American Business." *Forbes*, 21 March. http://www.forbes.com/sites/jjcolao/2012/03/21/jobs-act/.

Collins, James C. 2001. *Good to Great: Why Some Companies Make the Leap—and Others Don't*. New York, Harper Business.

Collins, James C. and Jerry I. Porras. 1994. *Built to Last: Successful Habits of Visionary Companies*. New York, Harper Business.

comScore. 2011. "Average Time Spent on Social Networking Sites Across Geographies." *comScore Data Mine*, 7 June. http://www.comscoredatamine.com/2011/06/average-time-spent-on-social-networking-sites-across-geographies/.

Constine, Josh. 2012. "Pinterest Hits 10 Million U.S. Monthly Uniques Faster Than Any Standalone Site Ever -comScore." *TechCrunch*, 7 February. http://techcrunch.com/2012/02/07/pinterest-monthly-uniques/.

Conversocial. 2012. *The Company You Keep: Perceptions of Social Service*. Available from http://www.conversocial.com/resources/research.

Covey, Stephen R. 1989. *The Seven Habits of Highly Effective People: Powerful Lessons in Personal Change*. New York, Free Press.

Delany, Colin. 2011. "How Social Media Accelerated Tunisia's Revolution: An Inside View." *Huffington Post Blog*, 10 February. http://www.huffingtonpost.com/colin-delany/how-social-media-accelera_b_821497.html.

Deloitte. 2012. "Core Beliefs and Culture: Chairman's Survey Findings." http://www.deloitte.com/view/en_US/us/About/Leadership/1fe8be4ad25e7310VgnVCM1000001956f00aRCRD.htm.

Deming, W. Edwards. 1982. *Out of the Crisis*. Cambridge, MIT Press.

DesMarais, Christina. 2011. "Amazon Price Check Discount Has Competitors Crying Foul." *PC World*, 10 December. http://www.pcworld.com/article/245995/amazon_price_check_discount_has_competitors_crying_foul.html.

Dilawar, Arvind. 2011. "5 Great iPad Apps for Early Childhood Teachers." *Certification Map: Teacher Certification Made Simple*, 13 April. http://certificationmap.com/5-great-ipad-apps-for-early-childhood-teachers/.

Directorship. 2012. "Google Board Adds VMWare Founder." 13 January. http://directorship.twittweb.com/Google--working.

Dittmar, Jeremiah. 2011. "Information Technology and Economic Change: The Impact of the Printing Press." *Vox*, 11 February. http://www.voxeu.org/article/information-technology-and-economic-change-impact-printing-press.

Downes, Larry and Chunka Mui. 1998. *Unleashing the Killer App: Digital Strategies for Market Dominance*. Boston, Harvard Business School Press.

Drucker, Peter F. 1946. *Concept of the Corporation*. New York, John Day Company.

Drucker, Peter F. 1954. *The Practice of Management*. New York, Harper & Row.

Drucker, Peter F. 1983. *Concept of the Corporation*. New York, New American Library.

Drucker, Peter F. 1993. *Concept of the Corporation*. Piscataway, Transaction Publishers.

Drucker, Peter F. 2011. *Technology, Management, and Society*. Boston, Harvard Business Review Press.

The Drucker Institute. 2012. "About Peter Drucker." http://www.druckerinstitute.com/link/about-peter-drucker.

Early Connections: Technology in Childhood Education. n.d. "Learning & Technology." http://www.netc.org/earlyconnections/preschool/technology.html.

Edelman Trust Barometer. 2012. *2012 Edelman Trust Barometer: Global Results* [Presentation slides]. 19 January. http://trust.edelman.com/trust-download/global-results/.

Elliott, Stuart. 2009. "Tropicana Discovers Some Buyers Are Passionate about Packaging." *The New York Times*, 22 February. http://www.nytimes.com/2009/02/23/business/media/23adcol.html?pagewanted=all.

Enterprise Integration Act of 2002. Public Law 107–277, 107th cong. (Nov. 5, 2002). http://www.gpo.gov/fdsys/pkg/PLAW-107publ277/pdf/PLAW-107publ277.pdf.

Ericsson. 2012. *Traffic and Market Report on the Pulse of the Networked Society*. June. http://www.ericsson.com/res/docs/2012/traffic_and_market_report_june_2012.pdf.

experience. n.d. In *Dictionary.com Unabridged*. http://dictionary.reference.com/browse/experience.

Farber, Dan. 2012. "Twitter Hits 400 Million Tweets per Day, Mostly Mobile." *CNET*, 6 June. http://news.cnet.com/8301-1023_3-57448388-93/twitter-hits-400-million-tweets-per-day-mostly-mobile/.

Farley, Tom. 1998–2006. "Telephone History Page 4: 1876 to 1892." *PrivateLine.com*. http://www.privateline.com/TelephoneHistory2A/Telehistory2A.htm (accessed 13 November 2012).

Fiegerman, Seth. 2012. "Biggest Social Media Disasters of 2012." *Mashable*, 25 November. http://mashable.com/2012/11/25/social-media-business-disasters-2012/.

Field of Dreams. 1989. [Film] Directed by Phil Alden Robinson. USA, Universal Pictures.

Firger, Jessica. 2012. "Occupy 2.0: Protesters Go High-Tech." *Wall Street Journal*, 17 March. http://online.wsj.com/article/SB10001424052702304459804577285793322092600.html.

Fischer, Claude. 1992. *America Calling: A Social History of the Telephone to 1940*. Berkeley, University of California Press.

Fisk, Donald M. 2003. "Compensation and Working Conditions: American Labor in the 20th Century." *U.S. Bureau of Labor Statistics*, 30 January. http://www.bls.gov/opub/cwc/cm20030124ar02p1.htm.

Flynn, James R. 2012. *Are We Getting Smarter? Rising IQ in the Twenty-First Century*. Cambridge University Press.

Flyvbjerg, Brent and Alexander Budzier. 2011. "Why Your IT Project May Be Riskier than You Think." *Harvard Business Review* 89(9), 23–25. Available from http://hbr.org/2011/09/why-your-it-project-may-be-riskier-than-you-think/ar/1.

Forbes. 2012. "The World's Most Innovative Companies." September. http://www.forbes.com/innovative-companies/list/.

Ford, Henry and Samuel Crowther. 1922. *My Life and Work*. Garden City, Doubleday. http://www.gutenberg.org/dirs/etext05/hnfrd10.txt.

Fountain, Henry. 2012. "Yes, Driverless Cars Know the Way to San Jose." *The New York Times*, 26 October. http://www.nytimes.com/2012/10/28/automobiles/yes-driverless-cars-know-the-way-to-san-jose.html?pagewanted=all&_r=0.

Friedman, Thomas L. 2005. *The World Is Flat*. New York, Farrar, Straus & Giroux.

Frost and Sullivan. 2006. *Meetings Around the World: The Impact of Collaboration On Business Performance*. Whitepaper. Available from www.frost.com.

FTI Consulting. 2012. *Allstate/National Journal Heartland Monitor #13 Key Findings* [memorandum], 25 May. http://www.allstate.com/Allstate/content/refresh-attachments/Heartland_Monitor_XIII_Summary.pdf.

Gallup Consulting. 2010. *The State of the Global Workplace: A Worldwide Study of Employee Engagement and Wellbeing*. http://www.gallup.com/strategicconsulting/157196/state-global-workplace.aspx.

Gilder, George. 1993. "Metcalfe's Law and Legacy." *Forbes ASAP*, 13 September. http://www.gilder.com/public/telecosm_series/metcalf.html.

Gilmore, James H., and B. Joseph Pine II (editors). 2000. *Markets of One: Creating Customer-Unique Value through Mass Customization*. Boston, Harvard Business School Press.

Gino, Francesca, Linda Argote, Elia Miron-Spektor, and Gergana Todorova. 2010. "First Get Your Feet Wet: When and Why Prior Experience Fosters Team Creativity." *Organizational Behavior and Human Decision Processes* 111(2), 102–115.

Goodell, Jeff. 2011. "Steve Jobs in 1994: The Rolling Stone Interview." *Rolling Stone*, 17 January. http://www.rollingstone.com/culture/news/steve-jobs-in-1994-the-rolling-stone-interview-20110117.

Goodwin, Bill. 2012. "Gartner Identifies Trends in CIO Spending in 2012." *Computer Weekly*, 23 January. http://www.computerweekly.com/news/2240114141/Gartner-CIO-spending-2012.

Google. n.d. "Transparency Report." http://www.google.com/transparencyreport/.

Google. n.d. "Transparency Report: Canada." http://www.google.com/transparencyreport/removals/government/CA/?metric=requests&by=reason&p=2011-12.

Google. n.d. "Transparency Report: India." http://www.google.com/transparencyreport/removals/government/IN/?metric=requests&by=reason&p=2010-12.

Google. n.d. "Transparency Report: Thailand." http://www.google.com/transparencyreport/removals/government/TH/?metric=requests&by=reason&p=2011-12.

Google. n.d. "Transparency Report: Vietnam." http://www.google.com/transparencyreport/removals/government/VN/?metric=requests&by=reason&p=2010-12.

Gordon, Robert J. 2012. *Is U.S. Economic Growth Over? Faltering Innovation Confronts the Six Headwinds*. National Bureau of Economic Research (NBER) Working Paper 18315. http://faculty-web.at.northwestern.edu/economics/gordon/Is%20US%20Economic%20Growth%20Over.pdf.

Goudsblom, J. 2004. "Fire, Human Use, and Consequences." In N. J. Smelser and P. B. Baltes (editors), *International Encyclopedia of the Social and Behavioral Sciences*. London, Elsevier. pp. 5672–5676. doi: 10.1016/B0-08-043076-7/04203-0.

Ha, Anthony. 2012. "Zappos Labs: Retailer's San Francisco Office Searches for Disruptive New Ideas." *TechCrunch*, 22 June. http://techcrunch.com/2012/06/22/zappos-labs/.

Harvard Business School. n.d. "Our History." http://www.hbs.edu/about/history.html.

Harvard Magazine. 2012. "Harvard, Extended." July–August. http://harvardmagazine.com/2012/07/harvard-extended.

Heartland Monitor Poll. 2012. *NEW POLL: Americans Using Social Media Are More Engaged Consumers and Citizens, But Remain Skeptical of Social Media Trustworthiness* [press release], 7 June. http://www.allstate.com/Allstate/content/refresh-attachments/Heartland_XIII_press_release.pdf.

Heidemann, John, Lin Quan, and Yuri Pradkin. 2012. *A Preliminary Analysis of Network Outages During Hurricane Sandy.* Technical Report ISI-TR-2008-685, USC/Information Sciences Institute. http://www.isi.edu/~johnh/PAPERS/Heidemann12d.pdf.

Helliwell, John, Richard Layard, and Jeffrey Sachs (editors). 2012. *World Happiness Report.* The Earth Institute, Columbia University. http://www.earth.columbia.edu/sitefiles/file/Sachs%20Writing/2012/World%20Happiness%20Report.pdf.

Henderson, Charles R. 1901. "The Scope of Social Technology." *American Journal of Sociology 6*(4), 465–486. http://www.jstor.org/stable/2762288.

Hendler, James and Jennifer Golbeck. 2008. "Metcalfe's Law, Web 2.0, and the Semantic Web." *Web Semantics: Science, Services and Agents on the World Wide Web 6*(1), 14–20. doi: 10.1016/j.websem.2007.11.008.

Hensley, Russell and Stefan M. Knupfer. 2005. "Reducing Waste in the Auto Industry: Carmakers and Parts Suppliers Can Capture Huge Savings, But Only by Working Together More Closely." *McKinsey Quarterly*, June. http://www.mckinseyquarterly.com/Reducing_waste_in_the_auto_industry_1622.

heterarchy. n.d. In *Dictionary.com Unabridged.* http://www.thefreedictionary.com/Heterarchy.

hierarchy. n.d. In *Merriam Webster.* http://www.merriam-webster.com/dictionary/hierarchy.

Hill, Kashmir. 2012. "British Airways Won't Be Google Image Stalking You Unless You're a V.I.P." *Forbes*, 9 July. http://www.forbes.com/sites/kashmirhill/2012/07/09/british-airways-wont-be-google-image-stalking-you-unless-youre-a-v-i-p/.

Hof, Robert. 2011. "Zynga IPO Goes SplatVille. What Went Wrong?" *Forbes*, 16 December. http://www.forbes.com/sites/roberthof/2011/12/16/zynga-ipo-goes-splatville-what-happened/.

Huffington Post. 2011. "Banned or Challenged Classic Children's Books." 28 September. http://www.huffingtonpost.com/american-library-association/10-surprising-childrens-b_b_976704.html#s369908&title=Little_Red_Riding.

Huffington Post. 2012. "Julia Bluhm, 14, Leads Successful Petition for Seventeen Magazine to Portray Girls Truthfully." 5 July. http://www.huffingtonpost.com/2012/07/05/julia-bluhm-seventeen-mag_n_1650938.html.

Hunt, Katie. 2012. "China Tightens Grip on Social Media with New Rules." *CNN*, 28 May. http://www.cnn.com/2012/05/28/world/asia/china-weibo-rules/index.html.

Institute of Directors in Southern Africa. 2002. *King Report on Corporate Governance for South Africa 2002.* http://www.mervynking.co.za/downloads/CD_King2.pdf.

Institute of Directors in Southern Africa. 2009. *King Report on Governance for South Africa 2009.* http://african.ipapercms.dk/IOD/KINGIII/kingiiireport/.

International Monetary Fund (IMF). 2012. *World Economic Outlook: Growth Resuming, Dangers Remain.* April. http://www.imf.org/external/pubs/ft/weo/2012/01/pdf/text.pdf.

International Organization for Standardization (ISO). 2010. *Ergonomics of Human-System Interaction—Part 210: Human-Centered Design for Interactive Systems*. Available from http://www.iso.org/iso/catalogue_detail.htm?csnumber=52075.

International Telecommunication Union. 2011. "Key Global Telecom Indicators for the World Telecommunication Service Sector." 16 November. http://www.itu.int/ITU-D/ict/statistics/at_glance/KeyTelecom.html.

Internet of Things Consortium. n.d. "About." http://iofthings.org/#about.

Internet World Stats. 2012. "Internet Usage Statistics." http://www.internetworldstats.com/stats.htm.

Isidore, Chris. 2009. "GM Bankruptcy: End of an Era." *CNN Money*, 2 June. http://money.cnn.com/2009/06/01/news/companies/gm_bankruptcy/.

Jumpstart Our Business Startups (JOBS) Act. H.R. 3606, 112th cong., 2nd sess. (Jan. 3, 2012). http://www.gpo.gov/fdsys/pkg/BILLS-112hr3606enr/pdf/BILLS-112hr3606enr.pdf.

JUSE (Union of Japanese Scientists and Engineers). 2012. "The Deming Prize." http://www.juse.or.jp/e/deming/92/.

Kain, Eric. 2011. "Amazon Price Check May Be Evil But It's the Future." *Forbes*, 14 December. http://www.forbes.com/sites/erikkain/2011/12/14/amazon-price-check-may-be-evil-but-its-the-future/.

Kelly, Heather. 2012. "Self-Driving Cars Now Legal in California." *CNN*, 30 October. http://www.cnn.com/2012/09/25/tech/innovation/self-driving-car-california/index.html.

Kerner, Sean Michael. 2012. "Salesforce Keeps Adding New Products, Growing Revenues." *Enterprise Apps Today*, 21 November. http://www.enterpriseappstoday.com/crm/salesforce-keeps-adding-new-products-growing-revenues.html.

Kerris, Natalie and Steve Dowling. 2007. *Apple Reinvents the Phone with iPhone* [press release], 9 January. http://www.apple.com/pr/library/2007/01/09Apple-Reinvents-the-Phone-with-iPhone.html.

Kiron, David, Doug Palmer, Anh Nguyen Phillips, and Nina Krushwitz. 2012. *Social Business: What Are Companies Really Doing?* MIT Sloan Management Review Research Report. Available from http://sloanreview.mit.edu/offers-socbiz2012/.

Koeppel, Dan. 2011. "The Future of Light is the LED." *Wired Magazine*, 19 August. http://www.wired.com/magazine/2011/08/ff_lightbulbs/.

Kubo, Jon and Libby Smith. 2012. *Social Commerce IQ™: Retail*. 8thBridge, 11 December. http://www.8thbridge.com/downloads/SCIQ-Retail-2012.pdf.

Kucera, Danielle. 2012. "Amazon's Zappos Combines Pinterest and E-Commerce in New Site." *Bloomberg*, 28 August. http://www.bloomberg.com/news/2012-08-28/amazon-s-zappos-combines-pinterest-and-e-commerce-in-new-site.html.

Lam, Andrew. 2012. "From Arab Spring to Autumn Rage: The Dark Power of Social Media." *Huffington Post*, 14 September. http://www.huffingtonpost.com/andrew-lam/social-media-middle-east-protests-_b_1881827.html.

Lerner, Josh. 2012. "The Narrowing Ambitions of Venture Capital." *MIT Technology Review Online*, 6 September. http://www.technologyreview.com/news/429024/the-narrowing-ambitions-of-venture-capital/.

Lewis, Kyle and Benjamin Herndon. 2011. "Transactive Memory Systems: Current Issues and Future Research Directions." *Organization Science 22*(5), 1254–1265.

Lewis, Meriwether, William Clark, and Members of the Corps of Discovery. 1805. July 20 Journal Entry. In G. Moulton (editor), *The Journals of the Lewis and Clark Expedition*. 2002. Lincoln, University of Nebraska Press. http://lewisandclarkjournals.unl.edu/read/?_xmlsrc=1805-07-20.xml&_xslsrc=LCstyles.xsl.

LG. 2012. *LG To Unveil Next-Generation Smart Appliances at CES, AIMS To Redefine Housework* [press release], 5 January. http://www.lgnewsroom.com/newsroom/contents/61738.

Li, Gangmin. 2008. "Economic Sense of Metcalfe's Law." In *Proceedings of the First International Workshop on Understanding Web Evolution* (WebEvolve2008). Beijing, China, 22 April.

Li, Shan. 2011. "Furor Surrounds Amazon's Price-Comparison App." *Los Angeles Times*, 9 December. http://articles.latimes.com/2011/dec/09/business/la-fi-amazon-app-20111210.

Lovell, Julia. 2007. *The Great Wall: China Against The World, 1000 BC–AD 2000*. New York, Grove Press.

MacCulloch, Diarmaid. 2005. *The Reformation*. New York, Penguin Books.

Madden, Mary and Kathryn Zickhur. 2011. "65% of Online Adults Use Social Networking Sites." *PewInternet*, 26 August. http://www.pewinternet.org/Reports/2011/Social-Networking-Sites.aspx.

Maddison, Angus. 2010. *Historical Statistics of The World Economy: 1–2008 A.D.* [Data file]. http://www.ggdc.net/maddison/Historical_Statistics/horizontal-file_02-2010.xls.

Madrigal, Alex. 2012. "Know Your Internet: What is Pinterest and Why Should I Care?" *The Atlantic*, 9 February. http://www.theatlantic.com/technology/archive/2012/02/know-your-internet-what-is-pinterest-and-why-should-i-care/252835/.

Magretta, Joan. 2012. *Understanding Michael Porter: The Essential Guide to Competition and Strategy*. Boston, Harvard Business School Publishing.

Man, John. 2009. *The Gutenberg Revolution: How Printing Changed the Course of History*. London, Bantam Books.

Marks, David Francis. 2010. "IQ Variations Across Time, Race, and Nationality: An Artifact of Differences in Literacy Skills." *Psychological Reports 106*(3), 643–664.

Marks, Richard Lee. 1993. *Cortés: The Great Adventure and the Fate of Aztec Mexico*. New York, Alfred Knopf.

MaRS. 2012. "Case Study: Dell—Distribution and Supply Chain Innovation." http://www.marsdd.com/articles/dell-distribution-and-supply-chain-innovation/ (accessed 21 December 2012).

Marshall, Alfred. 1890. *Principles of Economics: An Introductory Volume*. London, Macmillan. http://socserv2.socsci.mcmaster.ca/~econ/ugcm/3ll3/marshall/prin/prinbk1.

Maslow, Abraham. 1943. "A Theory of Human Motivation." *Psychological Review 50*(4), 370–396. doi: 10.1037/h0054346.

Mayo, Elton. 1933. *The Human Problems of an Industrial Civilization*. New York, Macmillan.

Mayo, Elton. 1945. *The Social Problems of an Industrial Civilization*. Boston, Harvard Business School.

McGregor, Douglas. 2006. *The Human Side of Enterprise, Annotated Edition*. New York, McGraw Hill.

Meyerson, Rachel. 2012. "Three Reasons Why Your Deepest Desires Will Salvage Facebook's IPO." *Dachis Group blog*, 21 June. http://www.dachisgroup.com/2012/06/three-reasons-why-your-deepest-desires-will-salvage-facebooks-ipo/ (accessed 13 November 2012).

Miller, Joy. 2009. "The Telephone in the Early 1900's." *FiveJs blog*, 24 February. http://fivejs.com/the-party-line-the-telephone-in-the-early-1900s/ (accessed 13 November 2012).

MIT News. 2012. "MIT and Harvard Announce edX." 2 May. http://web.mit.edu/newsoffice/2012/mit-harvard-edx-announcement-050212.html.

Moffitt, Sean. 2012. *@SeanMoffitt*, 27 June [Twitter post; used with permission]. https://twitter.com/SeanMoffitt/status/218133981126856704.

Nadkarni, Ashwini and Stefan G. Hofmann. 2012. "Why Do People Use Facebook?" *Personality and Individual Differences 52*(3), 243–249. doi: 10.1016/j.paid.2011.11.007.

Nelson, Amanda. 2012. "15 Stellar Uses of Social Media Command Centers." *Salesforce.com Marketing Cloud Blog* [blog post], 11 December. http://www.radian6.com/blog/2012/12/15-stellar-uses-of-social-media-command-centers/.

Nelson, Dean. 2012. "More Mobile Phones Than Lavatories for a Booming India." *The Telegraph*, 14 March. http://www.telegraph.co.uk/news/worldnews/asia/india/9143545/More-mobile-phones-than-lavatories-for-a-booming-India.html.

Newman, Jared. 2012. "SOPA and PIPA: Just the Facts." *PC World*, 17 January. http://www.pcworld.com/article/248298/sopa_and_pipa_just_the_facts.html.

Newth, Mette. 2010. "The Long History of Censorship." *Beacon for Freedom of Expression*. http://www.beaconforfreedom.org/liste.html?tid=415&art_id=475.

Nielsen. 2012. *State of the Media: The Social Media Report 2012*. http://blog.nielsen.com/nielsenwire/social/2012/.

NM Incite. 2012. *The Social Care Imperative: Four Steps to Drive Brand Health and Customer Acquisition*. White paper. Available from http://nmincite.com/download-white-paper-the-social-care-imperative-2/.

Norman, Donald A. 1988. *The Psychology of Everyday Things*. New York, Basic Books.

Norton, Quinn. 2011. "Anonymous 101: Introduction to the Lulz." *Wired*, 8 November. http://www.wired.com/threatlevel/2011/11/anonymous-101/.

NPR Staff. 2012. "Stanford's Next Lesson: Free Online Courses for Credit and Degrees?" [*All Tech Considered* audio recording] 20 July. http://www.npr.org/blogs/alltechconsidered/2012/07/23/157132291/stanfords-next-lesson-free-online-courses-for-credit-and-degrees.

O'Donnell, Catherine. 2012. "New Study Quantifies Use of Social Media in Arab Spring." *University of Washington*, 12 September. http://www.washington.edu/news/2011/09/12/new-study-quantifies-use-of-social-media-in-arab-spring/.

OICA (Organisation Internationale des Constructeurs d'Automobiles). 2011. *World Motor Vehicle Production: World Rankings of Manufacturers 2010*. http://oica.net/wp-content/uploads/ranking-2010.pdf.

OpenNet Initiative. 2012. "About ONI." http://opennet.net/about-oni.

OpenSite.org. 2012. "Enemies of the Internet." *OpenSite blog*, 13 September. http://open-site.org/blog/enemies-of-the-internet/ (accessed 13 November 2012).

Orwell, George. 1949. *1984*. New York, Penguin.

Paladino, James. 2012. "Cloudforce 2012: Toyota Social Network 'Friend' Lets the Prius 2012 Tweet, FaceTime Chat Between Service Agents and Customers." *Latinos Post*, 20 October. http://www.latinospost.com/articles/5811/20121020/cloudforce-2012-toyota-social-network-friend-lets.htm.

Pepitone, Julianne. 2012. "Facebook IPO: What the %$#! happened." *CNNMoney*, 23 May. http://money.cnn.com/2012/05/23/technology/facebook-ipo-what-went-wrong/index.htm.

Peters, Thomas J. and Robert H. Waterman. 1982. *In Search of Excellence: Lessons from America's Best-Run Companies*. New York, Warner Books.

Philips. 2012. "Hue: Personal Wireless Lighting." http://www.meethue.com/en-US.

Pigman, Geoffrey Allen. 2007. *The World Economic Forum: A Multi-Stakeholder Approach to Global Governance*. New York, Routledge.

Plato. c. 360 B.C.E. *The Republic*. Translated by R. E. Allen. New Haven, Yale University Press 2006.

Poe, Marshall. 2010. *A History of Communications: Media and Society from the Evolution of Speech to the Internet*. New York, Cambridge University Press.

Pollard, Justine and Howard Reid. 2006. *The Rise and Fall of Alexandria: Birthplace of the Modern World*. New York, Penguin.

The Pony Express National Museum. n.d. "Pony Express Historical Timeline." http://ponyexpress.org/pony-express-historical-timeline/ (accessed 4 December 2012).

Porter, Michael. 1980. *Competitive Strategy: Techniques for Analyzing Industries and Competitors*. New York, Free Press.

Porter, Michael. 1985. *Competitive Advantage: Creating and Sustaining Superior Performance*. New York, Free Press.

Porter, Michael. 1990. "The Competitive Advantage of Nations." *Harvard Business Review* 68(2), 73–93. http://hbr.org/1990/03/the-competitive-advantage-of-nations/ar/1.

PricewaterhouseCoopers. 2010. *Set Your Future Free: IT's Role in Innovation Management*. May. http://www.pwc.com/us/en/increasing-it-effectiveness/assets/it-role-innovation-management.pdf.

Pyne, Stephen J. 2001. *Fire: A Brief History*. Seattle, University of Washington Press.

Radicati, Sara and Todd Yamasaki. 2012. *Social Media Market, 2012–2016*. The Radicati Group. http://www.radicati.com/wp/wp-content/uploads/2012/08/Social-Media-Market-2012-2016-Executive-Summary.pdf.

Rawls, Philip. 2011. "Huck Finn: Controversy Over Removing the 'N word' from Mark Twain Novel." *The Christian Science Monitor*, 5 January. http://www.csmonitor.com/Books/Latest-News-Wires/2011/0105/Huck-Finn-Controversy-over-removing-the-N-word-from-Mark-Twain-novel.

Robbins, Jhan and June Robbins. 1959. "Harry S. Truman Selects Six Great Turning Points In American History." *This Week Magazine*, 22 February. p. 8. Available from http://newspaperarchive.com/salt-lake-tribune/1959-02-22/page-91?tag=harry+truman&rtserp=tags/?ndt=ex&pd=22&py=1959&pm=2&pf=harry&pl=truman.

Romer, Paul. 2008. "The Concise Encyclopedia of Economics: Economic Growth." Library of Economics and Liberty. http://www.econlib.org/library/Enc/EconomicGrowth.html.

Roschelle, Jeremy and Stephanie D. Teasley. 1995. "The Construction of Shared Knowledge in Collaborative Problem Solving." In C. E. O'Malley (editor), *Computer Supported Collaborative Learning*. Heidelberg, Springer-Verlag. pp. 69–97.

Rosenthal, Jack. 2009. "A Terrible Thing to Waste." *The New York Times*, 31 July. http://www.nytimes.com/2009/08/02/magazine/02FOB-onlanguage-t.html.

Rushe, Dominic. 2011. "Zynga IPO Fails to Generate Stock Market 'Pop' on Disappointing Debut." *The Guardian*, 16 December. http://www.guardian.co.uk/technology/2011/dec/16/zynga-ipo-values-firm-7-bn.

Rusli, Evelyn. 2011. "LinkedIn Shares Soar on First Trading Day." *The New York Times*, 20 May. http://query.nytimes.com/gst/fullpage.html?res=9C03E1DC113BF933A15756C0A9679D8B63&ref=linkedincorporation&smid=pl-share.

Salesforce.com Marketing Cloud. 2012. "Engagement Console." http://www.radian6.com/what-we-sell/marketingcloud/engagement-console/.

Sandler, Linda, Brian Womack, and Douglas MacMillan. 2012. "Facebook Fought SEC To Keep Mobile Risks Hidden Before IPO." *Bloomberg*, 10 October. http://www.bloomberg.com/news/2012-10-10/facebook-fought-sec-to-keep-mobile-risks-hidden-before-ipo-crash.html.

Sanger, David, David Herszenhorn, and Bill Vlasic. 2008. "Bush Aids Detroit. But Hard Choices Wait For Obama." *The New York Times*, 19 December. http://www.nytimes.com/2008/12/20/business/20auto.html?pagewanted=all&_r=0.

Sarbanes-Oxley Act of 2002. Public Law 107–204, 107th cong. (Jul. 30, 2002). http://www.sec.gov/about/laws/soa2002.pdf.

Schultz, Howard. 2012. "An Open Letter: How Can America Win This Election?" *Starbucks*, 29 June. http://www.starbucks.com/blog/an-open-letter-how-can-america-win-this-election/1207 (accessed 7 November 2012).

Schumpeter, J. 2008. *Capitalism, Socialism and Democracy*, 3rd edition. New York, Harper Perennial Modern Thought.

Schwab, Klaus. 2010. "A Breakdown in Our Values." *The Guardian blog*, 6 January. http://www.guardian.co.uk/commentisfree/2010/jan/06/bankers-bonuses-crisis-social-risk (accessed 4 November 2012).

SEO Peace. 2012. "Infographics: Latest SEO Methods to Rank Higher & Avoid Over Optimization." 4 June. http://www.seo-peace.com/seo-buzz/infographics-latest-seo-methods-to-rank-higher-avoid-over-optimization/.

ServiceMax. 2012a. About ServiceMax. http://www.servicemax.com/about-us/.

ServiceMax. 2012b. Customer Videos. http://www.servicemax.com/customers/business-results-video.html.

Serwer, Andy. 2012. "Howard Schultz: 'The American Dream Is in Jeopardy.'" *Fortune*, 3 July. http://management.fortune.cnn.com/2012/07/03/starbucks/?section=money_tops.

Shackford, Stacey. 2011. "Our Facebook Walls Boost Self-Esteem, Study Finds." *Cornell University Chronicle Online*, 1 March. http://www.news.cornell.edu/stories/March11/FacebookMirrorStudy.html.

Sheff, David. 1985. "Playboy Interview: Steven Jobs." *Playboy Magazine*, 1 February. http://www.txtpost.com/playboy-interview-steven-jobs/ (accessed 3 November 2012).

Shih, Clara Chung-wai. 2009. *The Facebook Era: Tapping Online Social Networks to Build Better Products, Reach New Audiences, and Sell More Stuff*. Boston, Pearson Education.

Silverthorne, Sarah. 2011. "The Most Important Management Trends of the (Still Young) Twenty-First Century." *Harvard Business School Working Knowledge*, 22 February. http://hbswk.hbs.edu/item/6639.html.

Sloan, Alfred P. 1963. *My Years with General Motors*. New York, Doubleday.

Small, Albion W. 1898. "Seminar Notes: Methodology of the Social Problem. Division I. The Sources and Uses of Material." *American Journal of Sociology 4*(1), 113–144. http://www.jstor.org/stable/2761856.

The Social Network. 2010. [Film] Directed by David Fincher. USA, Columbia Pictures.

Social Security Administration. 2012. "Historical Background and Development of Social Security." http://www.ssa.gov/history/briefhistory3.html.

South African Institute of Chartered Accountants (SAICA). 2009. *Summary of Report on Governance for South Africa—2009 (King iii)*. http://www.auditor.co.za/Portals/23/king%20111%20saica.pdf.

Spears, Lee and Douglas MacMillan. 2011. "Zynga Declines in First Day of Trading after $1 Billion IPO." *BloombergBusinessweek Magazine*, 17 December. http://www.businessweek.com/news/2011-12-17/zynga-declines-in-first-day-of-trading-after-1-billion-ipo.html.

Spencer Stuart. 2011. *Spencer Stuart Board Index*. http://content.spencerstuart.com/sswebsite/pdf/lib/SSBI_2011_final.pdf.

Srinivasan, Ramesh. 2012. "Taking Power Through Technology in the Arab Spring." *Al Jazeera*, 26 October. http://www.aljazeera.com/indepth/opinion/2012/09/2012919115344299848.html.

Standards Australia. 2005. *Corporate Governance of Information and Communication Technology (AS 8015–2005)*. Sydney. Available from http://infostore.saiglobal.com/store/Details.aspx?DocN=AS073376438XAT.

Standards Australia. 2009. *Department of Broadband, Communications and the Digital Economy: Digital Economy Future Directions Consultation Paper*. February. http://www.dbcde.gov.au/__data/assets/pdf_file/0005/112388/Standards_Australia.pdf.

Steinberg, Brian. 2010. "Lightspeed Survey: Toyota's Loss of Consumer Trust Is Domestic Rivals' Gain." *Advertising Age*, 8 February. http://adage.com/article/news/toyota-s-loss-consumer-trust-domestic-rivals-gain/141967/.

Stelzner, Michael A. 2012. *2012 Social Media Marketing Industry Report: How Marketers Are Using Social Media to Grow Their Businesses*. Social Media Examiner, April. http://www.socialmediaexaminer.com/SocialMediaMarketingIndustryReport2012.pdf.

Surowiecki, James. 2005. *The Wisdom of Crowds*. New York, Anchor Books.

Swanson, Greg. 2012. "Early Childhood Education and the iPad." *Apps in Education*, 3 July. http://appsineducation.blogspot.com/2012/03/early-childhood-education-and-ipad.html.

Sum, Andrew, Ishwar Khatiwada, Allison Beard, Joseph McLaughlin, and Sheila Pama. 2009. *The Great Recession of 2007-2009: Its Post-World War II Record Impacts on Rising Unemployment and Underutilization Problems Among U.S. Workers*. Center for Labor Market Studies, Northeastern University, June. http://www.northeastern.edu/clms/wp-content/uploads/Great_Recession_of_20072009.pdf.

Tam, Donna. 2012. "Facebook Processes 500 TB of Data Daily." *CNET*, 22 August. http://news.cnet.com/8301-1023_3-57498531-93/facebook-processes-more-than-500-tb-of-data-daily/.

Taycher, Leonid. 2010. "Books of the World, Stand Up and Be Counted! All 129,864,880 of You." *Google Inside Search blog*, 5 August. http://booksearch.blogspot.com/2010/08/books-of-world-stand-up-and-be-counted.html (accessed 13 November 2012).

Taylor, Alex III. 2009. "Toyota's New Man at the Wheel." *Fortune Magazine*, 26 June. http://money.cnn.com/2009/06/23/autos/akio_toyoda_toyota_new_president.fortune/index.htm?postversion=2009062605.

Taylor, Frederick W. 1911. *The Principles of Scientific Management*. New York, Harper and Brothers.

Taylor, Jerome. 2010. "Google Chief: My Fears for Generation Facebook." *The Independent*, 18 August. http://www.independent.co.uk/life-style/gadgets-and-tech/news/google-chief-my-fears-for-generation-facebook-2055390.html.

Telligent. 2012. *2012 Market Survey Report: Do Brits Really Believe in the Social Enterprise?* Available from http://telligent.com/resources/m/white_papers/1353367.aspx.

Toyota. 2011. "Toyota Concept New 2011 Fun-Vii Tokyo Motor Show." http://www.youtube.com/watch?v=c4h-SRXaEcQ&feature=youtube_gdata_player.

Türk Telekom Group. 2012. "Global Developments in the Telecom Sector." http://www.ttinvestorrelations.com/turk-telekom-group/investing-in-turk-telekom/global-telecom-sector.aspx (accessed 13 November 2012).

UNESCO (United Nations Educational, Scientific and Cultural Organization). 2012a. *Adult and Youth Literacy: UIS Fact Sheet*, September. UNESCO Institute for Statistics. http://www.uis.unesco.org/literacy/Documents/fs20-literacy-day-2012-en-v3.pdf.

UNESCO (United Nations Educational, Scientific and Cultural Organization). 2012b. *EFA Global Monitoring Report; Youth and Skills: Putting Education to Work*. http://unesdoc.unesco.org/images/0021/002180/218003e.pdf.

UNESCO (United Nations Educational, Scientific and Cultural Organization). 2012c. "Learning with Mobile Technologies." 19 December. http://www.unesco.org/new/en/education/resources/online-materials/single-view/news/learning_with_mobile_technologies/.

Ura, Karma, Sabina Alkire, Tshoki Zangmo, and Karma Wangdi. 2012. *A Short Guide to Gross National Happiness Index*. Centre for Bhutan Studies. http://www.grossnationalhappiness.com/wp-content/uploads/2012/04/Short-GNH-Index-edited.pdf.

Van Belleghem, Steven, Dieter Thijs, and Tom De Ruyck. 2012. *Social Media Around the World 2012* [Presentation slides]. InSites Consulting. http://www.slideshare.net/InSitesConsulting/social-media-around-the-world-2012-by-insites-consulting.

Wallace, Brenden 2012. "Why Wall Street Likes LinkedIn More Than Facebook." *Forbes*, 4 August. http://www.forbes.com/sites/ciocentral/2012/08/04/why-wall-street-likes-linkedin-more-than-facebook/.

Wal-Mart. 1988. *1988 Annual Report*. http://media.corporate-ir.net/media_files/irol/11/112761/ARs/1988AR.pdf.

The W. Edwards Deming Institute. 2012a. "Biography." http://deming.org/index.cfm?content=61.

The W. Edwards Deming Institute. 2012b. "Resume 1993." http://deming.org/index.cfm?content=622.

Wegner, Daniel M. 1987. "Transactive Memory: A Contemporary Analysis of the Group Mind." In B. Mullen and G. R. Goethals (editors), *Theories of Group Behavior*. New York, Springer Verlag. pp. 185–208.

Wegner, Daniel M., Toni Giuliano, and Paula T. Hertzel. 1985. "Cognitive Interdependence in Close Relationships." In W. J. Ickes (editor), *Compatible and Incompatible Relationships*. New York, Springer-Verlag. pp. 253–276. http://scholar.harvard.edu/dwegner/publications/cognitive-interdependence-close-relationships.

Weisenthal, Joe. 2012. "An Analyst Walked into Best Buy, and Discovered Firsthand How Amazon Is Destroying It." *Business Insider*, 17 October. http://www.businessinsider.com/analyst-amazons-price-check-app-is-creaming-best-buy-2012-10.

White House. n.d. "The Presidents." http://www.whitehouse.gov/about/presidents/.

Williams, Christopher. 2011. "How Egypt Shut Down the Internet." *The Telegraph*, 28 January. http://www.telegraph.co.uk/news/worldnews/africaandindianocean/egypt/8288163/How-Egypt-shut-down-the-internet.html.

Wohlsen, Marcus. 2012. "Amazon Changed Holiday Shopping Forever—Now App Showdown Is On." *Wired Magazine*, 20 November. http://www.wired.com/business/2012/11/black-friday-mobile-apps/.

Wood, Roy. 2012. "Self-Driving Cars." *Wired*, 5 October. http://www.wired.com/geekdad/2012/10/self-driving-cars/.

The World Bank Group, The. 2012. "GDP." http://data.worldbank.org/indicator/NY.GDP.MKTP.CD.

Wu, Suzanne. 2011. "How Much Information Is There in the World?" *USC News*, 10 February. http://news.usc.edu/#!/article/29360/How-Much-Information-Is-There-in-the-World.

Wu, Tim. 2011. *The Master Switch: The Rise and Fall of Information Empires*. New York, Vintage Books.

ACKNOWLEDGEMENTS

Throughout my career, I've been fortunate to work with a lot of very smart people from all over the world. From my clients to my colleagues, this book stands on the shoulders of all of the teams that I have had the pleasure to be a part of, and all of the people from whom I've learned over the years. Thank you, one and all!

I would also like to specifically thank the following people for their help and support in the writing of *Social Inc.* Wendy Amstutz from Whitespace LLC, a long-time colleague and friend, your support and advice made *Social Inc.* better than I could have made it on my own. Thank you also to economist Maureen Maguire for her insights and support on the econometric side of *Social Inc.* To my editors at the Kauffman Fellows Press, Anna F. Doherty and Leslie F. Peters, thank you for your attention to detail and thoughtful insights.

My gratitude also goes to publicist Lynn Goldberg and to Jim Levine. Lynn and Jim have worked with some iconic authors and brought some landmark thinking to market; I'm humbled to a part of their team. For their coaching and advice I thank Bill Tobin, Dean Yoost, Peter Waller, Larry Arnoff, Fred Farivar, Todd Gold, and Ed Merino. For stretching my thinking around the realm of the possible I appreciate the insights of Carlye Adler, Andrew Schmitt, Mike Sigal, Owen Shapiro, Mark Bonchek, Steve Curtis, John Hotta, Ted Kao, Fay Feeney, Jeremy Frank, Stacey Epstein, Rich Pearson, Ken Schulz, Johanna Flower, and Patricia Hogan. For having my back, Mom and Dad, Rich McDonnell, Megumi Suzuki, and Spud Zukis.

A special thank you to Marc Benioff for his support and contributions to *Social Inc.* His vision and leadership have taken the software industry to new heights and his contributions to *Social Inc.* did the same.

Finally, thank you to my muse. Everyone needs a muse, not just as a writer but in life as well—my wife, Kimberly Zukis, is mine. It's been a fun journey and I'm glad we're on it together.

About the Author

Bob Zukis helps leaders and their companies find their future. He has spent the last thirty years living and working across 4 continents and 20 countries, advising hundreds of global leaders on the intersection between business management and information technology in the creation of corporate value.

Bob is now helping the world find its future with social technology. He is the Chairman and Social CEO of Saaskwatch Systems, where he is turning industries upside down with social technology and bringing the concepts in this book to life through a new approach to enterprise software.

He also is working to improve social and IT governance in the boardroom as a Senior Fellow, Governance Center for The Conference Board. Bob serves on the Advisory Boards of the University of California, Irvine Paul Merage School of Business' Center for Digital Transformation, Constellation Research, and Los Angeles Universal Preschool.

He holds an MBA, with honors, from The University of Chicago Booth School of Business and a BBA from Texas Tech University.

Bob lives with his wife Kimberly and their pack of rescued shelter animals in Manhattan Beach, California. A portion of the proceeds from *Social Inc.* will go directly to no-kill animal shelters and rescues around the world.

Made in the USA
San Bernardino, CA
29 April 2014